A SHOT IN THE DARK

Pop!

It was short, but distinct. The sound rang out clearly in the quiet neighborhood.

"Oh God, no!" Kent Whitaker heard his wife scream. He ran toward her, but he was too late. Tricia Whitaker bolted into the house to protect her baby boy. "Don't you—"

Pop!

Another crack. Nothing but silence from Tricia, then a moan.

"Help," she barely muttered.

"Dad!" Bart screamed, only to be interrupted by yet another . . .

Pop!

Bart sought out his target. A man dressed in black from head to toe stood near the family kitchen. Bart's adrenaline took over and made his decisions for him as he charged at the masked intruder. He grappled with the shooter but ultimately fell short.

Pop!

The Whitakers were left to die, writhing in their own thick pools of blood. . . .

Other books by Corey Mitchell

PURE MURDER

STRANGLER

EVIL EYES

MURDERED INNOCENTS

DEAD AND BURIED

SAVAGE SON

COREY MITCHELL

PINNACLE BOOKS
Kensington Publishing Corp.
http://www.kensingtonbooks.com

Some names have been changed to protect the privacy of individuals connected to this story.

PINNACLE BOOKS are published by

Kensington Publishing Corp.
119 West 40th Street
New York, NY 10018

All Kensington Titles, Imprints, and Distributed Lines are available at special quantity discounts for bulk purchases for sales promotions, premiums, fund-raising, and educational or institutional use. Special book excerpts or customized printings can also be created to fit specific needs. For details, write or phone the office of the Kensington special sales manager: Kensington Publishing Corp., 119 West 40th Street, New York, NY 10018, attn: Special Sales Department, Phone: 1-800-221-2647.

Pinnacle and the P logo Reg. U.S. Pat. & TM Off.

ISBN-13: 978-0-7860-2013-3
ISBN-10: 0-7860-2013-X

First Printing: June 2010

10 9 8 7 6 5 4 3 2 1

Printed in the United States of America

For Sabrina Mitchell.
Welcome home, sweet girl.

1

Nestled cozily inside their luxurious home in the tony neighborhood of Sugar Lakes, in the upscale small city of Sugar Land, Texas, just outside the crime-filled, polluted metropolis of Houston, the Whitaker family gathered for a special occasion. They were to celebrate the impending graduation the following day of their eldest son, Bart, from Sam Houston State University.

Outside, the pre-Christmas chill had finally started to kick in and the crispness permeated the neighborhood. Heron Way, the street upon which the Whitaker home resided, was bedecked with the ever-popular icicle lights. Doors were festooned with oversized evergreen wreaths, and life-sized wooden cutouts of most major Christian-based, Christmas-themed characters were erected, like a movie set for a Western.

Inside, the Whitakers huddled together in the warmth of their lovely home, so painstakingly tended to by the family matriarch, Patricia Whitaker, known to her family and friends as "Tricia." She made sure nearly every inch of their home was covered in Christmas knickknacks—from Santa snow globes, to fake snow, to little green candy canes laid everywhere with care. But there was an even deeper devotion in this household, more than mere secular Santa–ism. Tricia and her husband, Kent, were both deeply religious people who made sure that "Christ" remained in *Christ*mas in the Whitaker household. Kent and Tricia held tightly to their faith and made sure to incorporate their devotion into their everyday lives, whether they were attending church services and functions, or simply with how they comported themselves in their daily routines and dealings with other people.

Kent and Tricia also made it a point to teach the bountiful lessons of Jesus Christ and his Holy Father to their own two sons, Thomas, who preferred to be addressed by his nickname, "Bart," and his younger brother, Kevin. Both sons were outstanding in the eyes of their parents and both had made strides toward living a Christ-filled life.

"I'm so happy," Tricia whispered to Kent. He smiled back at his lovely bride, who, at fifty-one years old, looked as beautiful to him as the day they first met. He still felt a rush of warmth in her presence, and he knew he loved her more today than he had all those years ago.

"Me too," Kent replied. "I knew he could do it."

The couple stopped what they were doing and looked up at the portrait of their family, placed over the fireplace mantel. Their twenty-three-year-old son,

Bart, was ready to begin his adult life with a college degree in hand. He was brilliant, they said to one another, and now he would be able to step out into the real world and let others see his true intelligence.

"All right, Bart"—Kent Whitaker got his son's attention—"in honor of this wondrous occasion, your mother and I decided to get you something special to commemorate your hard work and dedication to finish your studies and earn that degree."

Bart stood next to the hearth and grinned. The handsome, though slightly pudgy, son beamed back in his parents' direction. He was dressed nicely in a casual pair of brown corduroy pants, a burgundy long-sleeved shirt, and preppy bowling shoes. He smiled in eager anticipation as to what it was his overly generous parents were giving him this time.

Kent handed Bart a wrapped gift, about the size of an old-fashioned small toaster oven. Bart thanked his father as he received the package. He stood near the family Christmas tree, which was already overflowing with gifts, even though Christmas was still more than two weeks away. He looked like a little kid whose parents would allow him to open one of his presents before Santa came.

Instead of diving right in, however, Bart played up the moment. He looked at the gift, held it up to his ear, and began to shake it vigorously. He smiled as he tried to guess what was inside. "Hmmmm, I'd say it's a coffee mug." His parents played along. His younger brother, Kevin, smiled as well.

"No, Bart, just open it," his mother playfully ordered.

"Yeah, c'mon, Bart. Your mother went to a lot of

trouble to find this for you," his father declared. "It's not every day one of our boys graduates from college."

Bart returned the smiles and hungrily tore into the package. After he removed the wrapping and the bow, he found himself holding a green box. The outside of the box looked like the interior of a fluorescent aquarium, complete with rocky coral shelves. He knew this was no ordinary box. He also knew it was no coffee mug.

Bart flipped the box over in an effort to try and figure out the best spot where to open it. As he did, he spotted *Rolex* on the opposite side. His eyes lit up. He had always wanted a Rolex watch, but he never had enough money to purchase one of the elite time-pieces.

Tricia's smile was wide enough to make every ortho-dontist happy as she watched her oldest boy unwrap his gift. She could not have been prouder—especially since she had always wondered about Bart and whether or not he could get his act together and be a solid contributor to the family. Now she knew that his com-mitment to his studies was all the proof she needed to know he was definitely on the path to a godly life and financial success. She could not have asked for any-thing more.

Once Bart realized what his gift was, he wasted no more time in getting to it. He opened the box, then removed another box from inside. He opened the second box and there it was: a shiny $4,000 Rolex watch. He was ecstatic. Bart had champagne tastes, and his parents never let him down.

Tricia leaned up against Kent and flashed him a loving smile. He nodded toward her and then turned to Bart. "Well, what do you think, Bart?"

Bart continued looking at the watch and then slowly shook his head to and fro. "I like it. I like it a lot." Bart smiled at his brother, Kevin, who returned the smile. "No, I love it!" Bart exclaimed.

The family spent another minute or so gawking at Bart's new symbol of success. After basking in the glow, Bart glanced at his new watch, which had the correct time already. "Hey, c'mon. We'd better get going. We don't want to be late for Pappadeaux."

The rest of the Whitaker family nodded in agreement and began to perform the "getting ready to go" shuffle of grabbing wallets, jackets, and gloves. Pappadeaux is a seafood restaurant chain that specializes in fried seafood and Cajun-style crawfish. It is owned by the Pappas family from Houston, who also own Pappas Bros., which serves steaks, Pappasito's, which serves Mexican food, and Pappas BBQ, which, of course, specializes in barbeque. There are several Pappas restaurants spread throughout the state of Texas, and they are hugely successful. The most upscale of all the Pappas' restaurants would definitely be Pappadeaux. There was one located near the Whitakers, out on Highway 59, near Highway 6, less than three miles from their home.

The four Whitakers piled into Tricia's TrailBlazer and headed out of their neighborhood.

They failed to notice the car parked on the back side street, directly behind their house.

Tricia made the short drive in very little time. The perpetually under-construction Highway 6 did not cause any problems for them, as work was being done in the opposite direction from the restaurant. In less than five minutes, the Whitakers pulled into the relatively empty parking lot, exited the TrailBlazer, and headed for the side doors of the restaurant.

No one in the family noticed the person sitting in the car who watched them as they entered Pappadeaux.

Inside the restaurant, the family was quickly seated as they had called in reservations. They perused the extravagant menus, made their selections, and gave their orders to the friendly waitstaff. Drinks were also ordered, delivered, and quaffed. It was all a very pleasant evening, with happiness and celebration the key themes for the Whitakers.

After stuffing themselves with crawfish, gumbo, and fried catfish, Kent Whitaker decided to order a celebratory dessert for Bart. A big production was made upon the delivery of the house special.

"Here's to you, Bart," Kent Whitaker toasted his oldest son. He could not contain his happiness. He had been worried that Bart would turn in the wrong direction and not make anything of himself. Thankfully, his son had proved him wrong. He was now on the precipice of greatness. "Congratulations on an amazing accomplishment. I only wish Lynne was here to share this special occasion with you." Lynne Sorsby was Bart's girlfriend. There had recently been talk of marriage proposals on the horizon.

"Thanks, Dad," Bart said, returning the salute. "I'll be talking with her later tonight when we get back home. She'll probably come over later, but she already had plans to go out to dinner with her folks."

Surprisingly, Bart had not thought to invite Lynne and her family to Pappadeaux to join his family for dinner. The whole celebration actually was thrown together at the last minute. Bart even had to call his father in to be sure he made it out to the restaurant. As a result, Lynne had already made plans that she could not back out of.

"Bart, honey, I just want you to know how proud I am of you, son." Bart's mom was beaming. "You stuck with it and now you are being rewarded for your tenacity and strong spirit. I wish you the best of luck, and know you will make a name for yourself, one day."

"Hear! Hear!" the other two Whitaker men chimed in. All four raised their glasses for a toast. Bart smiled at his mom as he lowered his drink.

"How 'bout some pictures?" Kent Whitaker asked. The proud papa pulled out his camera and snapped several shots of the boys and their mother, Kevin and Bart together, and Bart holding up his dessert plate. A good time was had by all.

Their appetites sated, Kent asked their waiter for the check, he paid, and they exited the now-bustling restaurant. It paid to eat early in a Houston restaurant. When the Whitakers stepped outside, the parking lot had gone from relatively barren to humming with SUVs and Mercedes Benzes. This time, Kevin asked his mom to drive her TrailBlazer. She agreed and the family members piled in and drove off the lot.

None of the Whitakers noticed that the same car from earlier was still in the parking lot. Nor did they see it as it pulled out and began to follow them home.

Kevin Whitaker pulled up to the entrance of their gated community. He punched in the security code to gain access into the neighborhood. The car behind them managed to squeeze through the gate as well, without having to enter its own code. They did not notice the vehicle as they turned the corner toward Heron Way and their home.

Kevin turned right into the Whitaker driveway and pulled his mother's TrailBlazer up close to the attached garage. The family got out of the SUV, locked their doors, and shut them. Tricia was the first out and also the first to head toward the front porch and into the front-door entrance. The porch light beckoned like a shining star in the cold night.

Kevin quickly walked around the truck and scooted past his mother. He always liked to be first to the door, and the one to open it up. Kent followed behind Tricia. Bart, however, made a beeline for the street and his Yukon, which his parents had bought for him while he was at college.

"I forgot my cell phone in the truck," Bart tossed back to his family. "I need to call Lynne so she can come on over."

Kent looked over at Bart, smiled, and followed his wife.

As Kent Whitaker rounded the corner, he looked up and saw his youngest boy, Kevin, unlock the front door and enter the house. He had no idea that when Kevin went inside, there was someone standing directly in front of him. He also had no idea that Kevin smiled at the person who was standing inside their home.

Pop!

It was short, but distinct. The sound rang out clearly in the quiet neighborhood.

"Oh God, no!" Kent Whitaker heard his wife scream. He ran toward her, but he was too late. Tricia Whitaker bolted into the house to protect her baby boy. "Don't you—"

Pop!

Another crack. Nothing but silence from Tricia, then a moan.

"Help," she barely muttered.

Kent Whitaker went after his wife. He unknowingly stepped over a loose garden hose on the front porch, only to see his wife and youngest son, both lying inside the foyer of their home. Both were bleeding badly. He could not tell if Kevin was moving or not. He could see that his wife was still alive as she began to take huge gasps of air.

By this time, Bart Whitaker began to run up the driveway to see what was happening inside his parents' home, the home he and his brother had grown up in.

"Dad!" he screamed, only to be interrupted by yet another . . .

Pop!

As Bart dashed through the front yard and hastily made his way onto the front porch, he was greeted with the ghastly vision of his father lying on his back with blood pouring out of his body. Instinctively Bart ran past his father to get inside the house. He only momentarily looked down to see his mother, gasping for air, lying in an ever-widening pool of blood. He barely caught sight of his brother farther in the house. He did not appear to be moving.

Bart sought out his target. A man dressed in black from head to toe stood near the family kitchen. Bart's adrenaline took over and made his decisions for him as he charged at the masked intruder. He grappled with the shooter and had every intention of disarming him. Unfortunately, his attempt of heroism fell short.

Pop!

The fourth gunshot crack of the night tore through the frigid air. It was much louder to Bart this time as he and the gunfire were both indoors.

The masked intruder then dropped the gun and took off running through the laundry room, which led to a door that led outside to the backyard. The man took off running by the swimming pool, leaped over the Whitakers' wooden fence, and headed for a small car parked on the street directly behind the Whitakers' home. The shooter and driver slowly drove off with the car's headlights off.

The Whitakers were left to die, writhing in their own thick pools of blood.

2

December 10, 2003, 8:18 P.M.
Stanley Residence
Heron Way—Sugar Lakes Subdivision
Sugar Land, Texas

Directly next door to the Whitakers' home on the east side, their relatively new neighbor, Clifton "Cliff" Stanley, sat in his recliner in his family's living room. He was having a relaxing evening watching television.

Cliff was very fond of his new neighbors. He and his wife, Darlene, had moved into the home just six months earlier. The couple had two sons, Brandon and Dane, who had gone off to college.

Cliff's job as a vice president of a regional insurance marketing company was quite demanding and kept him very busy. Thus, he enjoyed the little time he was able to spend with Kent and Tricia Whitaker. Cliff met Tricia the day he and his wife had moved in. He described her as "just a very, very sweet person."

The Stanleys and Whitakers developed a quick, pleasant friendship. They went out to lunch together, had dinner a few times, and even made it out to the theater once on a double date. Cliff Stanley worked out of his home, so he became closer to Tricia, who was a stay-at-home mother at the time. She had previously taught at nearby Lakeview Elementary School and was acting as a volunteer there on occasion. At night, when Kent would return home from his job at the Bartlett Construction Company, the couples would "congregate out in the front yard" and catch up on the day's events.

Cliff Stanley knew the Whitakers were in for a big weekend. Their oldest son, Bart, whom he had never met, since Bart lived up north in Willis, Texas, was about to graduate on Saturday. Stanley could tell that Tricia was very excited and happy about the impending ceremony. "She was very hopeful, very upbeat and optimistic for [Bart's] future."

Cliff and Darlene sat downstairs in the back of their comfortable home, on this particular night. The couple relaxed and watched television. They were also excited to have their eldest son, Brandon, home from college for the holidays. Their son had been upstairs in his room when he peeked in on his parents in the living room.

"Was that on the TV?" Brandon asked his parents.

"What?" Cliff asked his son.

"I heard yelling and shooting," Brandon stated.

The Stanleys were watching a family show. "No, it wasn't on this TV," Cliff replied.

Brandon walked down the steps and insisted, "Then it's outside. Something's going on outside. I swear I heard a shooting outside."

Cliff and Darlene looked at one another quizzically.

Cliff rose up to take a look. He and Brandon headed for the front door to see if something was going on.

When he walked out of his home, Cliff first looked over in the direction of the Whitakers' house. It was natural instinct. Look toward those you are closest with in hopes that everything is fine with them. Unfortunately, everything was far from fine at the Whitaker household.

Cliff spotted Kent Whitaker sprawled out on the concrete front porch next door. He couldn't tell whether he was dead or alive. Kent's head was pointing back toward the Stanley house in an awkward position. Suddenly Cliff saw his friend lurch sideways and mutter something.

"I'm bleeding . . . ," Kent Whitaker pitifully mewled. His voice was barely audible.

"Kent," Cliff called out to his friend. "Are you okay?"

"I'm bleeding, Cliff," Kent cried out much louder. "Help!"

Cliff immediately headed in the direction of Kent Whitaker, his own safety not crossing his mind. The thought that a man with a gun might still be on the premises did not enter into his consciousness. He simply understood that his friend was in trouble and needed his help.

Cliff made his way toward Kent. As he came upon him, Cliff looked up and saw Tricia directly in front of the entryway to the house, about six feet away from Kent. She was in a kneeling position with her head on the front porch, near the slight step leading into the house. Her legs and lower body were pointed outward toward the street.

Brandon Stanley followed directly behind his father.

When Cliff witnessed the carnage before him, he yelled back at his son, "Go back inside and call 911! Now!" Brandon took off back to the house to make the call.

Cliff turned his attention back to the bleeding Whitaker parents. He looked at Kent and asked, "What happened?"

Kent looked at his friend with pleading eyes and re-iterated, "I'm bleeding, Cliff."

"Okay, buddy. Just hang in there. Let me see what I can do," Cliff attempted to calm his neighbor.

Cliff hustled back to his house, stormed inside, and began yelling to Brandon, "I need something to stop the bleeding! Bring me something so we can bandage Kent up!" He waited as long as he could, but his son never came out with anything to staunch the flow of blood.

Cliff tore out of his house and returned to the Whitakers. He ripped off his T-shirt and placed it on Kent's left shoulder. "Kent, hold on to this. It will keep the blood from rushing out too fast," he ordered. He could tell by the looks of Tricia that she needed his help much more than Kent. "Just hold on tight."

Cliff edged forward, closer to Tricia. She was moaning in pain, but still conscious. "What happened?" he asked her.

Tricia Whitaker looked up at him, pale and bedraggled, and said, "Someone shot us. You need to go. He could still be here." She began to moan again—only this time, it seemed more drawn out and painful than before. Cliff could sense that she was going downhill rapidly. Unfortunately, he was afraid to move her body in case her blood had already started to clot up;

he didn't want to break up the clots and cause her to bleed even more.

Instead, Cliff began to pray. Tricia Whitaker continued to moan in agony. He looked up from Tricia into the house, where he spotted someone who he thought was Kevin Whitaker. He always thought a lot of the youngest son who had returned from his first semester in college at Texas A&M University. Cliff thought Kevin was "a special kid."

It was difficult to tell if it was actually Kevin or Bart, since it was dark inside the house. There was a light on in the foyer, which provided him with his only illumination. Cliff was unsure how that person was doing; that is, until he heard a pitiful sound emanating from the victim. Cliff would later describe it as a "death rattle." It was marked by "very ragged moaning." Cliff knew that the boy, whom he could finally make out as Kevin, was breathing his final breaths.

Cliff was unable to get to Kevin because Tricia was blocking the entrance to the front door. Besides, he could tell that Kevin was very close to dead. Cliff bent his head and said a silent prayer for Kevin.

The nineteen-year-old son of Tricia and Kent Whitaker stopped breathing.

Cliff knew he needed to get assistance for Kent and Tricia. He quickly moved back and leaned over Kent to see how he could help. He took over holding the bloody T-shirt used as a bandage and held it firmly in place. He then heard the front door to his house open and saw his wife, Darlene, stick her head outside.

"Clifton, get out of there!" she shouted frantically. "The killers might still be inside their house!" She was frightened to tears and was determined that her husband not join the list of fatalities.

Cliff Stanley had not cared about the possibility of a shooter or shooters still hiding out inside the Whitaker home. Regardless, he continued holding the temporary bandage on Kent's gushing wound.

Kent then looked up at his neighbor and said, "Cliff, they really could be inside there. I don't want you getting shot."

Cliff snapped to and realized that both his wife and Kent were right. He needed to get the hell out of there. But instead of fleeing, Cliff decided he needed some protection of his own. He went to get his shotgun.

"I'll be right back, Kent."

Cliff darted up from his wounded neighbor and bolted back toward his home. He went inside, determined to find his weapon, which he did. He began to load the shotgun with bullets when his wife stepped in front of him. She was scared.

"If they pull up," she said in reference to police officers, "and they see you with that shotgun, they'll probably shoot you, too. They might think you are the one who shot the Whitakers."

Cliff knew his wife was right. He felt so frustrated. It seemed as if there was nothing he could do for his friends. He decided it was best to put down his own weapon; however, he knew he had to do something. Instead, he returned back to the Whitakers' front porch and attempted to comfort Kent.

Cliff then heard the screech of police sirens.

The whole scenario took less than ten minutes. To Cliff Stanley, it seemed like a lifetime. "Everything seemed to be moving in slow motion," he recalled.

Sugar Land police officer Kelly Gless was the first to arrive at the scene. He slowly exited his vehicle to assess the situation. He was very cognizant of the fact that the shooter or shooters might still be in the house or in the nearby vicinity. Officer Gless noticed Cliff holding a bloody shirt up against Kent Whitaker.

"Sir, could you please step away from that man?" Gless asked Cliff.

"I'm their next-door neighbor. I found them like this," Stanley assured the officer.

"That's fine, sir," Gless responded. "I need for you to step away from that man, and please stand on your driveway."

Cliff immediately complied, looked at Kent one more time, then retreated back to his yard.

More police cars pulled up onto Heron Way. The revolving lights on top of the vehicles intermingled with the red, green, and white Christmas decorations throughout the neighborhood. It looked like a spinning holiday season kaleidoscope.

Darlene came out of the house to join her husband. Cliff began to pray out loud so Kent could hear him. Cliff and Darlene clutched each other and worried about their newfound friends.

An ambulance pulled up to the location immediately thereafter. The emergency medical technicians (EMTs) jumped out of the truck and quickly examined the scene. The prognosis was grim, especially for Tricia Whitaker. One of the EMTs phoned in a request for a Life Flight helicopter. Tricia would need immediate surgical attention at the nearby Memorial Hermann Sugar Land Hospital. Her chances of holding on were slim.

3

December 10, 2003, 8:20 P.M.
Sugar Land, Texas

"All units, we have a reported shooting [on] Heron Way in the Sugar Lakes Subdivision," the voice over the dispatch called out to Sugar Land police officer Kelly Gless. Though Gless was actually patrolling in District 1 of Sugar Land, and Heron Way was located in District 2, he realized he was very close to the district line. The six-year veteran relayed that he would head for the scene.

When he arrived at the address, Gless was surprised to be the first police officer on the scene. He spotted a man on the front porch of the house, frantically waving his arms at him. Gless cautiously exited his vehicle and approached the front porch. As he worked his way up the walkway to the front, he noticed an injured woman lying on her stomach in the doorway. She was moaning and in obvious pain. The man was clutching his right shoulder, which was bleeding.

Officer Gless then looked inside the foyer and saw

the body of a young man. At first, there did not seem
to be any movement from the young man, but then
his arm began to twitch spasmodically. That stopped
and the arms rested, outstretched. Gless could see
that the young man had suffered some sort of serious
chest wound and had bled profusely.

"Help my wife," Kent Whitaker pleaded with Officer Gless. "Please help my wife."

Gless directed his attention to Tricia Whitaker. She
was gasping for air.

"Ma'am, have you been shot?" Gless asked the
barely coherent mother.

Tricia was not able to respond to the officer.

"Ma'am, have you been shot?"

Again, nothing.

Since Gless was on the scene by himself, he was at a
distinct disadvantage in case the shooter or shooters
were still inside the residence or on the premises. Instead of barreling into the house and chasing down
the shooter, Gless determined his safest bet was to wait
until help arrived. He then left the front porch and
took cover behind the hedge at the front of the porch.

"Unnnnggghhhh!" A terrible moan emanated
from the young man in the foyer. Gless knew he
needed to summon help for the boy and the woman
immediately. He grabbed his receiver and put a call in
for a Life Flight rescue helicopter. It was only a matter
of time before it would be too late.

"Please, Officer. I have another son inside," Kent
Whitaker cried out to Officer Gless in reference to
Bart. "He went inside after the shooter, and I haven't
seen him. Please, please check on him."

Gless motioned to Kent to stay still and to be quiet.
Eventually Gless was joined at the Whitaker home

by two more police officers. After their arrival, even more officers appeared. They were able to create a three-man search team to enter the house to see if they could locate any survivors, any more victims, and/or the shooter or shooters.

Officer Gless stayed outside to secure the perimeter around the Whitaker home.

One of the three men on the search team was Phillip Prevost, a fourteen-year veteran who had spent his last seven years with the Sugar Land Police Department (PD). When he got the same call for a shooting at 8:20 P.M., he took off, Code 3, which means with "lights and sirens." He hurried off to the scene, but he turned his siren off by the time he reached the freeway. He did not want any criminals to hear his approach. He then pulled into the Sugar Lakes Subdivision and headed toward Heron Way. He turned all the lights off on the cruiser as he got closer to the house. He then parked his car three houses down the street and ran toward the Whitaker residence. (It is Sugar Land PD protocol not to park directly in front of a location where a shooting has occurred so as not to become one of the shooter's next victims.)

Officer Prevost spotted Officer Gless. He glanced over and caught sight of Kent Whitaker, who was apparently standing up by this time. Provost then spotted Tricia Whitaker. He could hear the blood gurgling inside her chest and throat. Prevost then spotted Kevin Whitaker inside the house. He approached the house to see if he could help the young man.

Officer Prevost was aware that the fire department had probably been called. They would not enter the house if there was a chance that an armed shooter could be inside. Prevost knew the people lying down in their own pools of blood needed immediate medical attention, so he went about clearing out the house in order to assure the fire department.

Prevost walked up to the front door, with his gun drawn. He glanced down at Tricia Whitaker and precariously stepped over her prone body. Once he got inside, he also had to straddle Kevin's body to make any forward progress.

Once Prevost made his way past Kevin, he spotted a small table in a living area. It was dark inside and difficult to see, but he was able to make it out, nonetheless. On the other side of the table was a well-worn sofa. In between the sofa and the small table was another person, Bart Whitaker. He was lying on the floor and in obvious pain. He was also on top of a cordless telephone.

Officer Prevost could see that Bart Whitaker was doing okay, so he advanced through the rest of the house. Once he made his way into the kitchen, he spotted a gun on the floor. He could instantly tell it was a Glock, because he used two of them himself. According to Prevost, he "did not have time to secure the weapon." Instead, he released the magazine and stuck it in the breast pocket of his shirt. He removed a live round, which was in the chamber, and stuck that in his left rear pocket. He then placed the gun back in the same position as he had found it.

Prevost checked all the way to the back door. He scanned the laundry room and could determine that no one was hiding in there.

Prevost then made his way up the Whitaker staircase to the second floor. He noticed a set of car keys on one of the steps and also lots of Christmas decorations, such as a giant green stocking and a stuffed polar bear with a Santa Claus cap on the banister.

The officer was joined by two more Sugar Land PD officers, Clifton Dubose and John Torres. All three men explored the upstairs to make sure it was clear. It appeared as if there was no longer an intruder inside the house.

Prevost made a very obvious and unusual observation—all of the dresser drawers had been pulled out, in at least two rooms. Normally, in a robbery situation, such a sight would not be unusual. What made this unique was that the drawers had been pulled out the exact same length. It did not appear to be ransacked, but rather someone's poor attempt at what they thought a robbery would look like. Most everything else in the upstairs rooms looked relatively undisturbed. Some usual big-ticket items—such as DVD players, laptop computers, videogame consoles, and more—had not been stolen. Prevost noted this was not the usual garden-variety robbery scene. He smelled something fishy about the whole ordeal.

After scanning all of the upstairs rooms, Prevost and the other police officers nodded to one another that everything was clear. The green light to the fire department could now be given, and the emergency medical technicians could enter the home and begin assisting the victims. Once Prevost was certain there were no longer any armed shooters inside, he radioed that everything was clear.

Prevost began to case the inside of the house for signs of anything out of the ordinary. He looked for any evidence of a break-in, like a jimmied window or a damaged door lock, but he found nothing. No glass was discovered on the floor from a shattered window, and no doors appeared to have been kicked in. The point of entry was not leaping out at the patrol officer.

Prevost made his way over to the den, where he looked for the young man between the coffee table and the sofa. Bart Whitaker had moved himself toward the kitchen and closer to the gun on the floor. Prevost walked up to Bart to check on him.

"Are you okay, son?"

Bart nodded. "I'm okay."

Prevost was joined by Officer Arthur Freeman. As Prevost began to talk to Bart, he pulled out a micro-cassette recorder from his jacket pocket. He liked to keep it with him at all times while on duty. It allowed him to keep track of all his encounters while out on patrol. The officer turned the recorder on and began to ask Bart if he knew what had happened.

"We were coming in from dinner and I went to my car to get my phone," Bart began speaking, albeit in an understandably dazed manner. It appeared as if he was in shock. "I was walking up the driveway and I heard some *pops*. I ran in and somebody was running this way." He pointed toward the laundry room. "I ran in, they turned, and someone shot me."

"What did they have on? Could you see any clothes?" Officer Prevost asked.

"I couldn't tell." Bart shook his head, as though disappointed. He did not want to let anyone down.

"And they ran out the back door?"

"That way." Bart nodded and pointed toward the back door.

Officer Prevost pointed toward the gun on the kitchen floor. "Where did this gun come from?"

"When I hit him"—Bart nodded, recalling his valiant

attempt to apprehend the shooter—"I don't know if he dropped it, or what."

"You hit this guy that was running?"

"I tried to grab him. I don't know if I hit him or not, but I came after him."

"Do y'all keep a gun in the house?" Prevost inquired.

"Yeah, my dad has a gun," Bart responded. "My brother has one, too."

"Both of those guns upstairs?"

"No, my dad's is in a closet in there." He pointed toward another room downstairs.

"What kind of Glock is [it] that your dad has?"

"My dad doesn't have a Glock. My brother does."

"Do you know where your brother keeps his gun?" Prevost asked the drained-looking oldest Whitaker boy.

"No." He shook his head. "Probably in his room."

Bart looked over Officer Prevost's shoulder. He spotted his brother, Kevin, lying still in the foyer. Kevin was not moving. "Oh God!" Bart cried out. "What's going on in there?"

Prevost leaned over in an attempt to block Bart's view. "They're just trying to help everybody." The officer tried to keep Bart's attention focused on him. He did not want the young survivor to get too emotionally wrecked by the sight of his dead brother. Prevost was determined to get the freshest account possible from one of the surviving victims at this crime scene. It was pertinent to help him solve the shooting. "They got a lot of people working on it, okay?" He continued to soothe Bart's jangled nerves.

"Did y'all keep the gun in the house?" Prevost asked in an attempt to redirect Bart's attention.

"Yes, yes," Bart nodded. "That's—that's my brother's gun."

"Okay, Bart. You're doing great," Prevost affirmed. "Bart, did you know the guy who was in the house? Could you see his face?"

Bart began to shake his head again. "No, no. It was dark." He became frustrated. "It happened too fast. I don't know."

"Could you tell if he was black or white or . . . ?" Prevost inquired.

Bart paused. "He kind of, I don't—he made a noise. I don't know. He kind of sounded black to me. I don't know." Bart began to writhe in pain. The bullet had entered his shoulder and hurt tremendously.

"Just lay still, buddy." Prevost comforted the older brother. "Just lay still."

Prevost motioned over to one of the EMTs to take a look at Bart's wound. The technician began to move Bart's injured arm and ask him if it hurt or not.

Bart winced in pain. "It hurts." He also became more concerned for his family. "Please tell me they're okay."

"They're working on them," one of the EMTs responded.

Bart began to hyperventilate. The images rushing through his head were coming fast and furious. His breathing became too rushed. The technicians made sure he breathed through his nose and tried to calm him down.

How could he calm down with the lights on outside, his brother apparently dead, just ten feet away from him, and his mom and his dad out of his line of sight? He had no idea if they were even alive. Technicians and police officers littered the living room with their presence. It was all just too overwhelming. One of the EMTs stuck a needle in his arm.

"Okay, sweetie," she gently reassured Bart. "I'm going to start an IV on you before you get ready to move, all right?"

"Yeah." Bart nodded, even though he was not truly sure what she had just said to him. "I can't feel my arm."

"That's because you're breathing too fast, sweetie. Just squeeze my hand," she suggested to him.

Right about that time, Officer Freeman stepped up next to Officer Prevost and began to ask Bart some additional questions.

"Hey, bud"—the large police officer hovered over the average-sized injured young man. "I know you're in pain, but I need to know if that pistol," he asked, pointing toward the Glock on the kitchen floor, "is that your brother's?"

"It's actually registered in my name," Bart answered, "but it's my brother's."

"Where did y'all keep that pistol?" Freeman followed up.

"I don't know." Bart attempted a shrug. "In my brother's room, I guess. It's upstairs. You go to the top of the stairs and turn left."

Bart then basically retold the entire incident to Officer Freeman. One piece of new information was that his parents usually went through their front door whenever they came home.

Officer Freeman made sure to keep asking Bart questions so as to keep him alert. "When did you finish your finals?"

"Today," Bart acknowledged.

"How many finals did you have today?"

"Two," Bart muttered.

"My little brother goes to Sam Houston." Freeman kept up the patter. "He plays football over there. Did you go to any games this year?"

Bart shook his head no. "I'm not a big football fan."

"Oh, really? Man, everybody went to a couple of games." Freeman continued chatting with Bart, trying to keep Bart's mind off the chaos that surrounded them, and to get Bart's breathing under control.

"I went last year. They didn't do too well this year," Bart responded.

Freeman chuckled and nodded his head in agreement. "No, no, you're right. They need a new coach, don't they?"

"They need a lot of things." Bart chuckled as well.

Freeman kept talking to the young man. He found out what time Bart finished finals, what time he had arrived at his parents' home, and what time the family left for Pappadeaux.

One of the EMTs broke in to let Freeman know they were transporting both Kent and Bart to Hermann Hospital via a Life Flight helicopter.

Freeman began to ask Bart questions about Kevin's gun. Bart began breathing heavily. "Are you all right, man?" the officer queried.

"No." Bart emphatically shook his head. He seemed about to have a panic attack.

"Yeah, you are," Freeman said, attempting to calm him down.

It didn't work. Bart began hyperventilating again.

"Come on now," Freeman spoke to Bart. "You've got to control your breathing. Be strong. Control your breathing for me, all right? That's all you've got to do."

Bart seemed to calm down.

Freeman talked to Bart and learned he was about to graduate from college.

Meanwhile, the technicians scurried around the house as fast as they could, while tending to Kent and Tricia Whitaker. The scene was a surrealistic nightmare awash in high, saturated flashing colors, and a barrage of bodies—not meant to fit in the small front area of the Whitaker house—were part of the grisly tableau.

Freeman and another officer lifted Bart onto a gurney to prepare to ship him out. Bart had no idea where his mom and dad were. He could no longer see Kevin and had no idea what state his little brother was in.

Officer Prevost walked back over to Bart before they shipped him out. He looked him over once and turned away. Something seemed a bit off about the young man, but, of course, he had just been shot, as had the rest of his entire family. Prevost internally decided to give the guy a break and move on to the next problem that needed solving.

According to Kent, he had no idea how anyone in his family had fared during the ordeal. He had asked anyone who would listen, how they were. Despite the mass of people traipsing in and out of his home, no one would give him a straight answer—much less look him directly in the eye.

Finally he was able to catch the attention of one of the busy paramedics. "Please, can you tell me what is going on with my wife and kids?" Kent practically pleaded. The paramedic stopped what he was doing and addressed Kent quickly and quietly: "Sir, please let us do our job. You're in good hands, and lots of good folks are with the rest of your family."

Kent's initial reaction was one of muted relief. The

paramedic must have meant that everyone was alive and being attended to. Hopefully, everyone would be okay. He did not have the wherewithal to comprehend completely what the paramedic had really said, or, rather, not said.

Suddenly the seriousness of the situation struck him like an eight-inch adrenaline needle to the heart. Kent's life would soon be altered immeasurably by a conversation he overheard between two police officers. In reality, the only words that mattered, or that he even recalled, were uttered by only one officer: "What do you want to do about the DOA?"

As far from lucid as Kent was, he knew exactly what they meant by DOA—one of his family members was "dead on arrival," and he had no idea who. He then began to worry that there might be more than one dead family member.

Kent then recalled hearing the Life Flight helicopter rip through the night sky like a million machetes serrating an Amazon forest. Kent was able to glimpse a gaggle of paramedics as they hurried a body onto a gurney, and out to the front sidewalk.

"Sir, they are taking your wife on the helicopter first," one of the many police officers relayed the good news.

Kent's heart soared with joy. His lovely, incredible wife, Tricia, was alive, and they were going to do whatever they needed to do to take good care of her! He was overjoyed.

As soon as Kent was overcome with elation, he realized that some other horrible event had occurred. Since she was alive and there was a potential DOA on the scene, it meant only one thing—at least one of his precious sons was dead. Kent's relief was suddenly countered with an almost unbearable sense of guilt and grief as he knew he would never again speak to at least one of his boys. To make matters even worse, Kent had no idea if it was Bart or Kevin. He had no idea which of his sons he would not get to see graduate from college, which one would never get married, never have children and raise a family, nor to whom he would get to say "good-bye" and "I love you" one final time.

The fear of his new reality sent Kent into a fit of convulsions. His temperature dropped and he began to shiver.

"I'm freezing," he barely managed to mutter to one of the paramedics. "Can you get something to cover me up with?" His last ounces of strength seeped out of each of his pores as he knew that one of his sons had been murdered.

"Sir, please just be still. As soon as your wife's helicopter takes off," one of the paramedics reassured him, "there will be another to come pick you up."

No sooner said than done. The second Life Flight helicopter swooped into place, picked up its cargo, and hauled Kent off for an eight-minute ride, which seemed like an eternity.

According to Kent, all he could think about during that arduous, lonely passage was a recent, similar trip he had taken with his two boys, only the end result had been much more upbeat and positive. The three Whitaker men had set out for an adventure of white-water rafting on the Arkansas River. Their trip also included Kent's and the boys' first trip in a helicopter.

The difference between the two rides was astounding. The first, of course, brought excitement and peaceful memories mixed together. The latter brought nothing but misery and numbness.

4

December 10, 2003, 8:30 P.M.
Whitaker Residence
Sugar Land, Texas

Detective Marshall Slot got the call for a shooting on Heron Way in the Sugar Lakes Subdivision. It was an unusual occurrence in Sugar Land, but the ten-year veteran detective knew he needed to get over there as quickly as possible. He wrote a note so his wife and kids would know he would be gone, grabbed his keys, and headed over to the Sugar Land police station to pick up his camera and pocket digital recorder.

Detective Slot arrived at the Whitaker house, slightly after 9:00 P.M. When he pulled up to the street, he witnessed a Life Flight helicopter ascending out of the neighborhood. He had no idea who was inside the rescue vehicle; however, he knew it must be serious.

Slot exited his car, walked up to the front porch, and noticed several Sugar Land police officers on the scene. When he entered the house through the front door, he saw the prone body of a young man. It was obvious the man was deceased.

Slot turned to one of the police supervisors on the scene to get the lay of the land, and as much detail about the crime scene as possible. Slot asked another officer to give him a walk-through of the Whitaker house. The detective scanned every room and made special note of the awkward way the drawers were pulled out in the rooms. The manner in which they were pulled was an obvious red flag to the seasoned detective. His first thought was that he was staring at a staged robbery.

While upstairs in the Whitaker house, Detective Slot made his way into what looked like a young college student's bedroom. It was bedecked with sports equipment, desktop computers, and a framed Texas A&M poster, which had not yet been hung up on the wall. There was even a sheathed ceremonial sword propped up in the corner of the main room.

A quick stroll through the bedroom led Slot into a smaller room with a sloped ceiling. It was readily apparent that this was someone's game room. A couple of videogame consoles lay on the floor next to at least ten videogames in their cases. College textbooks were laid out on a table, and even more Texas A&M posters were found.

As Slot worked his way farther into the game room, he spotted something a bit out of character. He noticed a couple of boxes of bullets, along with a fairly large black metal box. He could see that the box appeared to be some sort of safe. Upon further inspection, he noted that the safe had been pried open with some sort of metal device. The door to the safe had been bent back, and the black paint had been scraped off around the edges.

Slot made his way back downstairs and to the back door, which was unlocked. He also noticed a window had been cracked open slightly; however, he could see no signs of entry through it. He noted that all of the outside screens for the windows remained intact. Slot also observed that the majority of the knickknacks inside the house, as well as the recent Christmas decorations, were mostly left undisturbed.

Once Detective Slot completed his walk-through, and felt sufficiently updated on what had occurred, he exited the home through the back door, so as to let the crime scene technicians perform their tasks. Outside, the detective continued to search for evidence of escape by the shooter or shooters. The only potential pieces of evidence he spotted were some loose pickets on the family's backyard fence. He could not determine for sure, though, whether they were loose prior to or after the break-in and shooting.

Detective Slot exited the backyard and made his way around to the front yard. There he encountered Deputy Keith Pikett, from the Fort Bend County Sheriff's Office. Pikett was the canine handler for the sheriff's department. His specialty was scent-tracking dogs. Pikett was working with three bloodhounds in an attempt to track down the shooter.

Slot stood back as Pikett and his four-legged fellow officers did their magic. The animals made their way over to a Yukon SUV, parked in the street directly in front of the Whitaker home. Slot walked over to the truck, when he noticed a plastic evidence number stand near the right back tire. It was difficult to see in the dark, but he saw a black glove next to the evidence indicator placard. It lay in between the bumper and the curb on the street. One of the police officers walked up to Slot and informed him that he had discovered the glove moments earlier.

Slot continued to work the crime scene at the Whitaker house. He sent Detective Billy Baugh out to check up on Kent, Tricia, and Bart Whitaker. He had no idea that Tricia Whitaker would not make it to the hospital. She passed away while on board Life Flight en route to Memorial Hermann Sugar Land Hospital.

5

December 10, 2003, 10:00 P.M.
Memorial Hermann Sugar Land Hospital
West Grand Parkway South
Sugar Land, Texas

According to Kent Whitaker in *Murder by Family,* where he detailed the night of the murders, he was joined at the hospital by both of his parents. He described being surrounded by doctors and nurses as well, and realized no one would tell him anything about his other family members. When he asked about Tricia, Kevin, and Bart, he was told by a nurse that he and Bart would be undergoing surgery. No mention was made of Tricia or Kevin. Their omissions worried him.

According to Kent, he spoke with his parents. "Mom, I think there's a good chance that Tricia and Kevin are dead." He then looked toward an administration representative for confirmation. "Isn't that so?" he queried, worried what the true answer would be. The representative stared back at him, an eternity frozen between two strangers. She broke the hold with a slight nod, up and down.

"It is," she quietly muttered.

Soon thereafter, Bart was airlifted into the hospital as well. Kent was informed that Bart had been rather heroic in his attempt to tackle the shooter and had been shot in the shoulder in the process. His oldest son was in a state of shock about the events that had just occurred, but he would be all right.

Both Kent and Bart were ably tended to by the Memorial Hermann staff. Both men had suffered a broken arm and were both set in temporary casts. According to Kent, the bullet he had taken had "entered my right shoulder and traveled through the arm muscle, striking midhumerus and shattering the bone."

Bart had been shot in the left arm, which had also been broken.

The arms of the Whitaker men weren't the only things to be set and healed that night. According to Kent, a self-described very religious man, he "felt God's presence and comfort" in his hospital room the night of the murders. As a constant stream of well-wishers respectfully marched in and out of his hospital room, he claimed that "Scriptures of comfort came to mind" and described it as if "God gave me a shot of Novocain" to deal with the pain of the complete and total upheaval he was now about to embark on.

Miraculously, on the same night his beloved wife, Tricia, and his equally beloved youngest son, Kevin, were murdered, Kent Whitaker decided to invoke a "conscious act of will." He forgave the shooter.

Not wanting to be burdened with the additional emotional turmoil wrought by anger, Kent made an emphatic decision to forgo anger and hatred. Instead, he decided to turn his faith over to God. According to Kent, he stated, "I wanted whoever was responsible to come to Christ and repent for this awful act."

Kent's decision to forgive startled even himself. Earlier, he felt the normal feelings of an individual who had a loved one ripped away from him—depression, anger, the desire to kill his wife and son's killer. He stated, however, that once he decided to forgive the killer for the murders, "This forgiveness astounded me." He believed the act saved his life and changed everything for the better.

6

The night after the murders, Detective Marshall Slot and his partner, B. W. "Billy" Baugh, paid a visit to Kent and Bart Whitaker at the hospital in their shared room, which had been upgraded from a double to a hospitality suite to hold their numerous visitors. Slot and Baugh were able to speak with both men about the previous night's fateful encounter. Detective Slot introduced himself to the two men and informed them that he would be lead detective on their case.

Detective Slot wanted to learn more about the Whitakers so he could possibly unearth a single clue as to why someone would rob them and attempt to kill their entire family. Kent and Bart recalled the events from the night before in as much detail as they possibly could.

They also spoke about their various backgrounds in education and employment. Kent informed Detective

Slot that he had been employed as an accountant for his wife's father's construction company for a number of years.

Bart spoke about his education and his impending graduation ceremony from Sam Houston State University, in Huntsville, Texas, which was to take place the following night. Bart added that he was interested in working in law enforcement and would be taking part in an internship with the Federal Bureau of Investigation (FBI) after graduation. He wanted to become a detective, just like Slot.

The detectives left the two grieving men to their own devices. Detective Slot expressed his condolences for the losses of Kevin and Tricia. He let them know he would be available for them at any time, if they thought of anything else that happened the night before, or if they could think of any reason why someone would want to cause them harm.

The Whitakers thanked Slot and Baugh and returned to healing and commiserating.

The following day, Detective Slot began to make a series of phone calls trying to track down as much information about the Whitakers and any of their acquaintances as possible. The detective mostly came up with dead ends, either with no information or simply that the Whitakers were well-liked and appeared to have no enemies.

Most of Slot's efforts seemed to bear no fruit. That is, until he received a phone call from the bursar's office of Sam Houston State University.

Detective Slot was stunned by the phone call he received. He knew he only had one option—he needed to speak to the oldest brother, Bart, at the hospital. The detective drove back up to Memorial Hermann and made his way toward the twenty-three-year-old's room. He walked into the room and saw Bart sitting up, watching television. Kent Whitaker was not in the room.

"Hello, Bart," Slot greeted the young man.

"Detective Slot"—Bart returned his gaze with a grin on his face—"any new information on the case, sir?"

"As a matter of fact, Bart, there is something that is quite puzzling to me."

Bart's expression changed to quizzical as he looked back at the detective. "What is it, sir?"

"Bart, I got a call not too long ago from your college, Sam Houston," Slot informed him.

"Yes, sir?" Bart looked confused.

"Bart, the bursar's office told me that you are not actually even going to school there. In fact, they said you only have enough credits to be a freshman," Slot calmly relayed the information. "Why would they tell me that?"

Bart sat, stunned. He looked defeated. He looked embarrassed. "I had a feeling you were going to find out, sooner or later," Bart replied with a knowing frown. He slowly began to shake his head and look down at his chest as he sat in his hospital bed.

"Bart, do you care to tell me what is going on?" Slot asked. "Can you tell me the truth, son?"

Bart paused interminably. Finally he lifted his head up and looked directly into Detective Slot's eyes. "I am not enrolled at Sam Houston State, Detective."

Slot did not press the issue with Bart. Instead, he made Bart go back over the details of the night of the murders. After he was done, Slot made his way over to Kent Whitaker's bed; Kent had since returned to the room, Slot waited until Bart left the room to speak to Kent.

"Hello, Mr. Whitaker," Slot greeted the mourning father. "How are you feeling today, sir?"

Kent Whitaker muttered, "Fine, I guess." The shock from losing his wife and youngest son had not settled.

"Mr. Whitaker, I have to ask you something about your oldest boy, Bart."

"Sure, go ahead," Kent replied.

"Did Bart tell you he was graduating from college this weekend, sir?" Slot asked.

"Yes, from Sam Houston State University, up in Huntsville. We were supposed to go to the graduation ceremony today, as a matter of fact. Why do you want to know that?" Kent asked.

"Sir, are you aware that Bart is not even enrolled at Sam Houston?"

Kent flinched at the statement. "No, that's not true. Of course, he's enrolled. How else could he be getting his degree?"

"Sir, Bart is not enrolled in school there. In fact, he has not been enrolled at Sam Houston for a number of years."

Kent sat stunned in his hospital bed. "That doesn't make any sense," he declared, dumbfounded. "That's why we went out to dinner. We were celebrating his upcoming graduation." Kent looked directly at Detective Slot. "This has got to be some kind of joke, doesn't it? This is just a cruel joke."

"I'm sorry, sir. Your son is not enrolled in college," Slot reiterated.

Kent sat silent and upright in his bed. He still was not sure if he heard the detective right. Even if he had, he was not sure what to make of the news. He knew his son had some trouble as a youth with telling the truth, but he knew his oldest child was a good kid.

Bart would never do anything to harm anyone—much less anyone in his family.

Kent Whitaker simply shook his head.

"Of course, sir, we are still looking into every angle to find out who killed your family," Slot reassured the stunned father.

Kent later admitted that when he heard the news about Bart's lies about college, he only had one thought: *This will derail the investigation into the police finding the real killer because they will focus on Bart as a suspect.*

Kent, of course, knew his oldest son had nothing to do with the murder of his own mother and brother, but this latest bit of information, coupled with a small-ish criminal record as a teenager, would temporarily delay things, as far as finding the actual murderer.

According to Kent, he decided he needed answers from Bart. An aching Kent glanced at Bart's side of the hospital room, where he spotted Bart asleep in his bed. He also noticed Bart's girlfriend, Lynne Sorsby, seated in one of the uncomfortable guest chairs. Lynne had been at the hospital since the morning after the shooting, and had not left Bart's side the entire time.

Kent nodded toward Lynne and then quietly asked her if he could have a moment alone with his son. Lynne cordially assented, stood up, and walked out of the room. Kent edged his wheelchair up next to his son's bed and began to speak.

"Bart, what were you thinking?" Kent whispered. "You weren't even in school? How could you lie to us about graduation?"

Bart sat up erect in bed at the sound of his father's voice. "Dad, I'm so sorry!" he bellowed out loud. "I didn't want to tell you because I knew how much you and Mom were looking forward to my graduation." He added, "I just figured I could work it out and take the classes next semester, and nobody would know."

Kent was livid. "Nobody would know! How would we *not* know? How would they let you graduate? How did you get into this mess in the first place?"

According to Kent, Bart had been a complete wreck since the shooting. He, too, was in a sling and bandaged up rather thoroughly. He had kept the drapes in his room closed so no light peered in whatsoever, and all he wanted to do was sleep.

Kent felt pity for his son as he listened to Bart's explanations for his scholastic situation, and why he felt the need to lie to his parents about it. Bart explained that he had been swamped at his job at the Bentwater Yacht & Country Club, in Montgomery, Texas, a palatial sporting club and restaurant located on Lake Conroe, which catered to some of the wealthiest individuals in the state of Texas. Several employees had quit during the summer and he had been forced to take over a majority of the duties to keep the restaurant afloat.

"Do you have any idea what you've done?" the once-mild-mannered father, now furious, asked his son. "Thanks to this 'little' lie about graduation, the police think you're a suspect!" Kent was incredulous. He told Bart that he believed the police now viewed Bart as the *only* suspect. "You weren't in school, you told everyone you were graduating, and they think you arranged to have us killed to cover it up. Can you see how stupid that was?"

Bart immediately snapped to and made sure his dad was fully aware he was in no way involved with the deaths of his mother and brother. "Dad, that's nuts! I didn't have anything to do with the shootings!" Bart tearfully apologized to his father for the ridiculous lie and reiterated that he did not want his parents to be disappointed with him for not doing well in college. "This will be okay," he reassured his father.

Kent, however, was not completely satisfied with Bart's response. "I'm so mad now, I could spit!" he bellowed out at his oldest son. "I've told you before—you cannot ever allow yourself to start lying again!" Kent reiterated that the police were now wasting time focusing on Bart because of his lies, instead of doing everything in their power to find the real killers.

Kent eventually relaxed and the two men made up, told one another that they loved each other, and mentioned that the police would get back on the proper trail soon enough.

Kent, however, had a niggling sensation that he could not shake. He was still very angry with Bart for having lied to him about his college career. One thing he did not ponder: *How could Tricia and I have not known Bart wasn't in college all these years?*

7

Kent and Tricia Whitaker's first encounter was on a blind date. "I walked into her house and I didn't know what I was expecting, but she came down [the stairs] and I thought, 'I've never been on a blind date like this before,'" Kent joyfully recalled. "We hit it off very well right from the start." Indeed, he was smitten by the beauty with long blond hair that draped below her shoulders. He realized within a matter of months that he had fallen deeply in love with her, and she had reciprocated his feelings.

Tricia and her younger brother, William "Bo" Bartlett, grew up near the South Loop in Houston. When she turned fifteen, the family moved over to the west side of Houston. Tricia and Bo attended Westchester High School. Tricia participated in the group Young Life, a Christian ministry that reached out to middle-school, high-school, and college-aged kids. She also loved to hang out with her friends and was even an avid waterskier. Tricia was a good student and very popular with her classmates.

Upon graduation from Westchester High School,

Tricia migrated north for college at Southwest Texas State University (now known as Texas State University) in San Marcos, Texas, the halfway point between Austin and San Antonio. She attended Southwest Texas for one year before she returned home for the summer. That was when she met Kent.

Having been smitten with her newfound love, Tricia knew she could no longer attend school in San Marcos, since she would have been nearly two hundred miles away from Kent. To remedy the situation, she instead opted to transfer to the University of Houston.

In 1974, Kent landed a job at Tricia's father's construction company, which was "in the commercial construction business in masonry." The company was founded in 1951 by Tricia's father, William Bartlett Sr., who ran a tight ship that turned into a lucrative venture in a short period of time.

According to Kent, he acted as the company's office manager and also its accountant. He mainly handled relations with the government and oversaw all of the accounting and contracts that came over the transom.

After dating Tricia and working for her father's company for more than one year, twenty-six-year-old Kent Whitaker and twenty-three-year-old Patricia Ann Bartlett decided to get married. They sealed their nuptials on June 21, 1975.

The happy couple enjoyed each other's company for another four years before they excitedly welcomed their first child. Thomas Bartlett "Bart" Whitaker was a New Year's Eve baby, born on December 31, 1979. The couple focused all their love and attention on

Bart, until four years later when they welcomed their second son, Kevin, into the family on March 19, 1984.

The Whitaker household was a growing hub of love and activity. Kent and Tricia worked hard to raise healthy, happy children. They went out of their way to make sure each son was cared for, paid attention to, and encouraged to be the best possible children they could be.

As the boys grew older, the family became closer. Kent played sports with the boys, and Tricia, a schoolteacher, worked with them on their studies. They exercised their minds, as well as their bodies. They also made sure to incorporate the boys into their religious beliefs, as they were very devout Christians.

When Bart and Kevin started having friends, the Whitaker household in Sugar Land was Grand Central Station for activity. Parents felt safe knowing their kids were with the Whitakers, and the kids enjoyed playing with Bart and Kevin and adored their parents.

By the time the boys were teenagers, they had pretty much anything and everything at their disposal. Nice clothes, a large two-story home, cars, skiing trips, girlfriends. All was good in the Whitaker household.

Bo Bartlett later described Tricia and Kent's relationship as something most couples would envy. "They would wake up in the morning excited just to talk to each other," Bo recalled. "Kent would even brush his teeth at the office before he went home just so he was more presentable to Tricia when he got home.

"He was so into my sister. That was his soul mate."

8

Saturday, December 13, 2003
Memorial Hermann Sugar Land Hospital
Sugar Land, Texas

Kent and Bart Whitaker were scheduled to have their surgeries, back-to-back, early that Saturday morning. According to Kent, his and Bart's injuries were practically mirror images of one another, with the damage to his right arm and Bart's in his left arm. Kent claimed to have teased the nurses into making sure they inserted the appropriate metal into the correct arms.

Both Whitaker men were to have titanium rods inserted into their arms which "over time the fragments would fuse together around it" and would take approximately three months to heal. Kent described himself and Bart as "real bionic men," after the '70s television icon Steve Austin, from the hit series *The Six Million Dollar Man*.

Both Kent and Bart came out of their successive surgeries without any further complications.

9

Sunday, December 14, 2003, 1:00 P.M.
Whitaker Residence
Sugar Land, Texas

Detective Marshall Slot returned to the scene of the double murder. This time, however, he was right behind Kent and Bart Whitaker. The two victims of the shooting had been picked up and driven home by Kent's brother, Keith. Slot hoped to get more information from the father and son as to what had occurred four nights earlier.

When Keith Whitaker pulled his vehicle alongside the front curb to his brother's home, Kent Whitaker was taken aback by the sight of several large yellow ribbons tied to many of his neighbors' trees, as well as around some of the trees in his own front yard. Tears welled up in Kent's eyes as he exited the vehicle and slowly made his way up to the front door of his home. He somehow managed not to break down as he walked past the spot where Tricia had fallen. As he cracked the door open wider, he was shocked to see that there was no blood to be found.

Kent walked inside, followed by Bart and Detective Slot. The latter was surprised to see that the entire foyer had been cleaned, from top to bottom. The scene looked nothing like it had the night of the murders. Extended family members of the Whitakers, as well as friends from the church, had come in during the preceding days after the police investigation had been completed and cleaned up the house. Slot described it as "pristine." The friends and family members wanted to make sure Kent and Bart came home to a nice, clean house that was seemingly devoid of any negative recollections from the gruesome scene, just four nights prior. They wiped up the blood-stains, removed tainted carpet, and placed everything back, including all of the Christmas decorations and tree, exactly where they had found it.

Kent and Bart's return home was not a time for mourning and organization. They were joined by Detective Marshall Slot and two other Sugar Land Police Department officers. Slot had prepared to conduct two separate walk-throughs of the crime scene by its two surviving victims. Slot first had Bart removed from the scene so Kent could provide a videotaped narrative of the events that occurred on December 10.

According to Detective Slot, Kent was very thorough in his reenactment of what happened. He was very animated, succinct, and was easily able to recall exactly what happened, at least from his perspective. Kent was very detailed in his depiction of the murders and attempted murders.

As the two men went over the details, Kent began to discover that certain items were indeed missing from his home. One was a Ruger .22 pistol.

In addition, after he rifled through his closet, Kent informed Slot that an envelope that contained cash was missing. He knew it was gone, because it had been strategically hidden on a shelf inside a small plastic VCR tape drawer. It would not be something someone would simply stumble upon.

Detective Slot then summoned Bart and asked Kent to leave.

Bart's walk-through was different than Kent's. On the videotape, Bart was much vaguer about the details of the crime. Detective Slot felt that Bart "was holding back," for some unknown reason.

Bart had his left arm holstered in a white hospital sling after his surgery. He was dressed casually in blue jeans, a brown sweater, and brown loafers. He began the walk-through videotaping session by turning off the light switch in the foyer so that the room was nearly pitch black.

Bart calmly walked out of the front entrance, where half his family had been murdered, made his way out onto the front porch, and then turned right onto the poorly lit driveway and headed toward the garage. He was reenacting what had occurred just after the family pulled into the driveway—after they returned from the restaurant, and before they headed inside.

Bart and three officers stood in the driveway as if they were seated in the car. Bart was in the back driver's side, next to his father. Kevin was the driver and Tricia sat up front in the passenger seat. As they imaginarily exited the vehicle, Bart calmly walked back up the driveway and pointed out where his Yukon had been parked in the street.

Though the murders had occurred only four nights before, Bart did not appear distressed in any way. Instead, he looked like he was giving directions to a lost tourist by pointing out some of the town's unique landmarks.

Bart directed the officers playing the roles of his family members to walk along the front of the house, while he made a beeline for the street to go to his vehicle. Bart turned around to the camera and replied, "I heard *Bang*. . . ." The complete lack of emotion could not have been more apparent.

Bart continued the reenactment by traipsing through the fallen dry leaves in the front yard. "I paused," he continued, "seeing my dad on the ground." Bart moved forward and then directed the officers where to lie on the ground so as to resemble his dead mother and dead brother. As he pointed out their respective fallen spots, again not a single ounce of emotion was evident on his face. It felt more like a choreographed dance as opposed to the supposedly most traumatic experience a young man could have ever gone through in his short life.

As Bart directed the officer playing Kevin where to lie down, he said, "You weren't that much in·the way, so maybe you were somewhere over here, instead."

Another officer played the suspect. When Bart spotted him, he said, "I saw you running," as though actually talking to the killer. "When I ran into the door"—he recalled his alleged heroic motion—"I could see you running away. I ran in this way." Bart headed into the dark living room. "I guess somewhere in here, I got shot. I fell back into the couch, onto the floor, and I remember I got up to use the phone to call 911."

10

Adam Hipp met Bart Whitaker at Clements High School in Sugar Land, Texas, back in 1996. Hipp was a junior, and one year older than Bart. The two boys were introduced to one another via a mutual friend from a journalism class they all shared. While working on the school's yearbook and newspaper, Adam and Bart became friendly acquaintances. They mostly hung out together on the school's campus and in class, but they seldom spent time together away from school, at first.

The two students, however, did seem to run in the same circle of friends at Clements. The two handsome young men considered their circle to be the elite among the rest of the students at Clements, an already wealthy school, thus making them the elite of the elite—at least in their own minds.

Despite such a high opinion of himself, Hipp apparently did not do well enough in school to attend a four-year college, such as Rice, Texas, or Texas A&M. Instead, he settled for a satellite school, the Sugar Land campus of Wharton County Junior College.

Meanwhile, Bart would advance to his senior year at Clements High School.

Bart and Adam became closer friends that same year. Their main bonding experiences would come during casual weight-lifting sessions. Adam had expressed his desire to work out and talked to Bart about partnering up with him. Bart suggested that Adam move his weight equipment into the Whitaker house. He mentioned a finished-out attic space, just off his room on the second story. It was unoccupied and would serve as a great locale for a makeshift gym. Adam was excited and quickly agreed to the arrangement.

Bart and Adam spent many days together lifting weights, usually two or three times a week. In between reps, the young turks talked about life, women, and, of course, their favorite subject—money.

Hipp recalled how most of their conversations went. "It seemed to be a common subject of how we both wanted to get ahead in life and be able to do things *now* versus when we were fifty or sixty." The two young men discussed "everything from the money that our parents had set away for our college accounts, and maybe different investments and monies that we had set aside for us."

As bizarre as the image of two young teenagers lifting weights and talking about finances might seem, it was all very normal to Bart and Adam. Both young men were pampered by financially successful parents, attended one of the most academically superior high schools, and considered themselves on the top rung of the social-strata ladder of Sugar Land. Precocious and presumptuous, Bart and Adam believed they were the top dogs in the pack and carried themselves in such a manner at all times.

"We were definitely over average," Hipp recalled in regard to his and Bart's financial and social statuses in Sugar Land. He described his family and Bart family's wealth as a barometer that "defines you as a class, separates you for what you have and what you don't have." Adam did not believe that he and Bart ever had to "portray" a wealthy and sophisticated image to their peers, because they simply just were. "I did not have to portray that, it's just who I was," and Bart too.

Over time, and thousands of reps of weights, Bart and Adam grew even closer. Their conversations took on a new life beyond just girls and money. They were mainly about Bart's family. Adam had taken an instant liking to the Whitaker family, as they always graciously welcomed him into their home and treated him like one of their own.

While Adam took a shine to the Whitakers, he noticed that Bart never seemed truly happy around his parents. "He got along somewhat with his dad," Adam recalled. "He identified himself, aligned himself, more with his father than with his mother." Adam also noted that Bart "felt estranged from his mother for various reasons." He just was not sure what those reasons were, because Bart would never completely open up to him.

Adam was able to glean a few reasons for Bart's discontent with his mother. "He felt she paid too much attention to his brother," Kevin. Hipp described this as very much "a sore spot" with Bart. According to Hipp, there were a multitude of reasons why this

ticked Bart off. Number one on the list was that Bart
believed he was, by far, Kevin's intellectual superior in
every way. Bart also believed Kevin was weak. He felt
he was too feminine, too much of a pushover. He did
not believe his little brother was tough. He did not believe he was a true man yet. Kevin was no superman.

Bart's mentality tended to follow that of German
philosopher Friedrich Nietzsche. According to the
Stanford Encyclopedia of Philosophy, Nietzsche's concept
of the "superhuman" first made an appearance in his
work *Thus Spoke Zarathustra, A Book for All and None*
(*Also Sprach Zarathustra, Ein Buch für Alle und Keinen*,
1883–85), wherein the famed philosopher described
*the spiritual development of Zarathustra, a solitary, reflec-
tive, exceedingly strong-willed, sage-like, laughing and danc-
ing voice of self-mastery who . . . envisioned a mode of
psychologically healthier being beyond the common human
condition. Nietzsche refers to this higher mode of being as
"superhuman"* (übermenschlich)." He believed it to
be *a doctrine for only the healthiest who can love life in
its entirety—with this spiritual standpoint, in relation to
which all-too-often downhearted, all-too-commonly-human
attitudes stand as a mere bridge to be crossed and overcome.*

Indeed, sometimes it appeared as if Bart and Kevin
Whitaker could not be any more different. Bart fash-
ioned himself to be an intellectual who was well-read,
worldly, and always impeccably dressed. Bart knew
these traits were going to shoot him into the upper
stratosphere of success in life.

On the other hand, at least in Bart's mind, Kevin
was beneath him. Kevin was the jock of the family who
loved to play baseball. Kevin was more interested in
making friends and being sociable than he was about
studying his academics. Kevin apparently got along

with his parents better than Bart did. He would willingly and eagerly participate in family events with his parents, while Bart usually made up some type of excuse to get out of such gatherings.

Another way the two brothers were distinct could best be described using Texas colleges as an analogy. Rice University is considered to be upper-crust, on par with a private Ivy League school in the state; while Texas A&M is the everyman college that focuses on blue jeans, pickup trucks, and sports. Without a doubt, Bart was Rice, and Kevin was Texas A&M.

Kevin enjoyed hunting and fishing. Bart could not stand them. Kevin was a blue-jeans-and-cowboy-boots kind of guy. Bart was the preppy. Kevin was destined to become an Aggie, the mascot for Texas A&M. Bart considered himself to be more of a Princeton guy, or a Stanford guy.

Though the two brothers professed their love for one another, Bart often complained about Kevin, saying that his younger brother was a "lazy, good-for-nothing bum," who always had everything handed to him.

Despite Bart and Kevin's differences, Adam always felt comfortable in the Whitaker household. He believed theirs was a warm and loving home, and that any problems that they may have had existed behind closed doors and were no worse than any other typical American family.

It was apparent to many that Bart believed he was truly better than most people, and he did not suffer fools lightly. In a later counseling session with Dr. Lynne Ayres, he informed her that he truly did not care about having relationships with other human beings. Yes, he had a girlfriend—yes, he loved his family—but he did not want to be bothered with other people's trivialities. As a result, most of the people who came into contact with Bart viewed him as "cold."

Bart did, however, believe he was a fixer. According to Ayres, he told her that if people wanted something done, they would often turn to him. "If they wanted anything done," Bart surmised, "they would come to me, because they would know the job would be done well." Ayres was not exactly sure what "jobs" people would hit Bart up for.

The young man also informed the doctor that he struggled with the responsibility that others placed on him. Since he was so reliable, he believed others leaned on him to fix their problems, but he could handle it. He referred to himself as "Atlas," because he was able to "hold the whole world" on his shoulders. Indeed, according to Greek mythology, Atlas personified the quality of endurance and was condemned to bear the heavens upon his shoulders. In addition, Atlas had been appointed the guardian of the pillars that held the Earth and the sky asunder. These roles were often combined, and Atlas became the god who turned the heavens on its axis, causing the stars to revolve.

Bart also assured Ayres that he was a master manipulator. He bragged about how he could charm his high-school teachers into giving him an A in their classes, even if he did not deserve such a grade.

Bart also spoke about his future aspirations. He claimed he wanted to join the FBI, and believed he would be an ideal candidate, as he assumed they would want agents "who can think like criminals."

After Ayres's single session with Bart, she was appalled by what she felt existed within the young man. She remarked that his "profile does not seem consistent with

ADHD (attention-deficit/hyperactivity disorder), but more consistent with irritability, intolerance for incompetence of others, and social disconnects."

In just one meeting, Ayres determined that Bart was egomaniacal, extremely narcissistic, and removed emotionally from everyone around him, including his girlfriend, brother, and parents. She felt he believed he was better than everyone else around him, including her. She described their encounter as a "very disturbing interview, especially social disconnections."

In 1924, two young men, Nathan Leopold Jr., nineteen, and Richard Loeb, eighteen, who subscribed to the Nietzschean "superman" philosophy distorted its meaning to fit their own wicked scheme. Leopold and Loeb, who met as teenagers at the University of Chicago, came from Chicago aristocracy, such as it was, and were basically bored out of their skulls. Each young man believed he was far superior to his peers. They were constantly seeking new thrills to plumb themselves out of the boredom that their families, their neighborhood, and their friends afforded them. These seemingly well-bred, well-mannered pinnacles of upstanding youth were anything but.

From all outward appearances, Leopold and Loeb were the type of young men that mothers wanted their daughters to marry, and fathers wanted their sons to grow up to emulate. Unbeknownst to everyone around them, the two young men's ennui led to a life of lies, deceit, and petty crime. The young men would occasionally lift belongings from their fellow college mates out of the others' fraternity houses. Having been bestowed with great financial wealth due to their families, neither young man was wanting for material possessions. Indeed, the majority of the goods they pilfered were almost always well below a value they were customarily used to. Leopold and Loeb stole from others because they wanted to experience a thrill they never had, and hoped it would spark a fire within them.

As with any junkie, however, the initial rush would soon wear off for the college students, and they needed an even greater fix. Not soon after they began their minor thievery spree, Leopold and Loeb decided they wanted to experience what they believed would be the ultimate thrill: the taking of a human life.

Leopold, definitely the more dominant of the two young men, convinced Loeb that the act of murder of an innocent human being would fall perfectly in line with what Nietzsche allegedly preached. According to Leopold, total dominance over another person could only come from the complete desecration and annihilation of that individual. Until you actually snuff the last breath out from another soul, you were never in complete control of that person, no matter how much power you may have seemingly exerted over them. In a correspondence with Loeb, Leopold wrote, *A superman . . . is, on account of certain superior qualities inherent in him, exempted from the ordinary laws which govern men. He is not liable for anything he may do.*

Leopold and Loeb took their twisted misinterpretation of Nietzsche's "superman" philosophy to the ultimate, horrifying conclusion when they picked out a so-called "inferior" human being to slaughter, fourteen-year-old Bobby Franks.

The stalking, abduction, and subsequent murder of Franks was all too easy for the misanthropes, and only served to reinforce their beliefs that they were above and beyond their fellow humans.

Eventually, however, Leopold and Loeb were discovered, arrested, and paraded in front of the national media for what was then considered to be the first "Trial of the Century." Though the phrase has now been overused, as this occurred before the Lindbergh Baby kidnapping trials and the O.J. Simpson/Nicole Brown Simpson murder trial, it was an apt description.

Indeed, Leopold and Loeb retained one of the highest-profile attorneys of the day, Clarence Darrow, noted defender of the study of evolution the following year with his defense of high-school football coach and substitute science teacher John T. Scopes in the infamous Scopes Monkey Trial. Darrow was an adamant opponent of the death penalty, and even though he was no longer an active advocate for the court, he took the young men's cases pro bono to make sure they received the highest-quality defense. He hoped to make the argument that every American citizen, regardless of how despicable he might be or how heinous a crime he might have committed, is fully entitled to top-level representation before the court—especially if that defendant's punishment might include execution at the hands of the people.

Despite Leopold and Loeb's adherence to their credo promulgated, as they believed, by Nietzsche and their ability to murder Franks with the utmost of ease, their ultimate convictions and life imprisonments blew out the biggest hole in their belief that they were supermen, that they were far superior in intellect and physical prowess to their fellow lowly mortal travelers.

11

Bart Whitaker never had a problem attracting the fairer sex. He was considered pleasantly handsome, attractive, but not threatening. He could be described as having a gentle face, though something was a bit askew. Bart's right eyelashes were discolored white, due to a genetic condition known as poliosis, which is a decrease in the melanin in hair. As a result, he resembled a reverse negative of Alex, Malcolm McDowell's character in *A Clockwork Orange*, a vicious tale about the effects of entertainment and society on a young ringleader of a gang of slightly dimmer sidekicks. In the film, Alex has heavy black mascara on his right eyelashes. The unique feature made Bart's somewhat decent looks stand out even more.

One of the young ladies who caught Bart's white-lashed eye was his journalism classmate Lynne Sorsby. The pleasantly pretty brunette, with shoulder-length hair, found Bart to be an intriguing, if somewhat quiet, boy. Of course, she was a whole year older than Bart, so he would have to prove himself worthy of her attention. Actually, Lynne was a very giving, sweet girl who readily made friends. She never held her family's status as owners of an extremely successful construction equipment rental company over others. She was as sweet, likable, and normal a girl as any young man could want, and any family would readily welcome her into their open arms.

Lynne and Bart developed a strong friendship during their time together in journalism class. They enjoyed learning, studying together, and simply talking to one another. Their courtship lasted nearly a full year before they became an official couple. Bart truly believed that Lynne was "the girl," and he made every effort in the book not only to woo her, but to keep her happy and content while they were together.

Their relationship flourished over time, and Bart eventually began to open up to Lynne more and more. He felt as if he could trust her with his most intimate thoughts and well-preserved secrets. He knew he could trust her with his life, and that she would never judge him harshly for any flaws he may have buried deep within. He decided to hit her with a doozy.

"I'm adopted," he whispered to her one afternoon, when just the two of them were together.

"What?" replied Lynne, taken aback.

"I'm adopted," Bart reiterated.

"You're not adopted," Lynne laughed and punched Bart in the shoulder.

"No, it's true. I'm adopted." Bart insisted.

Lynne hesitated. "Seriously?"

"I'm dead serious." Bart remained stone-faced. "I have no idea who my biological parents are. Kent and Tricia adopted me when I was a tiny baby."

Lynne had no idea what to say. She simply looked quietly at Bart, with a touch of sympathy infiltrating her lovely face. Despite hearing the words coming out of his mouth, she knew what he was saying was not true. He had a way of speaking rather "cryptically, so only he and one other person would catch the gist of the conversation." Maybe, she thought, that's what he was doing when he claimed to be adopted. Yet, she never called him on it. She merely wrote it off as one of Bart's eccentricities, and that he was simply being a goof. Besides, she knew Bart loved his family dearly and would do anything for them. Though they did not speak about their families very often when together, Lynne always noted how Bart seemed very close to his. He told her he worried about his little brother, Kevin, who always seemed to struggle in school. Bart was worried Kevin would not graduate and make it to college and become successful. He was "very protective of Kevin." Lynne also believed that Bart got along just fine with his parents and never noticed any "ill will" expressed toward them. He definitely "never expressed any violent or hateful comments about anybody in his family to me," Lynne emphasized.

Bart and Lynne spent most of their time basking in each other's glow. She did notice a few other not-quite-normal character traits about Bart, which she thought nothing of at the time. The main one being that she believed Bart was a good manipulator. Lynne described Bart as someone who can "convince people to think the way he wants to, or believe the things he wants them to" believe.

Lynne also made note of the type of people he befriended. It was "usually people with low self-esteem" or "people who didn't think much of themselves." She never considered herself to fall within that catcgory.

12

Bart Whitaker spent his summer before his senior year at Clements High School, literally *inside* Clements High School. Regrettably, it was not under the best of conditions.

Bart and two of his friends decided they were up for a Nietzschean adventure. The three teenagers felt bored and wanted to cause some mayhem. Led by Bart, they agreed they would break into Clements High School for a little vandalism and theft.

Bart and his friends gathered together at Bart's house to discuss the reconnoitering of the campus. Once they agreed that they should enter the building through a skylight in the roof, they took off for the school, beginning their "mission impossible." The three teenagers scouted the location two times before they decided to proceed forward with their criminal activity.

When they finally went through with the burglary, one of the friends had dropped out. Bart and the one remaining friend dressed all in black, with gloves and masks—the works. They made their way to the campus, scaled the side of the building, crawled through the skylight, and entered inside the school.

Bart and his friend scampered around inside the building. Bart's friend seemed nervous, while Bart remained a beacon of calm. As they worked their way around the school's interior, they found the mother lode—a classroom full of audio-visual equipment. VCRs, television sets, laser disc players, and computers were at their disposal. Bart honed in on two computers, which he and his friend packed up and readied for transport. As the two boys rolled the computers toward the exit, Bart heard a large door slam closed. Bart looked at his buddy and motioned that they take off without their bounty.

Later that same night, Bart convinced his two friends to go to the school to complete the burglary. Like good foot soldiers, they did as they were told. When they met up with Bart to show him their take, he was pleased.

But Bart wanted more.

The three boys continued their illegal escapades, and they decided to target Clements High School once again. They hit the school a second time about a week later. They brazenly entered on a rope through an open window. This time, they stole two televisions, a VCR, and a laser disc player. They stowed the hot items in the bed of one of the friends' truck, and drove back to the other friend's house.

The three boys had broken into a school three times, had burgled the place twice, and had not smelled a whiff of trouble for their efforts. They were excited by their rewards, and were starting to feel invincible.

Bart, however, already seemed bored. Yes, he found breaking and entering to be thrilling at first, just as it felt good to steal the items and get away with it. But something was missing. It just did not seem dangerous enough. Whatever the reason was for his committing the thefts, there was something deeper rooted in Bart that propelled him toward his next criminal endeavor.

The game plan remained the same; it was the location that changed. Bart wanted to make it a little dicier this time. He decided they would burglarize Lakeview Elementary School, where his mother taught school, and was much beloved by student and staff alike.

Near the end of July, at approximately 1:00 A.M., the three boys made the trip to the school. For whatever reason, either cockiness or boredom, they did not plan things out as they had at Clements High School. They simply drove up to the school, located an unlocked window, and crawled inside.

Bart played point man, keeping an eye out for police, while his two pals scoped out the goodies there for the taking. The other two boys made their way through the school with their tiny *X-Files*-like penlights, located an ideal computer and printer, and hauled them out to Bart's navy blue Ford Explorer. The boys hopped into Bart's vehicle and drove off to one friend's house, where they hid the stolen items.

But they were not done for the night.

They continued their criminal crawl at the Highlands Elementary School, located less than two miles from Bart's home in Sugar Land. Again they made no preparations, but rather simply entered the school's premises through an open janitor's gate and scaled a plastic pipe to clamber over the school wall. Once inside the perimeter, they resumed their usual roles. Bart played lookout, while the other two boys found a way into the building by prying open a roof hatch. Once inside, the two wormed their way throughout the school, looking for more loot. When Bart was certain that his friends were safely inside, he followed. The three boys joined up and looked around for the front office. Once again, one of the friends scaled yet another gate to get into the office. Once inside, he spotted two computers, which he took. Bart then ran outside and back to his Explorer and paged the two other boys when all seemed clear. The two friends on the inside hauled the computers out of the building, placed them in the back of Bart's SUV, and they sped out of the area.

The boys were not done yet. A few days later, they decided to hit another school. It was Commonwealth Elementary, located on Commonwealth Boulevard, less than six miles from Bart's home. For this excursion, one of the boys climbed on top of the roof of the school, but he could not find a way inside. He jumped back down and told the other guys about the situation. They chose to head straight for the front door of the school and break open a padlock with a crowbar to gain entrance.

This time, the boys stole three computers and took off.

The following day, Bart took the stolen goods to a nearby Public Storage, where they had rented a storage unit on July 15.

When asked why he participated in so much criminal activity, Bart would simply answer, "I did this for adventure."

* * *

Needless to say, several people were not happy about his adventures. The first was the staff at Clements High School. When Bart was discovered to have participated in two burglaries at their school, they took swift and immediate action by expelling him.

The other people who were not happy were, of course, his parents. Bart's mother, Tricia, seemed to take her oldest son's actions very hard, especially since Bart had committed one of his thefts at her place of employment. Tricia seemed devastated by her son's inability to make the right choice; she practically went into hiding. Afraid that she would go out into public and be ridiculed by her friends, Tricia uprooted many of her normal routines. She stopped shopping at her usual grocery store, because she did not want to face her friends and be supremely embarrassed. She even convinced the family to switch churches so as to avoid any more uncomfortable situations.

After Bart's arrest, his parents sought out help in the form of a psychologist, Dr. Brendan O'Rourke, a licensed doctor since 1982 after she had received her master's degree from the University of Houston graduate school. O'Rourke had worked as a high-school counselor after college, and before beginning her work as a psychologist. She was uniquely equipped to deal with the adolescent mind, and the trials and tribulations experienced by teenagers.

Kent and Tricia Whitaker had been referred to Dr. O'Rourke through a mutual friend. They hoped the doctor would be able to conduct sessions with Bart, determine what his problem was, and assess that he would be well enough to return back to Clements High

School. They were looking for a letter of reinstatement for their son from Dr. O'Rourke so he could complete his senior year of high school at Clements.

Unfortunately for the Whitakers, Bart's meeting with Dr. O'Rourke did not turn out as they had hoped. The doctor spoke with Bart about his bad behavior and how he felt about what he had done. The doctor also conducted a Millon Clinical Multiaxial Inventory test on Bart to help her come up with an assessment of the young man. The test is "ideal for use with individuals being evaluated for emotional, behavioral, or interpersonal difficulties."

After meeting with Bart ten times, Dr. O'Rourke's conclusions were definitive and damning simultaneously. *My impression*, Dr. O'Rourke laid out clearly, *is the court system will impose adequate consequences to punish Bart and to bring about a self correction.* In other words, she did not recommend that Bart return to school, but rather doing a little time in jail would do him the most good.

Needless to say, the Whitakers were not happy with the initial diagnosis.

O'Rourke further detailed her position on Bart's mental disposition. She described Bart as *an egocentric man who has an inflated sense of self-importance, combined with an intense mistrust of others.* She added, *He has a disputatious demeanor that invariably invokes exasperation and animosity in friends, relatives and co-workers.* O'Rourke admitted that many of these traits are fairly common among teenagers, but Bart seemed to transcend most of the *Breakfast Club* clichés of teenagerdom.

His guiding principle is that of outwitting others, O'Rourke's test results continued, *exerting power over them before they can exploit him.* Apparently, many of

Bart's interactions with his peers, his teachers, and his own family were a sort of competition, a test of wills to see if Bart would come out on top and not be bested by those around him.

Another portion of the test revealed that Bart *may embellish trivial achievements despite the contradictions of others and* added that he was *easily provoked.* Even more damning, *he may express sudden and unanticipated brutality.* So, to add to his general mistrust of others, was his need to best his friends and foes in everything, combined with a volatile personality capable of destructive behavior. But that was not the end of it.

One final result about Bart from Dr. O'Rourke's test was that he possessed a *narcissistic personality trait,* which is a severe mental personality trait that is characterized by a *pervasive pattern of grandiosity, need for admiration, and a lack of empathy.*

One of the more telling traits of a narcissistic personality is that the people who have it tend to view those around them as *tools to accomplish their goals.* Others are merely there for the true narcissist as a means to an end, as a way of achieving whatever goals he has in mind that he is unable to accomplish on his own. Dr. O'Rourke explained that narcissism is a common trait among most teenagers; however, *to have the disorder is different.* She further explained that Bart was not conclusively diagnosed as having the disorder, but he did possess several of the traits that made up the disorder. As a result, she believed that many of Bart's scores, which had flown off the charts, were abnormal. She reasoned since Bart had come from an allegedly strong, close family with strong values, and since Bart had no prior criminal history, that the results must be skewed for some unknown reason.

Indeed, instead of diagnosing Bart with narcissistic personality disorder, as was suggested by the Millon Test results, Dr. O'Rourke concluded that Bart had adjustment disorder, a far less intense condition.

According to the Mayo Clinic, adjustment disorder is *a type of stress-related mental illness. You may feel anxious or depressed, or even have thoughts of suicide. You may not be able to go about some of your daily routines, such as work or seeing friends. Or you may make reckless decisions. In essence, you have a hard time adjusting to change in your life, and it has serious consequences.*

Despite all evidence to the contrary, Dr. O'Rourke opted to pen a recommendation letter for Bart to return back to high school. It would prove to be fruitless, however, as the administration of Clements High School rejected Bart's appeal and he was not readmitted. Instead, he transferred to Fort Bend Baptist Academy, a private school, for his senior year.

13

Nearly a thousand people showed up at the cavernous Sugar Creek Baptist Church, just two miles from the Whitaker home. Sadly, it was not for a joyous occasion, such as the marriage of one of its parishioners or a baptism of a newborn. Instead, it was to mourn the deaths of two of Sugar Land's most beloved members, Tricia and Kevin Whitaker.

Family members, friends of the family, and complete strangers intermingled inside the church, most in tears. When Kent and Bart Whitaker entered, in slings as a result of their gunshots, some in attendance gasped as they caught sight of both men for the first time after the murders. Others cried upon their entrance, shocked to see them in their injured states. Kent and Bart took their seats in the front pews and attempted to listen to their friends sing the praises of Tricia and Kevin.

Family friend and church pastor Matt Barnhill likened the murders to an earthquake. "In some communities in California, they have earthquakes. This is Sugar Land's earthquake. Our lives are shaken and our sense of safety and well-being is shattered." The eulogy was especially difficult for the confident and calm pastor, as he was so close to the Whitakers.

John Flores, one of Kevin's best friends, spoke to the assembled masses about his buddy and Tricia. "They signified Christ in all that they did and all that they were."

Brittany Barnhhill, Matt Barnhill's daughter and Kevin's good friend, spoke directly to Bart about his younger brother. "I cannot tell you how much Kevin looked up to you." Bart was somewhat taken aback, but remained stoic. "He wanted so badly to be like you." Bart blushed and fought to hold back yet more tears.

Finally another family friend spoke to the crowd, asking for donations to a reward fund to help find Tricia and Kevin's murderer. He concluded by adding, "The killer is still out there."

14

Tuesday, December 16, 2003, 11:00 P.M.
Sugar Land Police Department
Highway 6 South
Sugar Land, Texas

Detective Marshall Slot was ready to call it a night. He continued to pursue all possible leads in the murders of Tricia and Kevin Whitaker. He had spent almost the entire day at the police station, working on the case. Slot began to pack up his equipment and just as he was leaving, a young man came up and introduced himself to the detective.

"I'm Adam Hipp, sir." The young, very tall man extended his hand out. Hipp spent the morning at the funeral for Tricia and Kevin Whitaker.

Slot reciprocated, shook his hand, and replied, "What can I do for you, son?"

"I need to speak with you about Bart Whitaker. You are the officer handling the murders of Tricia and Kevin Whitaker, aren't you, sir?"

"Yes, sir, that would be me," Slot answered. "Please

have a seat." The detective gestured to a well-worn chair in front of his desk. Slot put his briefcase down and took his own seat. "So, what do you want to tell me about Bart Whitaker, Mr. Hipp?"

"I know Bart did it," a nervous Hipp replied. "And I'm pretty sure I even know how he did it."

"Well, son, how would you know something like that?"

"Because he told me he wanted someone to kill his parents and his younger brother, two years ago, sir."

The young man had the detective's full attention.

"Go on," Slot encouraged Hipp.

15

Tuesday, December 16, 2003, 11:05 P.M.
Sugar Land Police Department
Sugar Land, Texas

Adam Hipp sat down across from Detective Marshall Slot's desk. He had driven all the way from Dallas the night before, late at night, because he felt compelled to let someone in an authority position know what Bart Whitaker had tried to do a few years earlier. He felt tormented by the knowledge, and knowing now that someone had killed Bart's mother and brother made him feel even more compelled.

"How did you find out that members of the Whitaker family had been killed, Adam?" Detective Slot asked in an attempt to calm the young man down and get him focused. The officer began to record their conversation.

"I got a call from my girlfriend." Hipp seemed to relax a bit. "She told me that she read on the Internet that something had happened in the Sugar Lakes Subdivision in Sugar Land. Since she knew I used to

live in Sugar Land, she asked me if I knew where
Sugar Lakes was."

Simultaneously Hipp received an instant message
from a friend through his AOL service. His friend informed Hipp that a shooting had taken place at Bart
Whitaker's house on Heron Way in Sugar Land.

The following day, Hipp was able to confirm the information via two news articles about the shootings he
spotted online from two Houston-based television
news stations' websites. From these articles, Hipp was
initially able to glean that the shootings took place at
the Whitaker house; that Tricia had died as a result of
the attack, and that one of the brothers was dead. The
articles did not specifically mention whether it was
Bart or Kevin who had died. Soon thereafter, the
online news sources did specify that it was Kevin who
was dead.

After speaking with his girlfriend and filling her in
on his past with Bart, Hipp realized he needed to speak
with someone in the Sugar Land Police Department.

After explaining to Detective Slot how he met Bart,
Hipp got down to business. "I used to go visit him up
in Waco, when he was going to school at Baylor.
Sometimes we would travel together to Austin over
at UT (the University of Texas) and visit his girlfriend,
Lynne," Hipp recalled. After high school, Lynne attended college at the University of Texas at Austin,
while Bart went to Baylor, in Waco, Texas.

In February 2001, Hipp remembered, Bart started
to bring up an unusual topic, to say the least. "He
started talking about killing his family."

Detective Slot leaned in closer to the young man.
"Did that surprise you?" the detective wanted to know.

"Not really," Hipp replied nonchalantly. "I knew he

had grievances with his parents and his brother." Hipp took a sip of water and continued. "In the beginning, it seemed to be all talk. I just thought he was talking shit, you know. Just trying to act tough."

"How did this come up in conversation?" Detective Slot inquired.

"It just sort of came up out of the blue. He practically spat it out. He said to me, 'Are you still interested in getting lots of money?' Of course, I said, 'Yeah, I'm always going to be interested in making a lot of money.'"

"Then what?"

"That's when he said we should kill his parents."

"How did you respond?"

"Like I said, I thought he was full of shit, so I just sat there and listened to him," Hipp continued. "He started laying out the details of how he was going to kill his parents and collect their insurance money. It seemed to me as if he had thought about this before, but had not spent much time thinking about the plan."

"What exactly was his plan?" Detective Slot asked the young man.

"He had wanted to set his grandparents' lake house on fire with the entire family inside," Hipp recalled. "There was no doubt that his intention was to kill every single person inside there."

"Whose lake house did it belong to?"

"It was Bart's mother's side of the family," Hipp answered. "The Bartlett family, his grandparents, cousins, everyone."

"What about his parents and brother?" the detective followed up.

"They were all supposed to be there."

"What'd you say to him?"

"Nothing. I just kind of nodded my head." Hipp nodded his own head yes. "I didn't take any of it seriously. I mean, it seemed to me at the time that *he* wasn't taking it seriously. It was definitely not well-thought-out, so I figured he was just venting off some steam."

Hipp explained how Bart planned to deflect attention away from himself. "He would be in the lake house when the fire was set. He would also make sure that he got burned in the process."

"Why would he want to get burned?" Slot asked.

"So as not to be suspicious for having survived the fire," Hipp replied.

"What was the motivation for wanting to do this?"

"His first cousins were in line to inherit the family company, Bartlett Construction Company," Hipp recalled. "He wanted to position himself to be in control of that business."

"He obviously didn't follow through with the plan that time, did he?" Detective Slot asked Hipp.

"Correct. He did not."

"So, did you guys ever talk about it again?"

"Yes, sir," Hipp replied. "He brought it up again, not too long afterward. He asked me if I wanted to help him and make some money. I told him no, and that there was no way I could do something like that."

"How did he react to that?"

"He didn't seem too pleased, but he kept talking about how he was going to do it, like it would convince me to change my mind or something," Hipp added.

"Did he say how he planned on killing his family?" Detective Slot needed to know.

"Yes, sir. He said it would be a fake robbery. That he would get his family out of the house, and that one of us would hide out inside. When they returned to the house, our other guy would shoot them as they came in. And Bart would get shot, too, to make it look real."

Detective Slot had difficulty keeping the stunned look off his face. This was the exact same story Bart told him the day after the murders. And now, here was an old friend of his corroborating the details, but implicating Bart directly in the murder of his mother and brother.

"Now, when did you say you guys first talked about killing Bart's family?"

"February 2001, sir," Hipp answered.

"Do you know any of the specifics on how he wanted to accomplish this?" Slot asked.

"He said his family would be out of the house, and he would provide someone else with a key and an alarm code to go into the house and stay in the living room and wait for his family to return," Hipp remembered. "He said it wouldn't be that hard to do, and that the shooter would just have to wait for the first two people to come in the door, all the way in, and they'd be able to shoot them at close range."

Slot sat quietly, checking to make sure that his tape recorder still worked properly.

"Bart said that after it was over, the shooter would take off through the back door, run through their yard, jump a fence, and meet up with another person who had a car ready to go."

Hipp began to unspool even more aspects of the supposed murder plot by Bart Whitaker. "He even told me where the shooter would stand, to make sure he maximized his efforts. He even talked about what kind ot clothes the shooter should wear. He suggested black clothing, along with a mask to hide the shooter's face."

"What did he say about shooting him?" Slot asked.

"He said he wanted someone to shoot him in the arm," Hipp responded. "He wanted it to be where it would heal, like muscle tissue or something. He mentioned it could be in different places, like the arm or shoulder, just so long as it was in a spot that could heal relatively easily."

"Was there supposed to be some kind of struggle?"

"Yes, sir. He was interested in making it look like he was in the position of tackling the shooter. Almost as if he were apprehending the shooter. He wanted it to look like the shooter had to shoot at him to try and get away."

"What else did Bart say about this?" Slot inquired.

Hipp paused and looked directly at the detective. "He basically warned me that I was not supposed to talk to anyone else about what he had said. He then added that if I were to talk to anyone else besides him about the plot, that either I or someone important to me might get hurt."

"He threatened you?"

"Not in so many words, but, yeah. He threatened me."

"What'd you do?"

"I just nodded and told him it was strictly between the two of us."

Detective Slot decided to change the direction of the conversation. "This plan did not, however, come to fruition, either, correct?"

"Correct," Hipp replied.

"So, was that the end of it for you two?"

"No, sir. There was a third plan."

"A third plan?" Slot asked incredulously.

"Yes, sir," Hipp responded. "For whatever reason, he decided to change it up a little bit. It was a further maturing of what we had talked about before." Hipp paused, took a deep breath, and continued. "Only this time, it was more geared to him wanting me to be the shooter. Having me catch his family early in the morning to do it."

"Was this the first time that he asked you to participate [directly] in killing his family?" Detective Slot asked.

"Yes, sir. For the earlier incarnations, I was simply his sounding board. Now he wanted me to be the triggerman."

"Now, when you say 'his family,' who all was he referring to?"

"Kevin, Tricia, and Kent."

"Tell me how he wanted you to kill his family."

"I was supposed to do it before Kevin would leave for school, or his dad left for work," Hipp recalled. "He told me if I was there before eight in the morning that the whole family would probably still be there, or I would catch his mom and brother on their way out to school." Hipp continued, "Bart told me, 'If my dad's there, then you can catch him off-guard as well. If not, I'll drive you over to my dad's place of business, and you or I can shoot him there.'"

"Did you take him seriously this time?" Slot asked.

"Since he was trying to get me involved, absolutely. Yes, sir. And I didn't want to have anything to do with it," Hipp protested. "He told me he was going to get the weapon, drive me from Waco to Sugar Land, and take me to his parents' house and his dad's place of business, in case we had to go there."

"How did he want you to do it?"

"Just shoot them as they walked out of the door."
Hipp shook his head in disbelief.

"Do you remember when you and Bart had these most recent discussions?"

"Yes, sir. It was April 2001."

"How much further did this plan go?" Slot asked.

"Like I said, I didn't want to have anything to do with it. Bart said he would call me when he was ready for us to do it, but I continually begged off," Hipp continued. "Finally, sometime in April, I got a call from him late one night. He told me I had missed his initial call to let me know it was going down. He then said that he had been on his way down to Sugar Land, but that something had come up and he had to turn around. He didn't tell me what had happened."

Hipp told Slot that he had been staying with his girlfriend at her apartment when he received the call on his cell phone from Bart. When she asked who it was, Hipp told her everything that Bart had tried to get him to do. The couple was scared and not sure what to do.

"I didn't talk to Bart again for, like, three or four weeks," Hipp recalled. "I was scared he was gonna go after my girlfriend or my family or something. After that, I did everything in my power to separate myself from him. I ignored his phone calls. I avoided any contact with him. I just made sure to focus on my studies and to graduate from Wharton County Junior College. I never really spoke to him again."

"So that was the last time you had any contact with Bart?"

"Yes, sir. And then I heard about his mom and brother getting killed. It just seemed too similar to what he had always talked about with me to be a coincidence. So I knew I had to talk to someone about it."

"Did you drive down here?" Slot queried.

"No, sir. I drove down here for Patricia and Kevin's funeral."

"Did you see Bart while you were there?"

"Yes, sir."

"Did you speak to him?"

"Yes, sir. I just told him how sorry I was to hear what had happened to his mom and brother."

"Did you say anything about his previous plans to kill his family?"

"No, sir. I just acted like someone who would be at a funeral."

After nearly two hours of conversation, Detective Slot decided to give the kid a break. They stood up from their chairs, stretched their legs, and got something from the soda machine. When they returned, however, Slot decided to bring up an unusual topic. "Are you aware that Crime Stoppers is offering up reward money for information leading to the arrest of the killer or killers in this case?"

"Yes, sir," Hipp replied. "I heard that there was reward money for helping to catch the killer."

"Do you know how much it is?" Slot asked.

"I thought I heard from someone that it was somewhere between twenty and twenty-five thousand dollars."

"Are you interested in the reward money?"

"No, sir. I'm not interested in that. My grandmother helps me pay my rent," Hipp responded. "She also helps me out by taking me out to eat a couple of times a week. My car is paid for, and my student loans are being taken care of."

"Well, that doesn't answer my question," Slot said pointedly. "Do you want the reward money?"

"Well, sir, I spoke with my girlfriend earlier today about it. I told her that the reward money should be much greater."

Slot was intrigued.

"I told her it should be more around one hundred thousand dollars," Hipp continued. "I figured the life insurance company stood to lose a heck of a lot more money on this."

"That still doesn't answer my question, Mr. Hipp," Slot countered. When he did not get a response back from Hipp, he added, "If you had this reward money, what would you do with it?"

"I don't know. I guess I would pay off the rest of my school loans and get those all cleared up."

Detective Slot made sure to soak up all of this additional information about Bart Whitaker. He stopped, looked up at Hipp, and asked point-blank, "Son, were you a part of Bart's plan to kill his parents?"

16

Fall 1998 to Spring 1999
Baylor University
Penland Residence Hall
South Fifth Street
Waco, Texas

John William "Will" Anthony was a bright-eyed, bushy-tailed newcomer to the state of Texas from the adjacent state of Arkansas. His first day on the campus of Baylor University was already an eye-opener. Even though he lived in Little Rock, somewhat of a metropolis, he had no idea what he was in store for in college.

Will was a bit of a self-proclaimed nerd. He loved movies, studying, and playing endless hours of video games. He was never good at making friends, and was worse than simply socially awkward. Needless to say, he was ecstatic to make fast friends with another fellow Penland Hall dorm mate, Justin Peters. The two young men shared the same passions of film, school, and video games. Will and Justin teamed up and became an inseparable duo.

It was only a matter of days before the duo became a trio.

One day during the first week of college, Will and Justin were returning to Will's dorm room when they heard the familiar beckoning sound of starcrafts destroying unforeseen worlds, punctuated by the unmistakable and inevitable groans to follow.

"Shit!" the boys heard emanating from across the hall.

Will and Justin decided to investigate. They crossed the hall to eavesdrop on their neighbor. Sure enough, the unforgettable sounds of lasers firing and people screaming could be heard. The two young men stood up straight and smiled at one another. Will rapped on the door.

Nothing.

Will knocked again.

"Go away, I'm busy!" hollered a male voice from inside the dorm room.

Will was persistent. He continued to knock.

"Hold on." The man inside sighed with exasperation. Suddenly the sounds of the video game dissipated. The door opened swiftly, as if a secret password had been uttered at a magic castle. "What do you want?" grumbled the occupant of the lair. The young man looked disheveled, and none too pleased to be disturbed of his quest.

"Hi, we heard your video game and—" Will began to speak before he was cut off.

"Look, if it's too loud, I'll turn it down." The young man smirked in disgust and began to turn away and close the door on them.

"No, no, no. That's cool," called out Will before the

man could shut his door. "We're gamers, too!" he added eagerly.

The man stopped, turned back toward the two young men, and simply said, "Cool. C'mon in."

Thus began the tight friendship of Will Anthony, Justin Peters, and Bart Whitaker.

Three gamers with a mutual passion—online video games. RTS—real-time strategy video games. Soon their time consisted of hanging out, watching movies, and playing video games together. "Basically being nerds," Anthony described later.

The three gamers had made other friends during their first year at Baylor, but they were by far the closest among the group. It was always games, movies, skipping class.

Will Anthony never really felt comfortable at Baylor. "I always believe I went there more for my family than for myself. I just never really fit in there." Bart and Justin also seemed to be cut from the same cloth. "I don't think either one of them felt comfortable at Baylor," Anthony recalled. "None of us fit in with the other students. You either had to be in a fraternity or you had to be really into a Christian lifestyle, what with being a big-time Baptist school and everything."

Will, Bart, and Justin used to sit around and talk about what they considered to be the hypocrisy of many of the Baylor students. "Just typical church bullshit," Anthony recalled. "These kids would be partying all week, skipping classes, doing drugs and getting drunk, or screwing around, and then when it came time to be the good little churchgoing monkeys, they were all bullshit. They acted like they never did anything wrong, and worse, they would look down on those who did not go to Baylor or those who weren't

Baptists. All that crap about going to Hell if you did not share their same belief systems. We just thought it was a load of horseshit."

In addition to the overwhelming religious aspect of Baylor, another facet that played an important part on campus was that of the fraternities. "None of us were in a fraternity," Anthony recalled. "And, of course, if you were not a part of the frat world, there was a whole 'nother group you were ostracized from."

Bart and the boys preferred one another's company and playing video games over everything and everyone else. Bart and Will, in particular, seemed to hit it off as time wore on. They spent many hours talking about their hopes, their goals, their dreams, and how they planned to achieve all of them. They also spoke about their families and friends back home and their other loved ones. They were very open about how they communicated with one another and were able to share practically everything with each other. They trusted each other implicitly.

Bart described his new friends as "people who were out of control" and "depressed and confused." He added that he was "less self-conscious around them." Finally he summed up their relationships as "Like attracts like. We just found each other."

Bart and Will's friendship grew as they hung out together more and more. Luckily, about halfway through their freshman semester, Will's roommate dropped out of college and moved out of their dorm room. Will asked Bart if he wanted to move across the hall and in with him. Bart readily accepted the invitation and the two developed an even tighter bond.

Will also had a love of music. Playing music was his dream, and that was what he really wanted to do with his life. He played his guitar for Bart and also let him know he played piano. He wrote many of his own songs, and Bart was quite impressed with his roommate's skills. Bart told Will about several friends of his in the music business down in Houston. He said he would introduce Will to them in hopes of providing a springboard for his musical aspirations. Bart was true to his word and took Will down to Houston to meet his friends; however, nothing came out of the meeting for Will. Nonetheless, Will was honored that Bart thought highly enough of his skills to make the introduction. He was impressed that Bart was a man of his word and not just someone who would blow smoke up his ass.

Over time, Bart and Will's relationship became close enough to where Bart felt he could confide more personal information about himself to his roommate. He mainly spoke about his family back in Sugar Land. He would often complain to Will that his parents tended to favor his little brother, Kevin, over him. He believed it was because Kevin struggled more in school and needed the extra attention. Bart often felt like he was neglected, since he was more intelligent and more capable of handling himself than Kevin.

Will could sympathize. He, too, felt like he could never live up to his family's expectations, albeit for different reasons than what Bart claimed. Will's older sister was always the star in the Anthony family, as far as Will was concerned, and as far as his parents were concerned. She had a very successful college career and had translated that success to even more rewards in the working world. Everything came easy to her—grades, interpersonal communication skills, earning a living. Meanwhile, Will's musical aspirations seemed to bring only disappointment for his family.

Bart and Will were two commiserating souls who "got" one another. They knew what it felt like to be on the outside peering in, even among their own family units. College life only shone the spotlight on their removal from the rest of the so-called "normal" world. Thus, they chose each other's companionship and their big-boy toys, such as video games and music as their escapes.

One aspect of Bart's family life that he occasionally spoke about was his parents' religious devotion. Bart did not consider himself to be a Christian, and he complained to Will that it was difficult not being one in his family. It further compounded his outsider status within his family.

Bart and Will skipped classes one day to play video games. It was a day just like any other during the spring semester at school. Suddenly Bart turned to Will and said, "I want to kill my parents."

Will laughed. "Yeah, me too." He continued focusing on the screen, where the video game held his real reality.

Bart continued playing as well. After nearly half a minute, he said it again. "I want to kill my parents." He glanced over at Will to see if there was any response. All he saw was a grin.

"I'm serious, dude," Bart insisted. "I want to kill my family." Bart smiled as he continued playing his video game. "What do you think would be the best way to go about doing it?"

Will laughed and shook his head. He knew Bart

had a warped sense of humor and was just yanking his chain. "You are one sick puppy, my friend."

Bart nodded. "Okay, if you were going to help me do it, what do you think would be the easiest way of doing it and not getting caught?"

Will decided to play along. "I'd say, having them run off a cliff in the car. Everyone would think it was an accident."

"Yeah, but you might leave paint marks on their car, or they might not even die from the fall," Bart countered.

"Well, what about a botched robbery?" Will asked.

"That would probably work much better, because you could have control of the crime scene," Bart added. "You could have someone wear dark clothes and gloves, so no one could tell what you looked like, and you wouldn't leave behind any fingerprints. And even if you did, you could wipe them down."

And on it went.

Bart would later describe these early discussions as "just another evolution of the game that me and Justin and Will were playing, which was to see who could be the worst."

Will glanced over at Bart. He liked Bart a lot. He was a bit warped, but he knew he was a good guy and a great friend. He simply laughed and repeated, "You are one sick puppy, Bart. One sick puppy, indeed."

Will and Bart remained good friends, and with Justin as well.

Unfortunately, their triumvirate would be broken up. Will's penchant for hanging out in his dorm room did not bode well for his academic career. His failure to attend class, much less take final exams, garnered him a one-way ticket out of Baylor after his freshman year. Will packed his bags and took off back home to Little Rock, Arkansas.

Apparently, Bart's magnetism had a great pull on Will. After working a miserable retail job several months, and still feeling left out of the loop in Little Rock, Will made a bold choice. He wanted to be near friends. He wanted to be near people who understood him. Those two people were Bart Whitaker and Justin Peters. Will packed his bags one more time and made the move back to Waco. He would not attend school at Baylor, but he would be back in the city where his true friends were.

Will spent lots of time with Bart. Just a few months after his return to Waco in the spring of 2000, Will noticed Bart was reverting back to talking about killing his parents.

"I need to talk to you about something," Bart informed Will one afternoon when he invited him over.

"Sure, man. What is it?" Will replied. He was concerned for his friend because Bart seemed stressed.

"Remember when I used to kid around with you and tell you how I wanted to kill my parents?" Bart quizzed Will.

"Yeah, of course."

"Remember how you always thought I was kidding around?"

"Yeah, yeah. Of course, you were kidding around."

"I'm not kidding around anymore," Bart stated as he looked Will directly in the eyes.

"Hmm?" Will muttered. He was not quite sure what his friend had just told him.

"I'm not kidding around," Bart said in a stern voice.

Will stopped. He looked at Bart closely. Then he burst

out laughing. "Dude, I swear to God, you are one sick motherfucker. You had me going there for a minute. Kill your parents. Your parents are nice, man. Plus, I know you wouldn't hurt a flea. It's not in you, man."

Bart waited patiently while his friend nervously ticked off the reasons why Bart was not going to kill his parents.

"Will, I know you think I'm a big joker, but I am dead serious," Bart declared. "I need to get rid of my parents. I need to have them killed, and I want you to help me do it."

Will stood dumbfounded, his mouth literally agape. He had no idea what to say. Finally he piped up with the only thing that came to mind. "Why do you want to kill your parents?"

Bart was ready for the inevitable question. "Because my parents are worth a lot of money, and I want to collect on their insurance."

Will seemed surprised that Bart had an answer so readily available. "How much money would you get?"

"They're worth more than a million dollars," Bart calmly responded. "I would assume at least that much, if not more."

Will knew Bart did not like his parents. He had no idea, however, that he would seriously entertain the thought of killing them for insurance money, or anything else for that matter.

"I need your help," Bart said to Will. "I need for you to help me do it."

"What?" a stunned Will replied. "You want me to help you kill your parents?" Will rubbed his temple, trying to comprehend what in the hell was going on here. Why in the world would one of his best friends truly consider killing his parents, and then, on top of it all, ask him to help him do it?

"Yes," Bart replied. "I need for you to help me pull this off." Bart looked at Will in all earnestness.

Will slowly shook his head in the negative. "No, no, no. No way, man. I can't help you do something like that. It's your parents, Bart. You don't hate them enough to kill them. Hell, man, everyone gets sick of their parents from time to time. Some people might even hate their parents. But not yours, man. They're like fucking Ozzie and Harriet, dude."

"I'm tired of all their bullshit, Will," Bart attempted to explain his position. "I told you before, they favor Kevin over me. They always side with him. And they are hypocrites. I can't stand all the do-gooder bullshit act that they put on. It's a front. They are nothing like what they portray themselves to be. They go around acting like they're all super Christian and shit, but it is all a lie. It. Is. A. Lie."

"Bart, man. I don't know, buddy. I don't know. I don't think I can—"

"You can do it, Will," Bart interrupted. "I know you can do it," he insisted.

"Why? Why, Bart?" Will asked. "I can see where you might want to do something, but they're your parents, not mine. What good is it going to do for me? Why would I do something so risky?"

"I already told you." Bart smiled at his pal.

"What?"

"Money. I'm going to get a ridiculous amount of money from my mom and dad's life insurance," Bart reminded Will, as though they were just discussing a simple business transaction between two friends. "I will give you enough money to make sure you can do what you want to do."

Will stopped to consider what Bart just told him.

Bart continued, "You can finally play your music. You can write songs and rehearse and start up a band and land some gigs. You can finally be what you always wanted to be—a working musician. You won't have to mess with going to school or moving back home to your parents. You can finally live your dream."

For the first time since Bart brought up the idea, Will seemed intrigued. Bart was obviously appealing to Will's own self-interests, and Will could not help but think of the possibilities if he had a large influx of cash. It was not as if Will needed the money, he was the son of a very well-to-do dentist. Furthermore, it was not as if Will's bank account had been emptied by his college tuition, because his parents had paid for his schooling. He did not even have to work while attending Baylor. Nonetheless, the allure of money was strong for him.

Despite Will's seemingly steady financial situation, he still had a desire to prove himself. He was determined not to leech off his family, and wanted to make it on his own. He had no idea how difficult it truly was going to be.

"I'll think about it," Will told Bart.

Bart Whitaker smiled. "Thank you, Will. Thank you."

17

Fall 1998
Baylor University
Waco, Texas

Bart Whitaker and Will Anthony's other friend at Baylor was a freshman named Justin Peters. Like Bart and Will, Justin was an intelligent young man with a hankering for video games and a rather bored disposition toward life. He was intelligent, almost too intelligent for his own good. He aced high school and was rewarded with National Merit Scholarship status. His college was covered. It all could have been so easy.

As with Will, however, Justin seemed more interested in hanging out with his new friends and playing video games. Justin was majoring in bioinformatics, "the use of techniques, including applied mathematics, informatics, statistics, computer science, artificial intelligence, chemistry, and biochemistry, to solve biological problems usually on the molecular level."

At least, that is what he told his family. In reality, he was majoring in EverQuest.

Justin was always a bit of an outcast. Too smart for his own good. He never really fit in with any of the cliques in school. He did, however, have one friend who thought the best of him, no matter what. Jennifer Japhet, Justin's best friend since seventh grade, was way out of his league. She was beautiful, intelligent, and popular with the guys and the girls. Everyone knew Jennifer, and everyone was crazy about her, including Justin.

Justin and Jennifer attended high school in San Antonio at a magnet school called Health Careers High School. It was geared toward high-achieving students who believed they might consider a career in the profession of medicine upon graduation. It is an extremely difficult school to get into, with high admission standards and a tough selection process. The students who attended Health Careers High School were usually self-motivated, had specific goals they wanted to obtain, and would usually meet their objectives.

There was another reason Justin was so fond of Jennifer. He had a physical handicap. His right arm had no attached tendon, thus rendering it nearly useless. Jennifer never made fun of his malady and never brought it up in conversation. She simply accepted Justin for who he was and how he looked.

Though she became good friends with Justin, Jennifer saw their relationship as purely platonic. Indeed, Justin viewed her almost more like an older sister rather than an object of his affection. When Jennifer and Justin graduated from high school, however, they both made plans to attend college at Baylor. Justin never let on that the sole reason he applied there was so he could be closer to her.

Justin and Jennifer, however, did not spend much

time together during their freshman year at Baylor. Jennifer had joined a sorority, and the majority of her time was split between her sorority sisters and her classes. Justin, on the other hand, found himself hanging out with Will and Bart playing video games.

Justin felt he had quite a bit in common with Will and Bart. They all loved playing video games, they had similar tastes in music, and they all enjoyed many of the same movies, mainly action and sci-fi flicks. The three young men made a point to attend a screening of the revolutionary hi-tech film *The Matrix,* and all three immediately fell in love with it.

During their sophomore year at Baylor, in the fall of 1999, after Will Anthony dropped out of school, Justin and Bart decided to move into an apartment off campus together. They were joined by Sal Davis, a friend of Justin's from high school, who also attended Baylor.

Justin's world came crashing to a brutal halt soon after he moved in with Bart. Justin's high-school girlfriend, whom he no longer dated, was killed in a freak automobile accident back in his hometown. Justin was devastated and completely beside himself when he heard the news. He was never fully able to pull himself out of the haze for several months. He went into a severe depression and locked himself away from the rest of the outside world.

Bart tried his best to help his roommate and friend during his time of need. It seemed like an unmanageable task, however, because Justin would hole himself up in his room in their apartment and not come out for days. He started to cover up the windows with thick brown paper, and never turned on any lights in his room. He had developed a mourning cave and was in no hurry to rush his hibernation.

Justin's depression continued, and it began to affect his grades at Baylor. He refused to attend class, and he was so discombobulated during the few that he actually made it to, he was unable to function and make passing grades.

Bart continued to try and help Justin out of his funk. One way was to get him out of the apartment and into another city. Bart decided to take Justin down to Sugar Land to meet his family. They made it there twice. Justin found Bart's parents to be very sweet, accommodating, and humble. He also believed Bart's brother, Kevin, was a very nice young man.

During these trips to Sugar Land, Bart began to pepper Justin with his own tales of woe—namely, how much he despised his parents and also his little brother. Bart's main complaint about his family was that they were hypocritical Christians. They acted all superior over non-Christians, when, in reality, they were far from the idyllic symbol of Christianity.

Bart's rumblings against his parents and brother continued when the boys returned to Waco. He kept harping on how much he did not like them. After having met them in person, Justin did not understand how Bart could feel that way. Justin did understand how a son could find resentment against his parents, especially if the majority of things that Bart said about them were true.

Around November 1999, Bart started in on Justin. "You know what I'd like to do, Justin? Kill someone and see if I can get away with it. Commit the ultimate crime and see if I could not get caught."

Justin knew Bart had a predilection for dark humor. He laughed in spite of himself.

"No, I'm serious," Bart continued. "Could you imagine what it would feel like to actually take another human being's life, and then have the intelligence and cunning to get away with it. That would be the ultimate high. Better than any stupid video game or murder in a movie."

Just as Will reacted when Bart talked about the ultimate murder theory, Justin believed Bart was simply messing with him. So, instead of acting appalled, Justin played along. "Yeah, man. What do you have in mind?"

Bart started telling Justin all the fun things they could do together if they only had money. They could take trips, go skiing, buy a yacht. "All we have to do is get some money," Bart declared rather nonchalantly.

"And how do you propose we do that?" Justin queried.

"Kill my parents," Bart stated emphatically. "Kill my parents."

"Kill your parents?"

"Yeah. We kill my parents," Bart said with a serious tone to his voice. "They have lots of life insurance money. They're dead—*bam!* The money is mine. I'll give you some of it, and we can do whatever we want to. It's that easy."

"Bart," Justin said. "You are crazy. You'll never be able to get away with killing someone close to you. Family members are always at the top of the list when it comes to suspects."

Bart nodded. It was a good point.

"You would need to kill someone else that you

weren't related to," Justin added, still playing along with Bart.

"But then there would be no way to get the money," Bart countered. "No, it definitely has to be my parents."

Justin shook his head and chuckled. "That is messed up." He still did not believe his roommate was serious. "But I like it." He had no idea whether Bart was serious and, frankly, he did not care.

Over the course of the next few months, Bart kept up the "kill my parents" litany with Justin. Bart had upped the ante, however, by asking Justin to help him accomplish his morbid task. Instead of telling Bart to stop, or calling the police on him, Justin continued to play along.

Finally, the following fall 2000, Bart's persistent talk about killing his family seemed to turn into a reality. For the first time, Justin finally began to realize that his roommate had not been joking around. He had never been *just* joking around. Justin could sense that Bart truly wanted to murder his parents. And he seemed to be okay with that thought. Justin explained his position thusly: "I was extremely unhappy, and I guess I figured I might as well be unhappy with money."

Bart never promised Justin a specific amount of money if he helped him kill his parents. Bart merely told Justin that his parents were worth more than a million dollars, and that if they were dead, he would collect the insurance money. Bart would then give Justin more than his fair share for helping him out.

Bart eventually let Justin know that he had also recruited Will Anthony into the fold. Justin had no problem with Will's inclusion, since he was good friends with him, too. He was actually closer to Will than he was with Bart, so he found it reassuring to know that all three were involved.

The three young men would usually gather at Bart and Justin's apartment to lay out the plans on how they were going to murder Bart's parents. All three would participate in the discussions, though Bart was usually the ringleader. Justin and Will, however, would attempt to pick apart his suggestions in an attempt to make the crime foolproof.

After several weeks of dissecting and rethinking strategies, a plan was devised. All three men were to travel down to Sugar Land. Will and Justin would follow Bart in a separate car. When they arrived, Bart would get his parents out of their house under the ruse of a celebration dinner.

Meanwhile, Justin and Will would hide inside their car behind Bart's parents' home. Once they were assured that the Whitakers were gone, Will would sneak into their home via a back window, which Bart would leave unlocked. Once inside, he would have access to a hidden gun kept in Bart's brother's room. Will would then wait, patiently, with gun in hand until the Whitakers returned from their meal. He would be alerted by Justin, who was equipped with a walkie-talkie, so he could let Will know when the family arrived. Bart actually would have the other walkie-talkie to clue Justin in whenever they would be leaving the restaurant.

It was also agreed upon that Will would be dressed in all-black from head to toe. This would prevent him from being described by any potential witnesses. Furthermore, Will was advised that he needed to make the inside of the house look as if someone had attempted to burgle the home. No specifics were mentioned as to how to do so. The purpose of the burglary scene would be to throw the police off the scent and make them think it was simply a botched burglary that escalated, unfortunately, to murder.

To draw attention away from Bart, Will was supposed to shoot him as well. Of course, he was not supposed to shoot to kill, only to maim, so he would shoot his former roommate in the arm. That way, Bart could say he struggled with the shooter in an attempt to apprehend him and subsequently remove any doubt as to whether or not he was involved in the killings.

Bart's brother, Kevin, was not to be a part of the murder, only Bart's mother and father.

The plans were agreed upon by all three young men in December of 2000. Bart decided that just before Christmas would be the best time to execute his plans. He convinced both men to be ready to go forward in just a matter of days.

Less than a week later, Bart made the call. The three friends gathered together at Bart and Justin's apartment and prepared for their excursion. They did just as they had planned. Will and Justin followed behind Bart in a separate vehicle, and they made their way down to Sugar Land. Bart called up the other two guys on the walkie-talkie and told them that they were all going to meet in the parking lot of the restaurant, where Bart would bring his parents. It was a slight deviation from the plan, but it made more sense, because no one in his parents' neighborhood would get suspicious seeing a strange vehicle parked on the side of the street with someone inside.

When they arrived at the restaurant, Bart got out of his truck and walked over to Will and Justin. "All right, this is the restaurant. I'll be bringing my parents up here in about half an hour Why don't you guys just hang out here until I call you, and then you can head over to my parents' house."

Will and Justin nodded.

Bart handed Justin the walkie-talkie. "Here you go. This way you can let Will know when we are returning home. Oh, and remember, don't answer my phone call. When you see my number on your phone, you will know it's time." Bart did not want a record of any completed phone calls from his cell phone in case police decided to pin the crime on him.

Justin took the walkie-talkie and stated, "Okay."

Bart tapped Justin's car door and said, "I'll call you when we are leaving."

As soon as Bart turned his back and headed toward his truck, Will pulled out the black clothes he was supposed to wear. He began changing into them.

The pair waited in silence.

Thirty minutes later, their calmness was broken. Justin's cell phone lit up with a loud, clanging sound. It was Bart. They must be ready to go, he thought. "All right, Will, let's go," he stated as he took a deep breath and fired up the engine.

Will said nothing.

Justin shifted the vehicle into gear and pulled out of the restaurant parking lot. The fact that this was the location of the Whitakers' last supper did not enter into his mind. He was on a mission. He was focused and he needed to stay alert.

The two young men made their way to the Sugar Lakes Subdivision. Both had been to Bart's parents' home in the recent past, so they were pretty confident on how to get into the neighborhood and past the security gate, and where to find the house.

Justin pulled onto Heron Way and drove down to the Whitaker residence. Once in front of the house, he looked at Will, nodded, and idled the vehicle. Will exited the vehicle and made his way to the backyard and the unlocked window, left open by Bart. Justin then drove the car around to the back of the Whitaker house and parked it so he could wait for everything to go down and then provide the getaway car for Will.

Less than two minutes later, however, their plans suddenly changed.

"Come get me!" Justin could hear Will's voice emanating from the speaker of the walkie-talkie. "Dude, come get me now!" Will sounded urgent, but he spoke in hushed tones.

"What are you talking about?" Justin asked. "It's only been two minutes. What the hell is going on?"

"Just. Come. Get me!" Will stated through clenched teeth.

Justin drove around to the front of the house. He pulled up to the curb and saw Will slink over to the vehicle. He looked rather conspicuous in the middle of the front yard dressed in all black. Will got into the car and said nothing. Justin drove off and out of the neighborhood.

Several minutes passed before Justin spoke up. "What happened back there?"

"Bart didn't turn off the house alarm," Will responded.

"What? What do you mean?"

"When I went to go open the window," Will continued, "the damn house alarm went off."

Justin found this unusual, since he did not hear any alarm sound. "I didn't hear anything."

"I'm telling you, man, it went off."

Justin doubted the veracity of his friend's story, but he did not press the issue. Instead, he drove the two of them all the way back home to Waco. When they arrived, Will silently packed his bags into his own vehicle and drove back home to Arkansas. He wanted nothing to do with Bart Whitaker ever again.

With Will's departure, Justin believed his nagging suspicions were confirmed—no alarm had gone off. Instead, Will got cold feet and had chickened out.

Justin was not looking forward to hearing from Bart, once everything settled down. He assumed his friend was wondering what the hell was going on, since there was no altercation.

Later that night, Justin finally heard from Bart.

"Justin, where are you?" Bart wanted to know.

"Back at school, Bart," Justin responded.

"Is Will with you?"

"No, he took off. He seemed pretty spooked about the whole thing," Justin told his roommate. "Bart, what happened back there?"

"I'm not quite sure," Bart replied. "We were eating dinner when my dad got a call on his cell phone from the security company. He said that they were telling him that the alarm went off in the house."

"Wow, so he wasn't lying," Justin exclaimed.

"Who? What do you mean?" asked Bart.

"Will. He said that when he opened the back window you left open for him, it set off an alarm. I thought he was full of shit and chickened out on you."

"How long did you guys hang out there, after it went off?"

"Not long. We took off immediately. Will did not want to have anything to do with it after that."

"Where is he now?" Bart wondered.

"He took off, man," Will answered. "Packed his stuff and said he was off to Little Rock. I don't think we will be seeing him for a while."

"Fuck!" Bart screamed. "I cannot believe this fucking happened to me! I wonder what he did to trip that alarm?"

Justin simply listened as Bart began to vent his frustrations.

"I can't believe this didn't work," Bart muttered. "I know I turned off all of the alarms in the house. I also know I opened that window and told him which one was the exact one to open. He must have fucked it up somehow!"

Again, Justin listened.

"I think you're right, Justin," Bart stated.

"About what, Bart?"

"I think Will chickened out and got cold feet. He had to have screwed this up somehow. Damn pussy!"

Justin had no idea how to respond.

Much later, Bart would claim that this failed attempt was merely a test he had devised to see just how far Justin and Will would be willing to travel with him. "Will was supposed to enter from the back door, only I never unlocked it. Nor did I [turn] the alarm off, my only other duty." He attempted to justify his actions and make himself appear to be the savior in the situation. "The game had gone on too far. I didn't turn it off."

Of course, he kept the ruse up in front of Justin. He wanted to be sure he still had one of the guys on his side.

"He'd better watch his back," Bart threatened in reference to Will. "If he tells anyone about what we planned together, he's going to be in some serious shit."

"Oh, Bart. You don't need to worry about Will," Justin tried to comfort him. "He won't say anything. I know he won't."

"How can you be so sure?"

"Because he's not a dumb guy. He knows we'd be in a world of shit if this came out, and he'd be included. He's not an idiot."

"I'm not so sure about that," Bart grumbled. "I can see that pussy talking and blabbering out the entire plan to someone."

Justin again had no idea what else to say.

"I might just need to tie up some loose ends," Bart surmised. "Make sure he doesn't talk."

Justin kept his mouth shut. He soon realized that he, too, could be considered a loose end by Bart. He did not want to incur the wrath of his friend.

18

Winter 2001
Hastings Books & Records
Bosque Boulevard
Waco, Texas

Bart Whitaker's boredom never ceased. Despite his failed attempt at murdering his mother and father, he found no joy in attempting to pursue a life of crime. Nonetheless, he would continue his run—albeit, with somewhat petty crimes in comparison.

One cold February night, Bart and Justin went out for a spell. As usual, Bart was bored and looking for some excitement. He decided he would find it at Hastings Books & Records, of all places.

Bart and Justin sauntered into the chain store, known mainly for its selection of music CDs and smattering of DVDs. It was after eleven o'clock, and Holly Hansard, the night clerk, who also looked bored, ignored the duo and went about her business of sorting CDs. Out of the corner of her eye, Hansard kept track of the pair's doings, as she did with most customers who entered the store, especially late at night.

Bart and Justin sauntered about the store, appearing to be interested in the latest releases in the CD rock section. Mindlessly thumbing the plastic protective cases, as if to appear to be looking, the young men then moved over to the DVD section.

Hansard had been with the store for a while and knew how to spot a shoplifter. She had no doubt what was coming next. Sure enough, she spotted Bart checking out the DVDs, when he quickly lifted two movies, *Ronin* and *The Way of the Gun,* and stuck them in his gray coat's pocket. Hansard saw the whole thing, but she waited until they approached the counter. Sometimes customers will grab items, stick them in the coats or pants pockets, but take them out and pay for them before leaving the store. She hoped this would be the case. Unfortunately, she would not be so lucky.

Bart and Justin made their way to the front of the store and noticed the female cashier move toward the register. There would be no sale made on this particular night. Instead of walking up to the counter and paying for the DVDs, Bart and Justin made a beeline for the exit. As Bart passed through the security railings, an ear-piercing alarm sounded. The incessant squeal triggered an impulse in the two young men that caused them to flee. Bart and Justin tore out of there, not even hearing Hansard's cries for them to come back and pay for their stuff. They leaped into Bart's car and took off.

They did not, however, expect Hansard to run outside with a pen and notepad and jot down a description of the getaway car, as well as its license plate.

Hansard knew the routine and knew what to do next. Call the cops, report the incident, tell her boss. It was never fun to be violated in any way. Her brave detective work, however, proved beneficial. Police were able to successfully pinpoint the vehicle as belonging to one Thomas Bartlett Whitaker.

A Waco police officer was able to run a check on the license plate and soon discovered that the vehicle actually belonged to Kent Whitaker, on Heron Way, all the way down in Sugar Land, Texas. The officer contacted the Whitaker household and spoke with Tricia, who confirmed that her son Bart attended school at Baylor, and that she would have him contact the police officer. Soon thereafter, the officer received a phone call from Bart, who admitted the theft of the DVDs. Bart also ratted out his good friend Justin Peters. Justin, however, claimed he did not take the DVDs, nor did he have any idea Bart had intended to steal from the store.

The officer asked Bart to come down to the station and make a statement. The officer wrote up a citation for theft, which Bart agreed to and signed. Bart then returned the DVDs to the officer, who later returned them to Hastings. Bart was arrested but immediately released.

Nothing more came of the arrest.

19

January to April 2001
Waco Park Apartments
South Fourth Street, Apartment #509
Waco, Texas

Less than one month after the trial run for murder, Bart Whitaker was at it again. He started bending Justin's ear about killing his parents, and that they no longer needed Will Anthony's help.

"I've got another friend who can help us out," Bart assured Justin Peters.

"Who?" Justin asked.

"You remember Adam Hipp from the cruise we all went on?" Bart said, referring to his friend from high school. The three of them, along with a few other friends, decided to take an expensive ocean cruise to the Bahamas during the break between Christmas and New Year's Day. It was Bart's way of dealing with the depression of the bungled attempt earlier in December.

Justin nodded affirmatively.

"I talked to him after the trip. He is definitely down

with the plan," Bart assured Justin. "There won't be any problems this time, like we had with Will." Bart added that "Adam [is] the obvious choice, because he [is] easily the most corrupt person I [know]." Bart tended to lay blame on others for his actions and, indeed, posited that it was Adam who was the ultimate "mask wearer" and informed Justin that Adam was "far more competent at lying than I ever was."

By this time, Justin Peters's depression had actually grown more acute. The death of his ex-girlfriend, being asked to participate in the killing of two innocent people, the failure of that plan, and then a lonely Christmas holiday, followed by a dull and uneventful cruise. He felt he had nothing to lose, and everything to gain, by helping Bart out with his plan.

"Cool," Justin simply replied.

It would be more than two months before they actually decided to move forward with a new plan.

Bart would later rationalize his relationship with Justin and the crime they were both willing to commit. "Both Justin and I were drowning, and we didn't know how to help each other." He added that the two young men together would "only make things worse."

Bart, Adam, and Justin met to discuss plans for murdering Bart's family. One of their more elaborate scenarios involved murdering Bart's parents and his brother at his grandmother's lake house in Conroe.

Bart concocted a plan wherein he would get his entire family inside the cabin, along with some cousins, aunts and uncles, and grandparents—mostly everyone on his mother's side of the family. Adam and Justin would somehow barricade the lake house with everyone inside, light the entire structure on fire, and only Bart would manage to escape alive from the harrowing inferno.

According to Adam, Bart had a specific reason why he wanted to kill his entire immediate family, as well as the Bartletts. It was because his mother's family actually owned the construction company, and he knew if he could eliminate all of the family members with an ownership in the company, then everything would go to him.

Adam would later claim that while he listened to Bart's plans on murdering his family, and even offered advice on how to make it work better, as well as offering to participate directly, he eventually agreed to do so only because of the "simple fact I was kind of interested to see how far he would take it, and to see if it was something that was legitimate."

The goal was to eliminate Bart's family and his cousins who stood to inherit the Bartlett Construction Company, so he could have it all. As a reward for their participation in committing the murders for hire, Adam and Justin would be paid a substantial amount of money. There was, however, no discussion of how much money either young man was going to receive for their part.

The three young men spoke several times about the fire massacre plan—possibly as many as six times—before they decided to scrap it. There was no guarantee that everyone else would actually die in the conflagration, and they believed it would be too easy for the authorities to pinpoint arson.

Soon the various scenarios discussed among the three young men would lead to arguments, as they could never agree on the proper plan.

Eventually Bart decided it was best to break out the

old chestnut—the bungled burglary attempt, which, of course, was the exact same plan that he, Justin, and Will had attempted earlier.

This time around, Bart would give Adam a key to his parents' house, as well as the access code numbers to their home alarm system. Adam was to unlock the door, disable the alarm system, and wait inside Bart's parents' home until two people came through the door. Adam would then shoot them.

Adam was then supposed to run out the back door, jump the fence, run through their neighbors' yard, and hightail it out of there by jumping into the get-away car commandeered by Justin.

Basically, it was the Bart/Will/Justin plan—except Adam would have the keys and the alarm codes. Seemingly, there would be no accidental triggering of alarms, as with Will. Bart had also suggested that Adam was to shoot him inside the house, to make it look like the killer was trying to eliminate the entire family, but Bart had attempted a heroic move to thwart the criminal. Bart and Adam discussed the various locations on Bart's body where he could take a bullet and suffer the least amount of permanent damage yet still appear to be legitimately wounded. Bart wanted it to be an area that could grow sufficient scar tissue to help heal the gunshot wound and, hopefully, he would still be able to maintain his mobility.

There were little to no specifics discussed, however, among the three aspiring criminals. No details on how Bart was going to get his parents to their house; no information on how Adam was to get a gun— nothing. No firing-range practice so Adam would be able to use the gun properly. They never returned to Bart's parents' home to walk through the various scenarios while they were away. Bart basically assured Adam and Justin that he would handle everything, and they should patiently wait for further instructions.

Adam later claimed when asked why he continued to talk about the plans for murdering the Whitakers, why he did not cease the discussions, or warn Bart's parents, was because he was afraid. He believed the deeper the discussions got, the more he was in over his head, and he feared that Bart would come after *him* if he tried to thwart the plans.

Jennifer Japhet, Justin Peter's friend from junior high and high school, attempted to reinsert herself into Justin's life over the previous two months. She began to call him on the phone more, would stop by to visit him, and generally attempted to engage him in the outside world.

Jennifer had a far more successful career at Baylor than Justin. In addition to her busy social calendar at school, she was also performing well with her studies. She was set to graduate in the spring of 2001, a semester early, with a degree in English Renaissance drama, which she described as "utterly useless." Jennifer knew, however, that she would have a job with her father's company when she graduated, which would allow her to put herself through a master's degree program in psychology.

Regardless of her busy schedule, Jennifer made it a point to reconnect with her friend Justin. She knew how depressed he had become after his ex-girlfriend's death and that he was struggling in school. She also knew that she did not like Justin's roommate Bart Whitaker.

Justin and Bart moved into the same apartment complex that Jennifer lived in during their second year at Baylor. That was the first time she had ever met Bart. She had heard about him from Justin, but she was never actually introduced to him until their second year.

Jennifer had also met Justin's other good friend at Baylor, Will Anthony. She was not a big fan of Will's, either. "Will wasn't necessarily the caliber of person I thought Justin would normally hang out with, in the past," she recalled. Jennifer remembered what it took to make it in their Health Careers High School back in San Antonio—the drive and passion that was necessary to succeed there. "I didn't see that in Will. He just seemed adrift."

Jennifer's feelings for Bart were not much better. "He just seemed to be kind of going to college," she explained. "He just didn't seem to have any goals at that time."

Jennifer was disappointed that Justin spent so much time hanging around his apartment with Bart and playing video games. "They had networked their apartment so they could all play video games on a network together." She felt they spent way too much time playing video games and slacking off. Jennifer was also extremely upset with Justin that he had skipped so many classes.

The Justin that Jennifer saw before her was not the same young boy she had met in seventh grade. Sure, he had always been a bit shy, and maybe even a tad socially awkward, but he always had drive and ambition. Justin was an intelligent man with plenty of skills to succeed in life, and she believed he was wasting away his time hanging out with Bart and Will.

Jennifer knew that a large portion of Justin's change in demeanor was a result of his ex-girlfriend's fatal car accident. She said of Justin's reaction to her death, "He sank into a really deep depression. He dropped out of school for the semester. He gained a lot of weight. He became very antisocial." She also noted that when he moved into the apartment with Bart, Justin "pretty much stayed in his room and painted it this really dark blue and always had the shades down."

Despite her misgivings about her good friend's current state, she knew he was someone worth fighting for: "Justin's a little shy. He's a little insecure being around people he doesn't know." Jennifer always managed to see the best in her friend. "He has a very good heart, and anytime I needed to talk to someone, even at three o'clock in the morning when I was upset, he's always been there for me."

One problem Justin had—in Jennifer's estimation—was that he was easily led astray. "He can definitely be the type of person who is easily influenced by others."

Jennifer sensed that Justin was being influenced by Bart Whitaker, and not in a good way. "His dropping out of school being the most obvious," the young woman recalled. "Smoking marijuana and drinking. He hadn't done those things before."

Jennifer also noted that Justin's once-infectious go-get-'em attitude had all but disappeared. "He took on a definite 'I don't care about what happens' attitude and 'I'm only out to do what's best for me' mentality."

In addition to the negative influence Bart exerted over Justin, Jennifer had problems with the way Bart comported himself. "Bart was really into intelligence, like spy-type intelligence. He was very paranoid that someone was out to get him." Jennifer added that Justin talked to her about Bart's state of mind. Bart believed that outside people were listening in on his conversations and that they had planted eavesdropping devices, or "bugs," all around Bart and Justin's apartment. "Justin used to never act like that," Jennifer added. "He was into EverQuest and medicine, not smoking pot and being afraid that people were out to get him."

On April 4, 2001, Jennifer Japhet made it a point to stop by and see her friend Justin Peters. Jennifer's sorority, Alpha Phi Omega, was holding a rush party to spark up interest for new inductees for the following fall semester. Her sorority was part of a national service fraternity that did volunteer work for people in need. The party was located in the meeting room at Justin's apartment complex.

Jennifer wanted to make sure Justin came with her to the rush party. She was hoping to introduce him to a crowd of people she believed were more along the lines of the types he should be hanging out with, instead of Bart Whitaker and Will Anthony. Maybe the positive influence of some of her sorority members would rub off on Justin. She also hoped that the concept of putting others' needs before one's own would resonate with Justin.

Jennifer pulled herself away from the party to seek out Justin. She made her way across the complex up to his apartment. As she approached the front door, she overheard loud voices coming from the living area in the medium-sized apartment. She hesitantly knocked on the door. She almost didn't think anyone heard her. Suddenly the voices stopped and a *woosh* of air hit her face as the front door was hurriedly opened.

Standing before her was Justin. "Hey, Jennifer. What are you doing here?" he asked in a less than pleasant tone of voice.

"I thought you'd like to go with me over to the Alpha party. They're having a rush and I thought you'd like to meet a few people," Jennifer stated, somewhat dejected by his decidedly rude greeting.

Justin stood in the doorway for a moment and did not respond. Finally he stepped aside and asked her to come inside.

Jennifer stepped into the apartment and realized she had incredibly bad timing.

Staring back at her, and not very happy about it, were Bart and a fellow Baylor student, Felicia Guel. Justin had met Felicia during their freshman year at college and instantly fell for her. He then introduced her to Bart, which turned out to be a big mistake for Justin. Felicia was much more interested in Bart than she was Justin, and she began to pursue the former. Over time, Felicia won Bart over, and the two became an item. They had been dating, on and off, ever since, even though Bart was still seeing Lynne Sorsby, who was away at college in Austin. Jennifer had listened to Justin talk about Felicia and Bart, and how much it ate him inside to see them together.

It was no wonder why Justin basically gave her the cold shoulder when he answered the door.

As Jennifer slowly entered the apartment, she could sense the tension in the air between the three of them. "When I walked into the room," Jennifer recalled, "everyone was staring at me. They were all very uncomfortable that I was there."

Jennifer assumed she had walked into the middle of an argument that somehow involved the alleged love triangle. She looked over to her friend to see if she could get his attention. "Justin, can I talk to you, please?"

Justin did not answer her immediately. Instead, he looked to Bart, who did not acknowledge him.

"Justin, can we go in your room and talk, please?" Jennifer insisted.

Justin seemed to snap out of his trance and quietly acquiesced. "Sure, Jennifer. Come on."

Jennifer and Justin slowly padded down the small hallway, which led to his room. Neither Bart nor Felicia said anything to Jennifer. Bart glared at her as she walked behind Justin.

Justin and Jennifer went into his room, and Jennifer shut the door behind them. "What's going on, Justin? Are you and Bart fighting over Felicia?"

Justin could not look Jennifer in the eye. Instead, he looked down at the floor, as if doing so would simply cause Jennifer to disappear.

This annoyed Jennifer. "Justin, what is going on?"

"It's nothing."

"What is . . . ?"

"I don't want to talk about it. . . ."

Jennifer was on the verge of getting pissed with Justin. She knew he was holding back something important. "Justin, tell me. Is it Felicia? Did she do something to you again?" Jennifer believed that Felicia was toying with Justin. In addition to Bart, she had dated another one of Justin's college friends, and it used to drive him crazy.

"No, Jennifer. It doesn't have anything to do with Felicia. At least, not directly," Justin responded, even though he was still visibly upset.

"Justin, c'mon. It's me. It's Jennifer. You know you can tell me anything." She hoped the nice touch would help.

"I'm driving to Austin," he sputtered.

That was not what she expected to hear. "Okay, what does that have to do with Felicia?"

"It's not about her. Okay, Jennifer?" Justin snapped.

"Well, why are you driving to Austin? You don't know anybody that lives down there. Why are you going there?"

"Just don't worry about it," Justin replied disgustedly.

"I am worrying about it, Justin. That's why I'm here. Now, tell me what the heck is going on."

Justin continued to avoid giving Jennifer a straight answer.

Her frustration was escalating. "I really want you to come with me to this party. It'll be good for you."

"No, no, I can't," Justin responded.

"Why not, Justin?"

"Because I'm actually driving to Houston."

Jennifer was completely confused now.

"I'm driving to Houston, not Austin," Justin told her the truth.

"But you don't know anyone who lives in Houston, either." Jennifer continued to cajole Justin. "What is so important to do in Houston that you can't hang out at a party with one of your best friends?"

Justin began to get agitated with Jennifer. "Because I have to do something, and I can't go to the party with you."

"Just come with me to the party. It'll be a good time. We'll have fun," she persisted.

Justin shook his head. "I have to drive to Austin first

to pick someone up, and then I have to drive down to Houston. I have to drive them down there with me."

"Why are you going to do that?"

"I have to drop them off at Bart's house," Justin uttered.

Jennifer was finally getting somewhere. And, as she expected, it had something to do with Bart. "Why aren't you taking Bart with you?" Jennifer asked, thinking it was strange that he would be doing such a big favor for Bart, but Bart would not even be there. "I don't understand what is going on."

Justin continued to hem and haw. "We have this plan, and I'm going to get some money out of this."

Jennifer waited for him to explain himself fully. When he failed to further explain, she demanded, "You need to tell me straight up, Justin, what exactly is going on here? I don't understand."

Justin finally realized his childhood friend was not going to let up. "We've got a plan," he started off slowly, "a plan to kill Bart's family."

Jennifer was stunned. It was the last thing she expected to hear. She thought maybe there was some kind of drug deal going on, or maybe they were messed up with some type of theft or something. But murder? Of Bart's family? It sounded completely insane.

"I'm driving to Houston, actually Sugar Land, and dropping off some guy Bart knows named Adam. Dropping him off at Bart's folks' house."

Jennifer was waiting for the punch line. She knew this had to be some horrible joke and she was being set up.

"Come on, Justin," she tried to laugh it off.

But instead of denials, Justin went on with a discussion of the plans. "Adam is supposed to wait inside the house until Bart brings his family home, and then he is going to shoot them." There was no guffaw from Justin. No punch to Jennifer's shoulder, followed by a hearty "Gotcha!" Justin was not laughing. He was not even stifling a smile. He was serious.

Despite all the visual evidence, Jennifer held out hope that there was an inkling of acting on Justin's part. So she, too, decided to play along. "Okay, well, why would you want to take part in something like that?"

"Money," Justin flatly responded.

"You don't need money," Jennifer responded.

"Insurance money. Bart's parents are worth a lot of money, and Bart promised me a cut of it."

Somehow, the mention of Bart and insurance money in the same sentence clicked for Jennifer. She knew now that Justin was not messing with her, but that he was actually going to participate in the murder of Bart Whitaker's parents. She decided to give it one more shot. "Quit lying to me, Justin. You cannot be serious about this."

"It's true," he countered. "We're doing it tonight."

"Justin, come on. This is utterly insane. You cannot be involved in this!" she exclaimed, her voice rising.

Justin shushed her.

"Don't shoosh me," she snapped at him. "You cannot be a part of this!"

"Jennifer, be quiet," he tried to calm her down. "Bart's going to hear you."

"I don't care if he does hear me!" she screamed at Justin from the top of her lungs, loud enough so that the people in the next apartment could hear her. Jennifer turned around, disgusted, and stormed out of Justin's room. She walked back into the living area, expecting to see Bart and Felicia, but they were not there. She could hear voices from inside Bart's bedroom.

Jennifer barged directly into Bart's room and spotted him and Felicia lying on his bed. "Bart, are you seriously going to let this happen?" she asked in a stern, shrill voice.

Bart sat up slowly and smiled at Jennifer. He then rolled his legs off the bed, placed his feet on the floor, and stood up. He leisurely walked toward Jennifer, put his hands on the sides of her shoulders, and leaned in toward her right ear.

"Everything is going to be okay," Bart whispered into Jennifer's ear. "You don't have to worry." His voice was calm—practically soothing. He pulled back, while still grasping her shoulders, to give her a closer look.

Jennifer reacted violently. She pushed him away from her, breaking the clutch he had on her shoulders. She was livid. "If anything happens to Justin," she practically screamed at Bart, "you are going to be sorry!"

Bart again smiled at the frazzled young woman. He then turned his back to her and walked out of his bedroom. He ignored her as he sauntered past.

Jennifer was stunned by his nonchalance. She realized it was a lost cause and took off. If she could help it, she did not want to be in Bart Whitaker's presence ever again. She quickly darted out of the apartment, not even giving Bart or Felicia a second glance. As she scooted out, she caught Justin's eyes momentarily. She could see him pissing his life away right before her. She began to tear up, but she knew it was best she go. She did not speak to Justin as she dejectedly stormed out of the apartment.

Jennifer knew she had to do something to help her

friend. It was obvious he was not going to listen to reason. She had tried everything she could think of to convince him to abort the plans, but Justin would not heed her warnings. Jennifer needed to talk to someone to figure out what she should do about Justin and his crazy plans. She did not return to her rush party, but instead she found her car and drove home to call someone.

Jennifer got home, called her boyfriend, and hysterically began to tell him what had happened. When she was done telling the story, his advice was simple and clear: "You have to call the police." He repeated it, "You have to call the police."

Jennifer obviously knew this was the only choice she had. She could not let someone go off and murder other human beings.

Back at the apartment, Bart was not happy. He walked into Justin's room and said, "What the hell was that all about?"

Justin looked defeated. "I'm sorry, man. That's just the way she is. She thinks she's my big sister or something, and that she has to protect me. She's always been like that with me." He seemed embarrassed.

Bart simply shook his head, perhaps unsure of how to react about someone caring so deeply for another person. "Regardless," he told Justin, "we need to get it in gear and do this thing right now."

Justin nodded, almost bobbing his entire body. "Right, right. Okay, I'm ready to do this, if you are."

Bart nodded in agreement. "I'll call Adam and let him know you are on your way to pick him up."

Justin nodded again. His heart raced as he realized what was finally beginning to unfold before him. "Let's go."

20

Justin sat in the car with the engine idling. He had no idea whose car it was, other than he thought that Felicia had somehow managed to steal it from a friend of hers. Felicia had managed to lift her friend's car keys, make a copy of the key, and give it to Bart, who, in turn, passed it on to Justin.

Justin Peters, a National Merit Scholarship recipient, was sitting in a stolen vehicle, with a gun, on his way to Sugar Land to help murder his roommate's parents. Not quite where he imagined himself just a few years earlier when he graduated from Health Centers High School in San Antonio.

Bart stood next to the stolen car, with Justin sitting inside in the passenger seat. "Are you ready?" he asked Justin.

"I think so." Justin's trepidation was apparent.

"It's going to be all right," Bart reassured his friend,

using the same tone he had tried in calming down Jennifer. "I'll call you later to make sure everything is going according to plan."

Justin nodded, threw the car into gear, and began to drive away from Baylor University, away from Waco, and away from any sense of normalcy he may have once recognized in himself.

He didn't get very far.

Less than three miles outside of the Waco city limits, Justin looked down at the car's dashboard. He could not believe what he was seeing. The gas tank was practically on empty. He realized he needed to hit a gas station soon, or he was going to be stranded on the open highway, late at night, in the dark, with no one to help him.

Justin knew Bart would be pissed, too, if he broke down. It would be the second time that his plan had failed to come to fruition. He did not think Bart would be as calm about failure a second time around.

Justin drove onward in search of a gas station. The late-night hour, however, made it a seemingly impossible task. Most of the outlying areas of Waco tend to shut down when the sun sets. It was way beyond that point. Furthermore, the majority of the available gas stations were still mired in the '60s and '70s, with full-service pumps. No credit card–accepting pump in sight. Justin drove past two full-service stations that were closed for the night. He could not believe this was happening to him.

Bart did not want the car filled up with gas while inside Waco. He was afraid a surveillance camera would have taken Justin's picture, and he would have been spotted and easily tracked down for driving a stolen car.

Justin drove on, as long as possible, until he ran out of fuel. He pulled over to the side of the freeway. Here he was, stuck on the side of I-35, in the middle of nowhere. Justin pulled out his cell phone and gave Bart a call.

"Bart, it's me, Justin."

Bart answered from the comfort and safety of their apartment. "Justin? What's going on?"

"You are not going to believe this, Bart." Justin tried to laugh it off.

"Is everything okay, Justin? Is there something wrong?"

"Yeah, I ran out of gas!" Justin sighed in exasperation.

"You have got to be kidding me," Bart replied. "Weren't there plenty of gas stations on the way out of town?"

"Oh yeah. Except they were all built in the 1950s and have owners who think it's still the 1970s and everyone needs a full-service inspection."

"Where are you?" Bart asked Justin.

"I'm on I-35, not that far outside of Waco. I don't know where specifically, because it's too dark outside and I couldn't see any noticeable landmarks or street signs to let me know where I am exactly."

"All right." Bart sounded a bit harried. "I'll come on out there and get you right now."

Justin assumed the plan had fallen through, and it would finally all be over. He was ready for it to end, to be quite frank.

Bart had other ideas. "I'll bring a gas can with some gas for you. We can fill up that car and get you on your way to the nearest gas station and get you back out on the road again."

Justin seemed a bit dejected, but he agreed. "Okay, I'll be in the car. I'm sure you won't miss me."

As Justin sat in the stolen car, with a gun inside, waiting for his roommate to come give him more gasoline so he could be on his way, his other friend sat in her apartment and fretted about what she should do. Jennifer knew that she had to tell someone about Bart and Justin's plans to kill Bart's parents. She just did not want Justin to get into trouble, because she knew this would be serious and would forestall any chance her friend had of getting his life back on course.

Jennifer knew she had to do the right thing, and that was to make sure the Whitakers were not harmed in any way. She nervously picked up her telephone and punched in 911.

The call was immediately picked up by a dispatcher. "Nine-one-one, what is your emergency?"

"I need to report a potential murder," Jennifer declared. "A friend of mine is about to take part in a murder, and I want to stop him."

"What's your friend's name, ma'am?"

"I'd rather not say. I just want to make sure these people don't get hurt."

"What are their names, ma'am?"

"All I know is their last name is Whitaker and they live in Sugar Land, Texas, just outside of Houston. They are the parents of my friend's roommate. His roommate wants them killed, and he's convinced my friend to drive down from Waco with a gun. Something about giving the gun to another guy, who will be hiding in the Whitaker house, and [will] kill them when they come home from dinner."

The dispatcher continued to take down the information about the alleged hit.

Unbeknownst to Jennifer, her boyfriend also called police about the murder conspiracy. He was not shy about giving out Justin's name.

After Jennifer contacted 911, she hung up and called Justin.

"Hello," he answered somewhat somberly.

"Justin!" Jennifer screamed. "Where are you?"

"I'm on I-35, why?"

"Justin, I just called the cops. They know what's going on."

"You *what*?" Justin was startled by the revelation.

"I called the cops, but I didn't give them your name," Jennifer replied, and tried to assuage his concerns. "They don't know you are involved, just that someone was trying to kill Bart's parents."

"Goddamn it, Jennifer!" Justin was enraged. "This has nothing to do with you! Why the hell do you always have to butt into my life?"

Again, it was not the response Jennifer had expected. Maybe a little thank-you would be nice. "I'd better get the hell out of here before the cops bust my ass" would have been even more preferable.

"Justin, I'm just trying to get you out of something you will never, ever be able to come back from, if you go through with this. You don't need to be doing Bart's dirty work for him. This is his problem, not yours."

"Well, now, thanks to you, it definitely is *my* problem. And once Bart finds out, he's gonna make damn sure it becomes your problem, too." Justin was incensed. "Damn it, Jennifer! Just butt out, okay?" Justin hung up his cell phone on his former best friend.

Jennifer stared at her phone and began to cry softly. She knew there was nothing more she could do for her lost friend, but sit back and wait.

Approximately twenty minutes after Justin spoke with Bart about running out of gas, and two minutes after hearing Jennifer tell him she called the cops, Justin's cell phone rang again. Needless to say, he was shocked by who was on the other line. It was Bart's father, Kent Whitaker.

Hello?" Justin answered his phone.

"Is this Justin?" Mr. Whitaker asked.

"Yes, sir."

"Justin, hello. This is Kent Whitaker, Bart's dad. How are you doing, son?" Kent sounded cheerful and pleasant.

Justin was stunned. The last person he expected to hear from was the man he was on his way to kill. "I'm—I'm okay, Mr. Whitaker," he stammered.

"Justin, I hate to bother you, but I think we are the victim of some type of prank call, son. Somebody from Waco called 911, and they called the police, and the police called us down here."

"Y-yes, sir," Justin stammered.

"They said something ridiculous about you and Bart, and I'm sure it's some kind of silly joke one of your college buddies is probably playing on you." Kent Whitaker chuckled. "Apparently, they said you and Bart were on your way down to Sugar Land and that y'all wanted to kill me and Bart's mother. Ha!" Kent laughed at the thought of his son and roommate participating in something so devious.

Justin played dumb. "What, sir? That's just ridiculous!"

"That's exactly what I said. I know you two boys like to have fun, but I also know you had nothing to do with this."

"No, sir. Not at all."

"Okay, then, Justin. Sorry to bother you. Maybe you can find out who put you two boys up to this? Well, you take care of yourself and have a good night."

"Yes, sir, Mr. Whitaker. I'll tell Bart you called. Good night, sir."

"Good night, Justin."

Justin hung up his cell phone and let out a huge sigh of relief. He could not believe he just spoke with Bart's dad. He had a bad feeling that everything was going to come crashing down around him. Sure enough, just as that thought entered his mind, his cell phone rang again. He was so deep into concentration that the shrill sound alarmed him.

"Hello?" Justin answered, and wondered who in the hell was calling him now.

"Justin Peters?" a stern male voice on the other end of the line asked.

"This is Justin."

"Justin, I'm with the Waco Police Department."

Justin Peters could not believe this was happening to him.

Less than ten minutes later, Justin looked through the window of the stolen car. He noticed a large blue Yukon SUV pull up behind him on the side of the freeway. It was Bart.

When Justin looked up at his rearview mirror, he could see Bart ambling toward him. He was carrying a one-gallon red plastic gas can.

Bart walked up to the driver's-side window of the

car Justin was sitting in and motioned for Justin to roll down the window.

"Here's your gas, man," Bart offered.

"It ain't gonna happen, Bart."

"Why not?" he asked, sounding slightly perturbed.

"Because," Justin responded, "I just a call from your dad. He knows."

The reaction back in Sugar Land, and Austin, was quite different. Bart's parents could not believe their son would plot to kill them. They simply chalked it up to a silly prank that had spun out of control, because they just knew Bart was incapable of such horrifying behavior. Lynne Sorsby, Bart's girlfriend, called the whole thing "ridiculous." She also knew that Bart would never plot to kill his family and that he cared for them too much. Like the Whitakers, she simply blew the whole thing off.

Bart, however, did not blow it off. He was so freaked out by the inclusion of the police that he took off in his car and ran away to Dallas. He was gone for at least three days before his family could track him down. When they finally got ahold of their son, he told them he was scared, confused, and worried that he was going to be blamed for something he had no involvement in. His parents, however, assured their eldest son that they knew there was no way any of this could be true, and that he would never do anything to harm them or anyone else, for that matter.

Once Bart received assurances that he was not going to get into trouble, he returned to Waco. Upon his arrival, he informed Justin that he was moving out. Nothing about the incident was discussed between the two young men. Bart simply packed up his possessions and moved out of the apartment. The two men never spoke again.

Soon thereafter, Bart decided to completely remove himself from the Waco scene. He informed his family that he planned to transfer to Sam Houston State University in Huntsville, nearly ninety miles north of Sugar Land. Bart claimed he wanted to get a job with the Federal Bureau of Investigation. He believed he would make a good homicide detective or even a criminal profiler, mainly because he could "think like a criminal." Sam Houston has a renowned criminal justice college, which appealed to Bart, so he decided to make the move. He packed everything up again and moved to Nacogdoches.

Of course, he failed to inform his parents that he had not even completed enough courses at Baylor to be considered to have finished his freshman year, even though he had already spent two years in school. Completely unaware of Bart's deception, the Whitakers funded their son's move and also purchased a $90,000 townhome, located less than one hundred yards away from Lake Conroe, in a tiny hamlet called Harbour Town, in Willis, Texas. This town was located less than thirty miles southwest of Huntsville and Sam Houston State.

Bart also landed a prime job as a manager of The Dining Room restaurant at the nearby posh Bentwater Yacht & Country Club. He made friends with a young neighbor named Chris Brashear. Bart even got Chris a job at the restaurant.

21

Steven Champagne and his mother moved to the small town of Willis, Texas, nearly fifty miles north of Houston, when he was only thirteen years old. The young man, a product of a divorced family, led a relatively unremarkable, yet fun, life. The thin, tall, attractive young man turned many a female head, and he never hurt when it came to attracting the opposite sex.

Steven graduated from Willis High School in 2001. He parlayed his diploma into admission at The Art Institute of Houston, where he intended to study graphic design and computer animation.

To make ends meet, Steven took a job with United Parcel Service (UPS) in Conroe. He would have to commute from Willis to Houston to attend college, travel more than forty miles to drive from school to UPS in Conroe, and then ten miles from work back to his residence in Willis. The constant commuting took its toll on the young man. His academic career suffered the most. As a result, Steven dropped out of school after just one year. He blamed the commute as his reason for quitting.

Spring 2003
Harbour Town
Windlass Lane
Willis, Texas

After having dropped out, Steven moved into a small townhome in Harbour Town, a cozy gated community between Willis and Montgomery, and only a stone's throw from Lake Conroe. The community was mainly littered with townhomes, such as Steven's, apartment complexes, and a few small residential homes. Steven could walk out his front door and hit one of four tennis courts directly in front of his residence or take a quick jaunt down to the lake if he so desired. Nearby there was also a park, a pool, a playground for kids, a spot to play volleyball, and a clubhouse. It was, however, a somewhat humiliating experience for the young man, as he had to move in with his mother to help cover the expenses.

One month after Steven's arrival in Harbour Town, he ran into another young man, who lived on his same street. It was rather unusual to see people Steven's age around the neighborhood, as the majority of residents were considerably older. Steven perked up whenever he saw the young man, because he thought he could stand to have a new friend, or at least a friendly face to nod to and say hello to occasionally.

After crossing paths several times, Steven decided to introduce himself to the other young man, whose named, he learned, was Bart Whitaker. They began to develop a friendship of nods, hellos, and the random bout of small talk. It turned out that Bart lived a couple of doors down from him.

Steven eventually learned that Bart was employed

as a restaurant manager at the Bentwater Yacht & Country Club, located on Bentwater Drive, on Lake Conroe, in Montgomery, only three miles from their townhomes. Tucked away near hundreds of acres of towering pine trees, near the Garden Pines eighteen-hole golf course, the club allows an escape for well-to-do Texans who can arrive via boat at the club's marina, or sneak in under the cover of the copper-domed buildings of the club itself. Members can participate in a wealth of extracurricular activities, including racquetball, golf, and boating, or take advantage of an indoor workout facility or relax with a European-style manicure and day spa. After the frolicking is done, members can steal away to one of two restaurants, including The Crescent Grill, for a more casual environment, and The Dining Room, for more elegant fare. The latter was well-known for its bay-window views looking upon the vast expanse of Lake Conroe. This was where Bart Whitaker worked.

Steven had always heard about the restaurant in the country club, but he had never eaten there. He told Bart that it must be a really cool place to work—much better than his latest job at the Streater Smith Mitsubishi car dealership in Conroe, where he sold new cars.

As Steven and Bart got to know one another better, they naturally began to open up to each other—at least a little bit. Steven told Bart how he ended up living in a townhome in Harbour Town with his mother.

Bart shared some of his background with Steven, but not much. He did, however, tell his new friend that he was attending Sam Houston State University in Huntsville as a graduate student, and that he was also teaching a few courses there (though he never specifically mentioned what classes he was taking or teaching). He said that he had an interest in the criminal justice courses that Sam Houston had to offer. He told Steven he wanted to become an agent for the FBI. Bart managed to go to school full-time, as well as hold down the demanding full-time position at the restaurant. Steven was impressed with the workload his new friend was willing to take on. It made his brief days at The Art Institute of Houston seem somewhat silly in comparison.

Steven used to see Bart coming home from work most nights, and he would try to catch up with his new acquaintance. Both young men used to hang out on their respective patios and talk to one another from across the way. Most of their conversations revolved around their respective jobs. Bart talked about how much he enjoyed his, while Steven lamented his.

One evening, Steven came right out with it and asked Bart if he could somehow get him a job at the country club restaurant.

"Yeah, I might be able to get you an interview," Bart answered.

"Man, that would be great," Steven responded. "I am really sick of trying to sell cars."

"Let me talk to my boss and see if he can hook you up with something," Bart reiterated. "I know he's always looking for good workers."

"I am definitely a good worker."

"Any idea what you might be interested in doing?"

"Bartending," Steven confidently responded. "It's something I think I'd be good at, and I've had an interest in it for a while."

Two weeks later, Bart came through on his promise to Steven. He was able to land him an interview for a job at Bentwater Yacht & Country Club. It wasn't a bartending job, but rather what they called a "house boy"—someone whose job it was to help set up the restaurant for special occasions, such as weddings, speaking engagements, or banquets. The house boy's job involved plenty of physical labor, with moving tables, setting up equipment for the dance floor, or whatever other chores needed to be dealt with to make the restaurant party-ready. Certainly not the most glamorous of positions, but Steven understood he needed to work his way up the food chain before he could land the more lucrative position of bartender.

Steven began his new job near the end of May 2003. He was extremely grateful to his new friend for hooking him up.

Once Steven began work at the country club restaurant, he learned something more about his new friend Bart. He had one hectic work schedule. As manager of the restaurant, Bart oversaw the waitstaff and also coordinated with the head of the kitchen staff to make sure the two entities worked in sync. It was imperative for a smooth-flowing restaurant to succeed that the heads of kitchen and staff were on top of their games, communicated well, and knew how to bust balls, when necessary. Steven was impressed with how organized Bart seemed, and also how well he could run his half of the ship.

Steven also noted that Bart put in lots and lots of hours for work, and was very dedicated to his job. As a result, Steven and Bart did not see each other very often outside of work and the occasional chat on their patios. Steven described their relationship, once he started working at the restaurant, as "very professional."

Steven felt Bart treated him very well at work. He was always friendly to Steven, and the two young men worked well together. Steven also noticed that Bart seemed to work really well with all of his employees, and he always treated those underneath him with courtesy and respect.

Steven began to feel more comfortable around Bart, Chris Brashear, and some of the other coworkers at the restaurant. Everyone worked the same shift, as the restaurant was only open in the evening and nighttime. The employees' shift lasted from 4:00 until 10:30 P.M. After several weeks of working, Bart finally asked Steven to join him and some of the other employees after their work hours. The group of employees/friends would usually head out to eat at a different restaurant after closing, or head on over to one of their houses for nightcaps and some cutting up with one another.

Steven especially enjoyed the get-togethers for their camaraderie and for the alcohol. He had been spending most of his spare hours going out to clubs and bars—practically every single night, sometimes with friends and oftentimes alone—before he began working at the restaurant, so this was just a nice, normal addition to his partying ways.

Though Bart was the one who invited Steven into his inner circle, he did not tend to go to the bars with the groups. He preferred, instead, to have his employees come over and hang out at his townhome, drink, and stay up until all hours of the night. Bart's reasoning for holding drunk court at his place was that it was much closer to work, everyone would not have to drive as far, and if they got too inebriated, they could always crash out at his pad. Also, he assured them, it would be much cheaper to drink at his place than to throw down serious cash at bars for ridiculously priced beer and overpriced, under-liquored drinks.

Bart, however, did not have a fully stocked refrigerator bursting at the seams with alcohol and beer. Instead, he made sure his employees picked up the booze after work at a nearby convenience store. Bart usually had a bottle or two of something lying around so he would not come off as a total cheapskate.

Bart's after-work parties became quite the tradition that summer. Usually, they occurred every single night, which Steven, of course, was thrilled about. There was usually a small assortment of employees and friends of employees who would saunter in and out of Bart's townhome, drinking alcohol, flirting with one another, and just having a general good time getting drunk and chatting.

Bart's little get-togethers seemed to run on bar hours. Most of the time, the festivities would start closing up shop around 2:00 A.M. On nights when Steven had a bit too much to drink, he simply made his way two doors down to his townhome, making sure not to wake up his mother in the process. On the nights when he was still raring to go, he would jump into his vehicle and scour the after-hours nightclub scene for some additional action. It became his nightly ritual.

In late July 2003, just as Steven began to run in Bart's circle, one of Bart's closest friends, Chris Brashear, stopped working at the restaurant. It wasn't until about a month after Chris quit his job at The Dining Room at Bentwater that Steven finally began to consider Bart to be a friend.

According to Steven, it was not the usual type of friendship he was used to. He became Bart's friend because it "seemed like he needed a friend," referring to Bart. "He always seemed distant, and to himself. It seemed like he needed someone to talk to."

One thing Steven picked up on, in regard to Bart, was that even though he was usually the host of the get-togethers, he never seemed comfortable in those surroundings. He recalled, "Anytime there were a lot of people around, he kept to himself and just hung back." Steven added about Bart that he "just always seemed like there was something he needed to talk about." Steven noted that Bart seemed comfortable and confident while at work, but when he was hanging with others, he did not seem as outgoing or friendly.

"He just seemed to be watching people," Steven recalled, "just keeping track of how they acted and their mannerisms." Steven found Bart's behavior a tad strange, but he never thought much more about it. He did add, however, that it always felt as if he was being watched by Bart—almost as if his friend was sizing him up for some unforeseen job interview. It made Steven uncomfortable, but then he would simply throw back another cold one and forget about it.

Steven also noted that Bart would observe the other houseguests and would not usually engage in much drunken revelry. Bart seemed to want to watch his peers interact with each other. He also noticed that when Bart did engage others in conversation, he was always impressed with his new friend.

"He seemed very educated and very intelligent," Steven acknowledged. "He could talk about a variety of topics and he always sounded like he knew what the hell he was talking about."

Bart's seeming intelligence also added to the air that he created for himself. "The image he portrayed was very successful and very confident." Steven was impressed with Bart's intelligence, his impeccable manner of dress, and the fact that the young man owned, outright, his own townhome. It was "just the way he carried himself, and the way he presented himself to other people," Steven stated, almost in awe.

Steven wanted to be Bart.

Despite Bart's eccentricities, Steven viewed him as a person that most everyone liked. "He just seemed to have a certain way that would make people like him. He had a charismatic way about himself, and I wouldn't say he would charm people, but, rather, he just seemed to be able to get people to like him. He is a likable person."

Steven believed Bart's ability to be liked came from his overall positive attitude he seemed to have about life. "He always seemed positive and happy."

Over time, however, Steven would discover one aspect of Bart's life that the latter was not happy about—his family. As the two young men became closer to one another, Bart finally began to open up a bit more. One day, when Steven and Bart were alone after their coworkers had left the after-work party, Bart sprang something rather unusual upon him.

"I'm adopted," Bart told Steven with a straight face.

Taken aback, not quite sure how to respond, Steven merely asked, "Really?"

"Yeah, my parents adopted me when I was a baby."

Steven simply nodded and did not make a big deal out of the new information. He would later hear Bart tell other people that he was adopted. It seemed Bart was tallying the reactions, devising some bizarre unknowable schematic of trust and inclusion based upon their responses.

"It almost seemed like he was baiting you," Steven

described his friend's behavior. "He would throw out a little bit of information to see if you would pick up on it. Then if you would ask about it, he would try to see if you picked up on what he was trying to get you to talk about."

Over time, Bart opened up a bit more to Steven about his family. But just a little. He would send out dribs and drabs of information during numerous short conversations, without revealing too much about his inner disgust he seemed to be harboring toward everyone in his family.

Based on their late-night conversations, Steven garnered that Bart was not happy that he had been adopted. Bart further let out that "he didn't like his brother, Kevin, at all," and also that "he didn't have a good relationship with his mother or his father."

Bart was always evasive with Steven as to why he actually did not like his family. He would allude to "things about how he and his brother didn't get along," but he would never go into any specifics. He simply just seemed to not like his brother, as far as Steven could discern.

Steven noticed that Bart especially did not like his father. "He and his father didn't ever get along," and as for the whole family, "he was not fond of any of them." Bart convinced Steven that the reason he felt such dislike toward his family was because he was adopted.

One summer night during a party at Bart's townhome, Steven pulled Bart aside to have a quiet, private conversation.

"How come you don't go by your first name, Thomas?" Steven asked Bart.

Bart seemed to snap to attention. "I don't like to

talk about it," he replied, ready to dismiss his friend and return back to the fun of the group.

"No, seriously, man. Tell me."

"Nah, it's just something my parents do, or did, to me when I was a kid," Bart begrudgingly answered. "I think it has to do with the fact that my mother's maiden name was Bartlett," he replied with a sneer on his face.

Steven and Bart continued to talk about Bart's problems with his family. Again, Bart was somewhat vague: "I just don't get along with them very well," he coyly replied.

Steven sympathized with Bart. "I felt like he was alone. He seemed like his family lived far away and he had moved on." He continued to listen to his friend bemoan his family life because he sensed Bart needed a friend.

Eventually Steven and Bart became good friends. In another later conversation, Bart truly opened up to Steven. He was complaining about his family when he turned to Steven and said, "Thanks, man."

"For what?" Steven wondered.

"For listening to me bitch about my family all the time. It's really good to get it off my chest, and I appreciate you listening."

"Don't worry about it, Bart," Steven reassured him. "That's what friends are for."

"No, I mean it," Bart insisted. "You're like the brother I never had."

"You already have a brother," Steven joshed back.

"Yeah, I know. But he's worthless. I don't really consider him to be my brother. I just cannot confide in him the things I have already shared with you. It's important to be able to trust someone with my innermost thoughts and secrets, and I cannot do it with Kevin. But I can with you."

Steven was a bit embarrassed. "Don't mention it, Bart. Really, it's no big deal. You can tell me anything."

"I know, Steven," Bart responded. "That truly means the world to me. It's important that we both have someone we can trust explicitly. Someone we both can confide in and trust."

Steven nodded as Bart carried on.

"You are my brother," Bart added, "through thick and thin." He sealed the deal with a firm handshake and a pat on the shoulder.

July 2003
Lake Conroe
FM Highway 830 Road
Willis, Texas

Bart met up with Steven after work, this time without their fellow employees.

"Hey, Steven. C'mon, let's go for a ride."

"Cool, where we going?" Steven asked.

"I'll tell you when we get there" was Bart's sardonic response, with a slight grin on his face. "I'd like to talk with you about something very important."

"Sure, man," replied the amiable Steven. "Let's go." Steven hopped into Bart's Yukon and Bart drove up northeast on Lakeshore Drive to nearby Highway 830, hit the elliptical roundabout, until they reached the lip of Lake Conroe. The drive was less than one mile away. Bart pulled the SUV up to the end of the road, killed the engine, and got out of the vehicle. Steven joined him.

Bart walked to the edge of the lake and looked up at the partial moon hovering above him, its incandescent glow reflecting back on his pale face.

"Are you happy, Steven?" Bart suddenly asked his friend.

Steven snapped to and answered, "Kind of." It did not seem very convincing, and he knew Bart picked up on it immediately.

"I mean really, truly happy?" Bart prodded.

"I don't know," Steven admitted.

"You know what makes me happy?" Bart shot back. "Not having to worry about anything." He smiled as he turned toward his friend.

Steven did not respond.

"I like being successful," Bart went on. "I like having money. I like knowing that I don't have to worry about anything."

Steven was not quite sure if Bart was finished talking about what made him happy, but after an interminable pause, Steven finally interjected, "Money makes me happy, too."

Bart nodded vigorously as he turned to his friend. "It's not just money, but the security that goes along with it. The knowledge that you can do whatever you want, whenever you want, however you want, is the ultimate power. It's the ultimate aphrodisiac." Bart began to circle around Steven, who stood still under the eerie moonlight—the wolf hypnotizing his wounded prey.

Steven nodded in agreement. He was not simply mesmerized by his friend; what Bart was getting at spoke to him directly. It truly was what he had always wanted, had always desired. The ability to know every morning he could wake up and not have a financial care in the world was the most important thing to Steven Champagne.

"It would not be that hard to make it happen," Bart declared.

Steven stood silently. He was intrigued by the direction of Bart's conversation.

"Do you want to be financially secure, Steven?" Bart inquired in a strong tone.

"Of course, Bart. Who doesn't?"

"Are you willing to do whatever it takes to make sure you realize your dream, Steven?" Bart insisted.

"I guess so," Steven replied.

"Well, you better be ready, because I am going to make that dream a reality, my friend. Just you wait and see."

An hour later, Bart and Steven jumped back into Bart's Yukon. Neither of them spoke another word on the ride home. Steven sat quietly, looking off into the pitch black through the SUV's passenger window, while Bart showed only a hint of a smile.

After the excursion to the lake, Bart and Steven began to spend even more time together. Many times, the two of them would simply hang out on Bart's porch, without their coworkers around. This was always the ideal time for Bart to begin making his plans for him and Steven.

Most of the time, Steven considered Bart to be a pretty straightforward guy. He believed Bart spoke clearly and said what he meant. However, Steven recalled, "There were times where you felt like he was leading the conversation in a [unique] direction, and you didn't quite know what he was after, or what he wanted you to say."

After Steven got to know Bart even better, the two

developed a shorthand way of communicating with one another, if they were around a group of people. They did not want the others to know what they were talking about, so they would speak in "cryptic terms." According to Steven, the two young men tended to act as if they were participating in a big inside joke. "We could be talking to another person and say something completely cryptic, that didn't really give away anything during the conversation to other people, but we knew exactly what we were talking about."

End of August 2003
Harbour Town
Willis, Texas

Just like they had with Adam Hipp and Justin Peters and Will Anthony, the conversations between Bart and Steven began to take on a darker, more sinister tone.

"I want to kill my parents." Bart snorted derisively toward Steven one night out on Bart's patio. No one else was around.

"I'm sure you do," Steven tossed back in a sarcastic tone.

"I'm serious," Bart declared.

Steven was unsure if his new friend was serious, or if he was merely gauging him for a reaction. He assumed it was the latter. Steven did not respond. Instead, he just nodded as if he understood and continued to let his friend get his feelings out in some healthy way. Inside, Steven believed Bart was joking. There was no way this smart, handsome, successful young man would ever get involved in something as risky, and off the radar, as murdering his own family.

When Steven did not respond immediately, Bart dropped the subject.

After that initial broaching of the topic, Bart turned his future conversations into more generalized versions of killing people. Bart's conversations examined the various methods of how to murder someone—and, more important, how to get away with it.

"There was one incident where he was describing how you can kill someone," Steven remembered, "and it could be totally random, and no one would ever know you did it." Steven remembered clearly how Bart talked about murdering one of their coworkers at the Bentwater Country Club, and how he would go about doing it without being detected.

According to Steven, their coworker "was addicted to drugs," and Bart "looked at him as if he was worthless. Like he was a drain on society." But Bart had a plan to deal with societal dregs. Bart told Steven, "You take him out into a field," referring to their coworker, "and shoot him in the head." Bart seemed rather non-plussed to Steven as he spoke of brutal execution. "There's no motive. No one would ever know you did it." He grinned slightly at the thought.

Steven looked at Bart and said, "You'd never get away with it."

"Oh, really?" Bart responded. "Why is that?"

"Because we work with the guy," Steven answered in a rational manner. "At the least, we would be questioned as potential suspects or witnesses, because we knew him and worked with him."

Bart did not say anything.

Over time, the random people that Bart wanted to

kill included his brother, Kevin. "It seemed like he started taking the feelings that he had toward people in general and placing them onto his family members," Steven opined.

Bart's main target of his frustration was his younger brother. According to Steven, "He felt like his brother was worthless, that he was just draining his parents of money."

Like most everyone else who encountered Kevin Whitaker, Steven liked the young man. "I had met him once over at Bart's place. They were playing poker. I saw him with Bart, and said hi." Steven also recalled one time when Bart asked him to pick Kevin up and bring him back to Willis. Kevin needed to drop off his car, and Bart was going to bring him back home, so Steven picked him up in the interim.

Steven did not quite fully understand Bart's hatred for his brother. To him, Kevin "seemed like a normal kid."

Bart's constant hinting around at killing his brother, and possibly his entire family, soon took a more serious turn. "He's worthless," Bart stated in exasperation. "He's just a lazy mooch that never earns his keep. I tell you, Steven, he's going to drain my family dry. I can't let him do it."

Steven, once again, just assumed Bart was blowing off steam.

"My parents have a lot of money," Bart declared to Steven, as if it were the first time he realized that fact. "I should just wipe out my entire family and collect all of the insurance money. Then I wouldn't have to worry about my annoying brother, and I would never need to worry about being financially secure ever again."

As usual, Steven kept his mouth shut.

"What do you say?" Bart asked his friend. "Are you in?"

"Am I in for what?" Steven asked, knowing full well where the conversation was heading.

"Are you in for making a lot of money and never needing to worry about whether or not you can pay your bills, or what kind of car you can drive?" Bart quizzed him again. He seemed somewhat giddy—at least for Bart, it seemed giddy.

"Of course," Steven assured him. "I want to be well-off and financially secure. Who wouldn't want to be?"

"Well, that's exactly where we can be in our lives," Bart declared, his excitement and momentum building. "And the way we can do it is to kill my family. I collect the life insurance money, and I would give you a cut for helping me out. You'll have more money in one fell swoop than you would if you worked at the restaurant for the next twenty years."

"I don't know, Bart." Steven shrugged. "Yeah, I want financial stability, but these are your parents and brother you're talking about. You shouldn't joke around about stuff like that."

Bart stopped any further discussion of specifically killing his family. He did, however, continue to discuss various methods of killing people—and how best to avoid getting caught.

"So, hypothetically"—Bart smirked—"what would be the best way to kill a small family?"

"I don't know, Bart."

"What about a car crash?" Bart pondered. "Could we conceivably kill multiple people in a car crash?"

"Sure, you could." Steven nodded.

"But what would we have to do to make it happen?" Bart asked rhetorically. "We'd have to stage it so it would look real, obviously. Probably the best way would be to drive someone over a cliff, or to have their vehicle burn somehow."

And on and on, the conversation continued. Steven was still never quite sure if Bart was serious. His friend had such a dry and morbid sense of humor, Steven was unable to discern if Bart was simply messing with him.

As these morbid conversations continued over time, Steven never really questioned their morality. He simply wrote it off as Bart venting, and needing a friend to lend an ear. "I felt like he had anger inside him, like he needed a friend to confide in. I didn't feel like we were making plans to kill anyone. It was more about trying to help him."

Bart and Steven would often talk about what they would do with the Whitaker inheritance, if they were actually to receive anything. "I would like to buy a nice home in Houston," Bart declared. "And a couple of really nice cars." Steven said he wanted the same things, too.

After a few more casual conversations like this, Bart escalated the plans. "He started bringing more details to the table," Steven recalled. Bart started talking about "the times it should take place. Bart started talking about exact methods of killing, how we could do it, and how we could get away with it."

Bart was determined that the murders should occur during the Christmas holidays. "If we do it around Christmastime, it would look more like a botched burglary, like someone breaking into my parents home to steal Christmas gifts. That way, the police would be less suspicious and wouldn't think of it as a setup crime. We can do this, Steven."

It was then, and only then, that Steven knew that Bart was truly serious about killing his family. "It was when his conversations turned from 'this could happen' to 'we can do this,' I knew he was for real."

Strangely enough, Bart never came straight out and asked Steven to help him murder his family. But he would always include Steven in his hypothetical plans of plotting the murders.

The conversations picked up and were engaged in every day for several days. By the end of August, Steven Champagne realized that his new friend wanted his help to wipe out his entire family. Unsurprisingly, Steven was completely against the idea.

One night in the beginning of September, at a bar in Conroe, Bart finally came out and directly asked Steven to help kill his family.

"I need your help, Steven," Bart stated, almost as an afterthought. "I cannot do this without you."

"I know, Bart. I get it," Steven responded, somewhat annoyed. He felt like Bart was simply pestering him now, and he was getting upset.

"So, can I count you in?"

"No!" Steven declined vehemently. "I don't want anything at all to do with this!"

"C'mon, Steven, don't you want to rest easy, knowing that you have all the money you need?" Bart cajoled.

"Bart, I don't want to talk about this," Steven replied sternly. He was trying to concentrate on a game of darts.

Bart, however, persisted. "I know you want to try this. I know you want to see if we can pull this off," he interjected in between Steven's dart throws.

Steven tossed a dart, which went askew and stuck into the bar's wall. He turned around, obviously infuriated, and yelled at Bart, "I don't want to look over my shoulder for the rest of my life!" Other patrons in the bar stopped to take notice. "I don't want to have anything to do with it!"

Bart calmly nodded his head and ignored the nearby customers. He was certain they had no idea what the two young men were talking about.

Steven hoped his outburst would put Bart on the spot, that someone in the bar would know he was up to no good, and that Bart would finally let the whole thing disappear. He believed it worked when Bart finally dropped the subject, grabbed his things, and took off from the bar.

22

Just a few days before Bart and Steven got into it at the Conroe bar, Chris Brashear moved in with Bart at the townhome. Chris was going through a difficult patch in his life, mainly because he had lost his job at the Bentwater Yacht & Country Club.

Bart had a spare bedroom in his townhome, which he gladly offered up for Chris to crash in until he was able to pick himself back up.

Steven thought Chris Brashear was a "normal, regular young man." He also believed him to be a bit of a "slacker and a goof," based on Chris's wardrobe preference, which consisted of baggy T-shirts and baggy blue jeans. He also described him as "kind of laid-back," but "a hard worker" when it came to his job at the restaurant. It came as a surprise to Steven that Chris quit.

Steven liked Chris when they first met at Bentwater.

He noticed, however, that Chris seemed to have changed after spending time living with Bart. It was not necessarily for the worse, though. Steven noticed that Chris had begun to change his style and his personality to resemble Bart more closely. He dressed nicer, in what Steven deemed "preppy clothes," such as well-pressed slacks and button-down long-sleeved oxford shirts. He was wearing clothes that were much more expensive than what Steven was used to seeing him in, which he found unusual since Chris was no longer employed.

Steven also noted that Chris "started to carry himself in a more intelligent manner." He described Chris as being "more disciplined" and that he had been "speaking different, proper," or more intelligently. Steven also noticed how Chris was even beginning to mimic many of the things that Bart did or said. It was like watching a little Stepford buddy.

Steven definitely considered Chris to be more of a follower, not a leader. He was definitely a follower of Bart Whitaker.

With Chris living on the same street as Steven, the two young men began to spend more time together. Though Steven sensed that Bart was closer to Chris than he was to him, Steven and Chris became friends as well.

The two young men bonded over guitar. Chris knew how to play and Steven had always wanted to learn, so the two started hanging out a lot together, with Steven learning a few licks from Chris.

Bart always seemed to be working, so Chris and Steven were able to spend lots of time together, developing a friendship. Steven soon felt as if his relationship with Chris was even better than the one he had with Bart. Indeed, he considered Chris to be a better friend than Bart.

23

September 2003
Harbour Town
Willis, Texas

Steven Champagne stood in the middle of his patio, smoking a cigarette. He was simply enjoying a bit of peace and quiet for the evening. As he took another drag off his cigarette, he spied Bart and Chris heading in his direction. His two friends seemed somewhat serious. They approached Steven as if it were simply a regular evening together.

After some idle chitchat, Bart and Chris both stood erect and faced Steven. Bart spoke up first. "We need you to drive."

Steven looked at his friend quizzically.

"You need to be our wheelman and pick Chris up," Bart continued as he nodded toward his roommate.

"What are you talking about, Bart?" Steven responded with a question.

"Chris is going to do it, and I need for you to be the one who picks him up and makes sure he gets out of my parents' neighborhood, without getting caught," Bart almost commanded.

Steven had somewhat expected this conversation. Instead of speaking up and angrily denying his part in the scheme, Steven said nothing. His silence equaled acquiescence, and was as good as a yes in Bart's mind. The conversation ended almost as quickly as it had begun.

After several minutes of standing outside, Steven finished his smoke.

"Let's head over to my place," Bart stated. He was ready to iron out some details with his newest recruit.

Inside Bart's townhome, the two henchmen settled into Bart's plush couch cushions as he poured drinks.

Steven looked up at Bart as he returned with glasses in hand. "Chris has agreed to do it," Bart confirmed Steven's suspicions. "We want you to drive him there and to pick him up after it's done."

Chris also looked at Steven as if to gauge his reaction.

"You then need to drive Chris back here," Bart continued.

"Bart, I told you, man, I don't want any part in this." Steven declined the offer.

Despite having just believed that Steven had agreed, Bart was nonchalant about his friend's response. "I understand, Steven." Bart poured him another drink and added, "But there is going to be a large amount of money in it for you if you help us out." He nodded toward Chris. "I understand, Steven." Bart was practically cooing his assurances. "I'm sure you must be very confused about this whole scenario."

"No, Bart, I'm not confused," Steven answered, and the tenor of his voice rose. "I told you, I don't want to have anything at all to do with this!"

Bart tilted his head down and then lifted it up to

look toward Chris. The mute communication conveyed a bond between them. They both turned to look directly at Steven.

"You're already a part of this, Steven."

Steven felt like one of the pod people from *The Invasion of the Body Snatchers*. He was trapped, and had no way of escaping.

"You already know what we're going to do," Bart added ominously. "You've been conspiring to do this with me, just as much as Chris has. As far as the police would be concerned, you're just as much as involved in this thing as we are. You will be considered an accomplice as well. You might as well get on board with us."

Steven was stunned. He had always thought Bart just wanted to vent about his family. He thought he was being a good friend by lending an ear. Instead, he had been sucked into Bart's malefic plan of mayhem.

"You've been a part of this since day one." Bart was basically threatening his friend. "If we get caught, you will go down as well. And your sentence will be just as bad as ours, even if you don't participate directly in it."

The unveiled threat was now out on the table. Steven had no clue which way to turn. He was caught. As far as he knew, there was no way out.

As time went by, Steven never bothered to look up the law that Bart had quoted him. He never bothered to turn Bart in, or give an anonymous tip to the police. He simply believed his friend was telling him the truth about being a conspirator. As a result, he kept his mouth shut and became a willing participant in a crime that would destroy an entire family, and his own life as well.

"All right," Steven relented. "I'm in."

Bart nodded, a slight grin on his face. His crew was set.

24

The treacherous trio began to make specific plans as to how they wanted to kill Bart's family.

The plan was basically the same exact plans that Bart had devised before, but had failed with Adam Hipp, Justin Peters, and Will Anthony. Drive down to Sugar Land. Bart would convince his family to go out to dinner. Steven would follow them to the restaurant and notify Chris when they had finished eating dinner. Chris would lie in wait inside the Whitakers' home and kill the entire family upon their arrival. He would wound Bart in the process to make it appear as if Bart were innocent. Chris would then escape through the back door and hook up with Steven for their escape.

Bart began to make sure the tiniest details were attended to, to make everything go off without a hitch this time. He did not want any of them to use their regular cell phones, for fear of them being traced back to the crime scene. Bart planned out their routes from Willis to Sugar Land and back. He wanted everyone to stay off the tollway, known as Beltway 8, for fear that the ever-present eye-in-the-sky cameras would document their travels. They were to drive only on the freeways.

Bart informed the two young men that he would leave a door unlocked at his parents' house, thus allowing Chris instant access. Bart informed Chris that his younger brother, Kevin, kept a gun in a lockbox upstairs in his room. Chris was to enter the house, head upstairs, pry open the gun lockbox, and retrieve the weapon.

To Steven, it appeared as if Bart and Chris had already worked out most of the details of the ambush. Steven was merely along for the ride, so to speak. They informed him—in no uncertain terms—that he was the driver. His sole responsibilities were to get Chris to Sugar Land, watch the family as they ate, alert Chris that they were coming home, pick Chris up, and then deliver him back to Willis in one piece.

It sounded easy enough. Maybe he could do this, after all, he thought. Maybe, since he was not the one calling the shots or aiming the shots, he could justify his actions. Besides, he really could use the extra money.

He did, however, find it unusual that Bart never came up with a definite dollar amount for their participation in the killing of his entire family. Steven found it even stranger that he personally never asked Bart how much money he was going to be paid. He also thought it strange that Chris never specifically asked Bart how much money Bart would pay him, either. Steven simply figured that all three men would move in together and live life like rich bachelors.

* * *

Once the plans were set into motion, Steven tended to lay low. None of the three guys spent much time together, as they had done during the summer and early fall. "It was more secluded," Steven recalled. "We didn't hang around as much. It was just more of Bart checking in to make sure that we were not talking [to anyone else]. That we were still in on the plan." Bart would continually call Steven to make sure everything was all right and to see if there was anything he needed. Bart seemed to be checking Steven's "state of mind" to make sure his friend was "not running to the police."

Bart needed everything to be perfect, which meant he needed his crew to be focused and not willing to crack under pressure.

If anything, Bart's constant surveillance of Steven made the latter more nervous and paranoid. He recalled a bizarre phone call he received at work one day in October.

"Hello," Steven answered his cell phone. The number came up as Bart's.

"Today is the first day of the systematic destruction of your life," Bart mysteriously intoned. He immediately hung up before Steven could respond.

Steven had no idea what Bart's cryptic message meant. He only knew it just made him a bit more freaked out than he already was.

Steven began to receive more and more similar calls from Bart, who would never explain what he meant, or what he was trying to get at. "I believe he felt he had to prove that he was smarter than everybody else," Steven theorized.

Bart was not above physical intimidation, either. He confronted Steven one day in an attempt to make sure he was still on board. "Getting cold feet?" he asked his friend.

Steven did not answer.

"You know," Bart informed him, "I know where you live."

Steven took it as a joke. He knew Bart's sense of humor was usually very dry and somewhat morbid. He assumed Bart was merely messing with him a bit to lighten the mood. Again, he did not respond, merely nodded.

Bart looked Steven directly in the eye and, in a less than jovial tone, said, "I know where your mother lives. I know where she sleeps." He grinned, and left it at that.

Steven was not quite sure what to make of Bart's statements. He deduced, however, that if Bart was willing to go to great lengths to murder his own parents, he probably would not hesitate to bat a white eyelash to take out Steven's mother. Bart's thinly veiled threat against Steven's mother finally did the trick for him. He knew he was in way too deep.

"I took it as, if he was willing to kill his own parents, he would not hesitate to kill mine. Also, if I brought any more attention to what was going on, or if I opened my mouth, or if I called the cops," their lives would be at risk as well.

Steven Champagne was very afraid of Bart Whitaker.

25

Steven Champagne overheard Bart Whitaker screaming inside Bart and Chris's townhome. It was obvious Bart was furious about something. After a few moments, Steven walked into Bart's room to see what was going on. He first saw Chris in the bedroom holding a Glock. He was busy loading a magazine with bullets into it.

"Everything all right?" Steven asked.

"No! I'm fucking pissed!" Bart screamed.

"What's wrong, man?"

"That was my fucking dad. He can't make it out to dinner tonight."

Steven was confused. "What do you mean, Bart?"

"I wanted to do it tonight!" Bart barked.

Steven had no idea Bart was ready to set the plan into motion. He was shocked by the reality of what was transpiring. "Do what?" Steven asked sheepishly.

"Take care of my problem."

"So, what happened with your dad?"

"I told him I wanted to come home and go out to dinner, but he has to work," Bart fumed. "He said there was no way he could go out tonight. This messes up everything!"

Steven simply stood silent. He was somewhat taken aback by Bart's intensity. He now fully realized Bart was deadly serious about wanting to kill his family.

26

November/December 2003
Harbour Town
Willis, Texas

As the month of December rolled ever closer, the leaves had only just begun to turn colors. Winters in south Texas are demarcated by two things: deer-hunting season and the Texas/Texas A&M classic Thanksgiving football rivalry. Both events require lots of preparation and extensive planning to pull off successfully. So it was that Bart prepared for his own winter rite of passage.

As a target date came closer into view, Bart began to shore up the smallest of details with Chris and Steven. Bart purchased two disposable cell phones for Chris and Steven to use on their excursion. He assured both men that the phones were untraceable. Bart also informed his friends that he would provide them with Nextel Direct Connect walkie-talkie phones so they would be able to communicate with one another during the commission of the crime.

Bart also spoke with Steven about making sure his car would not be traceable, either. He planned on securing license plates from another vehicle to switch out on Steven's car. However, he did not want to make the change until the actual day of the murders.

27

December 10, 2003, 4:00 P.M.
Harbour Town
Willis, Texas

Steven walked over to Bart and Chris's townhome to prepare for their trip. Chris was dressed very casually in blue jeans and a T-shirt. Apparently, ninja wardrobe was not the sartorial choice for the ride down. He would change into an all-black outfit later that evening.

The young men were quiet as Steven entered. After a few moments, Bart broke the quietude by handing Steven a pair of license plates, which he had stolen from a nearby shopping mall's parking garage. "Here, you're going to have to put these on your car in case you get snapped by a freeway camera." Steven was actually driving his mother's white Toyota Camry.

Steven took the license plates but did not say anything.

Bart then distributed the disposable cell phones to

his friends. He added, "We need to be sure that we leave at separate times."

"Okay," Steven responded. "How come?"

"Because we live in a gated community, we need to make sure the cameras don't videotape both of our vehicles leaving at the same time," Bart assured him. "It will look more normal if we leave the neighborhood in a staggered fashion."

"Okay, that makes sense," Steven replied.

"Of course, it does," Bart stated authoritatively. "All right, Chris and I are going to take off in my SUV. We'll meet you at the parking garage next to Woodlands Mall." (This was located in Spring, Texas, approximately twenty-two miles from Bart's townhome.)

Bart and Chris packed their items together and headed outside to Bart's Yukon. They loaded the SUV and drove off, out of the neighborhood. Steven left almost twenty minutes later.

Steven pulled his mother's car into the parking garage near the mall, approximately thirty-five minutes after he left Harbour Town. He drove around until he spotted Bart's SUV. He then pulled beside the Yukon, from which Bart had exited. Bart handed Steven a screwdriver to replace the license plates. Steven replaced the plates and tossed the originals in the trunk of the Camry.

Bart and Chris drove off and continued their sojourn to Sugar Land. After Steven finished with the license plates, he drove his mother's car around the parking lot, wasting time. He finally pulled out a substantial amount of time after the other two, then began his trek south.

Bart and Chris were headed for the Sugar Lakes Subdivision in Sugar Land, where Bart's parents lived.

Bart's plan was to drop Chris off on the street behind
his parents' house; then he would pull his Yukon up
to his parents' curbside. Steven was to drive to the
Pappadeaux seafood restaurant, where the Whitakers
were to celebrate Bart's impending "graduation" from
Sam Houston State University.

The three young men drove more than seventy
miles south, on Highway 59. Chris and Bart peeled off
to the frontage road that led to Sugar Lakes Drive, to
head to the home where he was born and raised.

Steven, meanwhile, still had an hour to go before he
was supposed to be at the Pappadeaux parking lot, so
he continued south on Highway 59 and drove for a half
hour. He then turned the car around and made his way
back to the restaurant. Finally he took the feeder road
north, back up to Pappadeaux. He pulled into the
seafood restaurant's back parking lot and waited patiently with his cell phone in hand. Bart had decided
earlier that they would not use the walkie-talkies, as he
did not feel that they were going to be secure lines and
someone might overhear their conversations.

Steven sat quietly, yet nervous, as he waited for the
Whitakers to show up. Bart had informed him that they
would be pulling up in either a white or black Trail-
Blazer. Not the most detailed of descriptions as SUVs,
many of which look almost identical to a TrailBlazer,
oversaturated Houston and the Sugar Land area.

Inside Pappadeaux, the Whitakers were enjoying
themselves immensely. They kidded with one another,
enjoyed their seafood, and snapped pictures in full celebration. The waiter then brought out a large white
plate for Bart with a special graduation celebration
dessert of strawberries and whipped cream in a white

bowl. The word "Concratulations" [*sic*] was spelled out with chocolate syrup on the rim of the plate.

It was like any other night that the Whitaker family got together and feasted, only with the added bonus of Bart's big news.

Bart Whitaker played his role perfectly. No one inside the restaurant would recall any unusual behavior by the young man, nor would his father. Bart seemed as if it was just another normal fun day in a life filled with them.

The Whitakers' last supper was memorable for its camaraderie, yet not that unusual for the seemingly close-knit, loving family.

Meanwhile, back at the Whitakers' home, stress was the order of the day. Chris Brashear made his way inside and was making sure he was adhering to the script. The first part of his job was to rifle through the family's belongings, making it appear as if a burglar had broken in and stolen items from their home. Chris set about his chore by first going into Kent and Tricia's bedroom on the first floor, near the foyer. Chris walked up to their dresser and began to pull out the drawers, only instead of doing it haphazardly, as one would think a nervy burglar would do when desperately searching for some unknowable riches, he pulled each drawer out very methodically and almost all the exact same distance. So, instead of a chaotic scene, it was all very controlled-looking. He then continued the neat ransacking of drawers that led from the parents' bedroom into their large bathroom.

After Chris finished the first part of the plan, he glanced down at his hands. He had pulled on two gloves, to avoid leaving identifiable fingerprints inside the house. He only now realized that one of his gloves was missing. He had no idea when or where he had dropped it. He grabbed his cell phone.

"Hello?" Steven answered his phone while sitting in the Pappadeaux restaurant parking lot.

"It's me," Chris stated, out of breath.

"What's wrong?"

"I lost one of my gloves!"

"What do you mean?" asked a baffled Steven.

"Dude, I lost my glove. I have no idea where it is!" The panic in Chris's voice was apparent.

"Calm down." Steven attempted to soothe his accomplice. "Do you have any idea where it might be?"

"No, dude. I don't have a fucking clue."

Steven's patience was being severely tested. "Find it!" he snapped.

"Okay, okay. I'll go look for it right now."

"Call me when you find it!" Steven ordered, then disconnected the call.

Chris looked at the dead phone and started to search for his missing glove. He scanned the house, to no avail. He had no idea that he had dropped it earlier in the front yard, near the curb.

Steven sat nervously in the Pappadeaux parking lot, as he had no idea which dark SUV belonged to the Whitakers. He watched as group after group of people filtered out of the side door of the restaurant with their bellies sated. Steven began to fret, for he was certain they were not going to leave the building. As a result, he decided to focus his attention on one dark SUV, which he hoped was the right one. After more than an hour, he watched as four people exited the restaurant and made a beeline toward the

SUV. He did not realize immediately that the group of people was Bart and the rest of his family.

The concept that three of these four people would possibly be dead in the next fifteen minutes no longer dissuaded Steven. He had made a promise to his friend, and he was going to live up to his end of the bargain.

Plus, he really needed the money.

Steven watched as the Whitakers piled into the Trail-Blazer and drove out of the parking lot. He started his mother's Camry and followed the Whitakers home. When Kevin pulled the SUV into their driveway, Steven continued on, down Heron Way, until he came upon a stop sign at Meadowlark Lane. He turned right and then took another right, onto Cardinal Avenue. He drove until he reached the house located directly behind the Whitakers' home. He pulled the car up, alongside the curb, checked to see if anyone was eyeing him, realized they were not, and turned the car engine off, killing the lights. Then he sat and waited.

Suddenly his cell phone rang.

"Yeah?" he answered quickly.

"Dude, I think they're here." It was Chris.

"Yeah, they're pulling up right now."

Chris immediately hung up the phone.

Steven was not sure if Chris could still go through with it. He put his phone down in the passenger seat and waited. He assumed Chris was scared that he was going to leave him behind.

28

December 10, 2003, 8:00 P.M.
Whitaker Residence
Sugar Land, Texas

The Whitakers returned home to be greeted with gunfire.

Pop!

Pop!

Pop!

Pop!

Chris Brashear exited through the Whitakers' back door into their neighbors' yard. Surprisingly, Chris was rather cool with his gait. He strode confidently, yet briskly, toward Steven's mother's car.

Chris immediately opened the door and entered the vehicle.

"Is everything okay?" Steven asked his friend.

Chris appeared calm. He was not freaking out, just determined to get out of the Sugar Lakes Subdivision as rapidly as possible. "Let's go, Steven," he replied, and ignored the question.

Steven was not quite sure how to react. He did not hear any shots being fired, nor did he hear any screams. He was not even sure if the shootings had occurred. When Chris remained quiet, Steven drove the car off into the dark December Sugar Land night.

Chris made sure that Bart left his Glock in the glove compartment. According to Steven, Chris "did not want to be without protection."

Neither young man spoke for the majority of the drive back to Willis. Chris began to rifle through his possessions to see what he had on him. He first pulled out his disposable portable cell phone. He then pulled out a small wad of cash.

"Where'd you get that?" Steven inquired as he saw the money.

"I found it in one of the closets in their house," Chris replied. He held on to the money. Chris also had a plastic water bottle that he drank from.

Steven continued to drive, until they came upon 610 Freeway and Interstate 45, approximately twenty-three miles from the Whitakers' home. He pulled the car underneath the freeway bridges, under the dark of night, grabbed his collapsible screwdriver, as well as his own license plates, and proceeded to switch them back. Chris got out of the vehicle to join him.

"So, what happened in there?" Steven wanted to know.

"I shot all of them," Chris responded coolly. He was not agitated, nor did he seem upset or particularly disturbed by what he had just stated.

"I was standing in the kitchen, in the dark," Chris continued on, "and I had just called you on the phone. Right after we hung up, I could hear someone fiddling with the keys to the front door, and the next thing you know, it was opening up. There was light coming in from the porch, and I could see Bart's brother."

Steven stopped what he was doing and focused on what Chris was saying.

"I saw Kevin walk inside, and he looked up and saw me." Chris paused. "He smiled at me! Can you believe that? He smiled at me, like he knew it was me and I was his friend, just there to greet him."

Chris stopped momentarily, kicked at the gravel, and resumed his recounting of the murders. "I walked right up to him and shot him at point-blank range, right in the chest. Then Bart's mom walked in, screaming, and I shot her at point-blank range also. I think I hit her directly in the middle of the chest as well."

Steven was transfixed by Chris's story. He almost could not believe it had happened.

Chris was on a roll. "I saw Kevin slump down to the floor, and he was immediately followed by their mom. They both looked dead to me right away." Chris seemed positive.

"The next thing I know, Bart's dad is near the front door, trying to come inside. I think I shot him in the shoulder or something. To be honest with you, I'm not sure if he was dead or not," Chris recalled. He sounded a bit nervous for the first time since the shootings.

"You don't know if Bart's dad is dead?" Steven replied, shocked. If Chris did not kill Kent Whitaker, then the whole plan would have been for naught. They needed all three of Bart's family members to die before Bart would receive any life insurance claims.

"No, man. I'm sorry," Chris pleaded. "I know I shot him pretty good. I just don't know if he's dead or not."

"What about Bart?"

"It went down just like we had planned it," Chris answered. "He ran into the house and acted like he was trying to tackle me, and I shot him in the shoulder, just like he wanted me to. That worked out perfectly." A friend later recalled that Bart had taken a martial arts course supposedly so he could sharpen his mind and learn how to take a bullet without completely falling apart.

All of a sudden, Chris was visibly exhausted and stopped talking. Steven finished changing the license plates, hopped back into the Camry, and they continued on their way back to Willis.

The two young men did not speak another word for the rest of the ride.

One hour later, Steven pulled his mom's Camry onto their street in Harbour Town.

Steven made a beeline for Bart's townhome car garage. Chris got out of the vehicle, closed the garage door, and grabbed a handheld vacuum cleaner. He crawled back into the car and began to vacuum out the back of the vehicle. Bart had earlier told Chris to do this in the event that he may have transferred something from the Whitaker home to the car—fibers, hair, pet dander, blood. Chris set to work.

Steven gathered together the screwdriver, a flashlight, the license plates, and a few other items. He bundled them together and handed them to Chris, so he could get rid of them.

Chris grabbed two duffel bags, which Bart had left behind in the garage, and began stuffing them with the items Steven handed over. When he finished, he threw both bags into the trunk of Steven's mother's car. Steven opened up the garage door and climbed back inside the vehicle, then pulled out of Bart's garage. Chris headed inside his townhome, while Steven drove to his driveway, parked the car, got out, and entered his townhome.

Steven walked inside and grabbed a glass of water. He could not believe that he had driven home a person who might have killed three people. He was neck deep in it now, and he understood the ramifications of his participation.

Steven finished off the cool glass of water and headed back over to Bart and Chris's place. He let himself in, and could hear the water running in the bathroom. He waited while Chris finished showering.

After about ten minutes, Chris stepped out into the living room. He had removed his black clothes and had changed into something more casual. Chris took the murder clothes and stuck them inside one of the duffel bags.

The plan, as conceived and ordered by Bart, was for Chris and Steven to stow everything they used at the murder scene into the duffel bags; then they were to drive over to the bridge on Lake Conroe. Bart wanted them to toss both duffel bags into the murky waters below.

They chucked the two duffel bags in the back of Chris's red Ford Ranger and began the haul, with Steven behind the wheel. Bart had asked them not to drive the Ranger to Sugar Land because it would have stood out due to its candy apple color. Chris begged off from driving, so Steven drove to the bridge on FM 1097 Road West, until they reached the top. He pulled the truck onto the shoulder and parked the car. The men got out of the vehicle. Steven moved toward the front of the truck to lift the hood, to make it look like they were stopped due to an engine malfunction, and hopefully not raise suspicions. While Steven tended to the engine, Chris removed the two duffel bags and tossed them over the side railing of the bridge.

Again, neither young man said anything as the deed was completed. They simply got back into Chris's Ford Ranger, and Steven drove back onto FM 1097, but with a different destination in mind. Instead of heading back to their townhomes in Harbour Town, Steven kept driving all the way to Houston. He pulled up to a local haunt known as The Ginger Man, a favorite college hangout for Rice University students, located on Morningside Drive, in Rice Village, near Rice Stadium, home to the perpetually hapless Rice Owls college football team.

Ensconced inside, Steven and Chris ordered the first of many beers. They were going to need some serious cooling off that only a cold brew could initiate. Beers paid for with the money stolen from the closet of the home of Kent and Tricia Whitaker.

Steven and Chris stayed at the bar for nearly three hours. They drank the entire time they were there. They never once mentioned what they had just partaken in. It was strictly a time for crawling inside the bottle.

Around midnight, Steven started to get paranoid. He was afraid that since they had been drinking that if they went out on the road and got pulled over by police officers, they would, at the least, get popped for a DWI. At the worst, they would get nabbed as accomplices to murder.

"We gotta go, man!" Steven blurted out.

"Calm down, Steven," a fairly inebriated Chris snapped back at him. "Be cool, man."

"No, we gotta get out of here," Steven responded.

"We've got to get the hell out of Houston right now. I don't want to get too drunk and have to drive all the way home. C'mon, let's get out of here." They paid their tab and left. Steven drove back toward Willis, but not until they first stopped in another bar, in The Woodlands, to continue their drinking binge.

Finally, at 2:00 A.M., as the bar was closed down, Steven and Chris were forced to head back to their homes. Steven pulled Chris's Ford Ranger into the driveway, and the two young men went to their separate residences to finally call it a night. They both went to sleep, even after having possibly participated in triple murder.

Surprisingly, both Steven and Chris slept well that night. They both went about the following day as if it were simply just another ordinary, run-of-the-mill day in their lives. They purposefully avoided watching the news on television, because they did not want to hear anything about the murders. Later that evening, Steven hooked up with his girlfriend to go out on a date. He called up Chris and invited him along. The trio headed out to another bar and began drinking again. Neither one of them talked about the previous night's events in front of Steven's girlfriend.

While sitting in the bar, nursing yet more drinks, Steven received a call on his cell phone from a close friend of his. The friend had called to tell Steven that he had heard his friend and boss, Bart Whitaker, had been shot, and that at least two of his family members were dead in Sugar Land. Almost simultaneously, Steven's mother also called him on the cell phone to share the same news. She had just watched a report on a local affiliate news broadcast and had immediately perked up when she heard the Whitaker name, since she knew Bart. Steven hung up his phone and played dumb in front of his girlfriend by telling her and Chris that Bart had been shot. The trio gathered their belongings and went back to Steven's townhome.

The following morning, Steven made a trip down to the hospital to check in on Bart. When he arrived, he noticed that many members of Bart's family were there, as was Bart's girlfriend, Lynne Sorsby. Steven had not seen Bart since he followed him from the restaurant to Bart's parents' house. He had no idea how Bart was doing. He realized that they would not be able to discuss what had happened because of the present company, so he simply played the role of the concerned friend.

The ensuing weeks after the murders led to upheaval in the three young men's lives. Bart, of course, underwent surgery; then he moved back to Sugar Land and into his former home with his father. The two men planned on supporting one another as they dealt with their grief over the loss of Tricia and Kevin. As a result, Chris Brashear was forced to move out of the townhome he had shared with Bart, and back home with his parents in Lake Jackson.

Bart did not want his townhome to go belly-up, so he asked Steven if he wanted to move in while Bart lived with his father. Steven, who was sleeping on his mother's couch at her place, jumped at the opportunity. He moved into Bart's townhome.

Bart Whitaker was handsome, intelligent, and had a sly sense of humor. *(Clements High School yearbook photo)*

Bart opening up his graduation gift from his parents on the night of the murders. *(Kent Whitaker)*

Kevin, Tricia, and Bart enjoy food and laughs at Pappadeaux Seafood Restaurant to celebrate Bart's impending college graduation.
(Kent Whitaker)

Bart with his very own celebratory dessert at the restaurant. *(Kent Whitaker)*

Kevin Whitaker, 19, enjoyed country music, cowboy boots, and Texas A&M University. *(Kent Whitaker)*

Tricia Whitaker, 51, was a former teacher who lived for her two boys. *(Kent Whitaker)*

Bart Whitaker, 23, the once-troubled oldest son, appeared to have gotten his act together. *(Kent Whitaker)*

The Whitakers' nearly $1 million home in the upscale neighborhood of Sugar Lakes in Sugar Land, Texas, just outside of Houston. *(Sugar Land Police Department)*

Bart's Yukon SUV with a black glove between it and the curb. *(Sugar Land Police Department)*

Black glove worn by the shooter and left at the scene.
(Sugar Land Police Department)

Front porch and entrance way into the Whitaker residence. Tricia was still alive and hanging out of the front doorway pointing toward the street.
(Sugar Land Police Department)

Kevin's right arm, bloody from clutching his abdomen after being shot.
(Sugar Land Police Department)

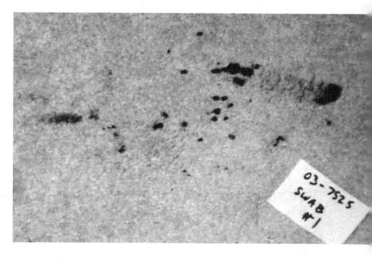

Blood left on the carpet near Kevin's body. *(Sugar Land Police Department)*

An EMT tended to an injured Bart Whitaker as he lay bleeding on the living room floor after accosting the shooter. *(Sugar Land Police Department)*

The shooter dropped the gun in the kitchen after colliding with Bart. *(Sugar Land Police Department)*

Close up of the gun used to kill Kevin and Tricia and shoot Bart and Kent.
(Author photo)

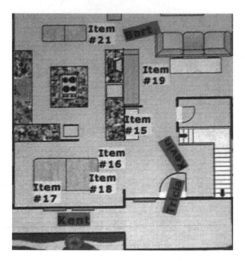

Map of the Whitaker house shows where all four victims were when they were shot. Bart claimed he leaped over his dying mother and dead brother to try to catch the shooter. *(Sugar Land Police Department)*

All nine dresser drawers in Kent and Tricia Whitaker's bedroom were pulled out at almost the exact same distance. Nothing inside the drawers was disturbed. *(Sugar Land Police Department)*

All five drawers in Kent and Tricia's bathroom were also pulled out at almost an identical distance and nothing inside was disturbed. *(Sugar Land Police Department)*

Officers went up the staircase festooned with Christmas decorations to locate more evidence. *(Sugar Land Police Department)*

Several boxes of bullets were discovered in the far corner of a playroom attached to Kevin's bedroom upstairs. *(Sugar Land Police Department)*

The gun safe located next to the bullet boxes was pried open by the
shooter and the gun inside was the one used in the killings.
(Sugar Land Police Department)

Detective Marshall Slot (left) being interviewed about the case.
He pursued the killer for more than two years. *(Marshall Slot)*

More than two years after the murders, Bart Whitaker's roommate, Chris Brashear, was arrested as the triggerman in the killings. *(Sugar Land Police Department)*

Two weeks after Brashear's arrest, Bart Whitaker's friend and co-worker, Steven Champagne, was arrested as the getaway car driver in the murder plot. *(Sugar Land Police Department)*

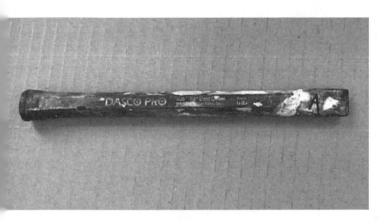

Champagne told Detective Slot where to find items used in the murders. At the bottom of Lake Conroe, divers discovered the chisel used to pry open the gun safe, along with one of the cell phones used in the commission of the crime (among several other items). *(Author photo)*

Bart after his arrest in Laredo, Texas, after he had been hiding out in Mexico for nearly a year. *(Sugar Land Police Department)*

Bart's mug shot after being charged with the murders of his brother and mother and the shooting of his father. *(Sugar Land Police Department) fill your heart with*

peace and happiness.

I'm not really sure if it is appropriate to communicate with you directly. I have wanted to for so long, though. I guess I just wanted to wish you Happy Holidays. I hope you are able to compartmentalize all the nastiness you are made to see on a daily basis, and concentrate on your family. More than anything else I've learned the past few years, they are what really matters. I suppose that sounds hypocritical, but even one as lost as I was can find my way home.

*"For God so
loved the world,
that he gave his only
begotten Son."*

—John 3:16

Praying for You,

[signature]

Christmas card Bart sent to Fort Bend Assistant District Attorney Fred Felcman, who believed it to be a threat. *(Author photo)*

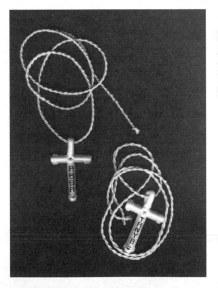

Bart spends his time in prison making cross necklaces out of dental floss *(Author photo)*

Kent Whitaker has forgiven his son for shooting him and having Kevin and Tricia killed. He says his faith in God led him to forgive Bart.
(Kent Whitaker)

Bart Whitaker on death row.
(Texas Department of Corrections)

29

After the murders, Bart moved back into the house where he grew up. Every day he would cross over the threshold where his family was slaughtered. He claimed he moved back home to help his father sort out everything and to be there for him, if needed.

More than one month after the murders, both Kent and Bart began their intensive physical therapy on their shooting wounds. According to Kent, his "was a mess." Apparently, the bullet that he was struck with "broke into high-velocity shrapnel" when it hit him "that shredded the muscle mass in [his] chest and upper arm before shattering [his] humerus bone." He added that he would "always have a hollow cavity beneath the bullet hole in my shoulder, where the tissue was destroyed beyond repair." Kent was kept immobile for nearly seven weeks, which led to "significant (and potentially permanent) loss in [his] arm's range of motion." Kent's painful therapy included rebuilding muscle mass by focusing on "scar tissue [that] had to be painfully stretched and pulled apart before it became too set." If he did not undergo the rigorous therapy, he might have to spend the "rest of [his] life with a severely restricted and weakened right arm."

According to Kent, the therapy could be torturous at times. Kent shared that he was assisted by a physical therapist who was a "huge guy who would have me lie on my stomach as he pried his fingers under my shoulder blade and . . . tried to pull it off. I felt like a Thanksgiving turkey as he yanked and pulled."

On the other hand, Bart's wound was much less severe, so his regimen was far less taxing and painful than his father's.

Kent believed the physical therapy sessions, combined with helpful gifts from God, would lead him on a healing path of recovery—of the physical, spiritual, and emotional kind.

30

January 7, 2004
Harbour Town
Willis, Texas

Steven Champagne lay in his bed, provided to him—generously enough—by Bart Whitaker. He was much later to rise these days. A combination of general malaise and guilt mixed together to create a certain sense of ennui, which seemed to glue his backside to the bed. He had no desire to wake up anytime soon.

He had no choice.

Steven was awoken by a loud rapping on the front door of the townhome. The disheveled young man tossed on some sweatpants and a T-shirt to go check and see who was waking him up so ridiculously early in the morning. He was definitely not a morning person, and whoever was making an early-morning house call was certainly not endearing themselves to him. He shuffled to the door, unlocked it, and opened it up to see the nonsmiling visages of two Sugar Land police detectives. Needless to say, Steven was caught off-guard and completely surprised.

"What can I do for you?" Steven asked the detectives.

"Good morning, sir, my name is Detective Marshall Slot, from the Sugar Land Police Department," the medium-sized lead detective, with the crew cut, proffered. "This is Detective Glenn White," he said as he nodded toward his fellow detective. "We'd like to come in and talk to you about the owner of this townhome, Bart Whitaker."

Steven appeared confused at first; however, he somehow managed to regain his composure. "Certainly, Detective," he acquiesced. "Please come on inside." He stepped back from the door to allow the two detectives unencumbered entrance. As the men stepped through the main opening, Steven asked, "Is everything okay with Bart?" He was trying to play it cool.

"He's fine, son," Detective Slot responded as he stepped inside.

"That's good," Steven acknowledged.

"I'm sorry, son. What is your name?" the detective asked.

"Oh, excuse me. I'm Steven. Steven Champagne. I'm a good friend of Bart's. I live just a couple of houses over."

"Sir, do you mind if I ask—if you live a couple of places over, why are you sleeping here in Mr. Whitaker's townhome?"

"Bart let me move in after his mother and brother were killed," Steven answered. He was keeping his cool much better than he thought he would be able to when this inevitable day came. "I guess that's why you guys are here, to find out who killed Bart's family? I still can't believe it happened." Steven invited the detectives to have a seat on the couch in the living room.

Detective Slot dismissed any notion of engaging in small talk. Instead, he got right down to business. "Mr. Champagne, are you friends with Bart Whitaker?"

"Yes, sir. I work under Bart at the Bentwater Country Club, as well as living two doors down from him."

"Where were you on the night of the murders?"

Steven lied and told the detectives he was "out at a bar" with "a friend from work" named Patrick. He just hoped the detectives did not decide to call up Patrick to verify his whereabouts that night.

"Very good, sir," Detective Slot thanked him. The three men continued to talk for nearly two hours. However, Steven became less nervous the longer he spoke with the men. They obviously had no idea who he was, and it was apparent to him that they did not consider him to be a suspect. They just asked him about his job, and mainly about anything he might have seen or heard about on or around December 10. Steven actually considered both detectives to be quite friendly toward him.

The rest of the time was spent mainly talking about Bart. Steven did not believe he gave up any valuable information on his friend. Of course, why would he? Giving up Bart would be like injecting the needle into his own arm. If Bart was willing to hurt Steven or Steven's mother for not even participating in the murder scheme, he had no doubt whatsoever that Bart wouldn't hesitate to rat him out to the police, given the chance. Steven hoped he never had to find out.

January 14, 2004
Harbour Town
Willis, Texas

One week later, Steven was suddenly jolted out of his slumber by the sound of his telephone. He picked it up and answered, "Hello?" He was barely coherent.

"Steven, it's Chris," he heard on the other end of the line. He had not spoken to Chris since the night after the murders.

"What's going on, man?" Steven asked. He was nervous and could tell his friend was scared. "What's wrong with you?"

"The cops were here!" Chris seemed terrified. "They think I'm involved in it, Steven. I think they know I shot Bart's mother and brother. I don't know how they know, but I think they know!"

For the first time since the murders, Steven was also terrified. It had all seemed a bit too surreal to him. Hearing the panic in Chris's voice raised the stakes for him. If the police were onto Chris, it would only be a matter of time before they set their sights on him.

"Chris, calm down. Tell me what happened."

"They were here, man! Two detectives just left my place. I don't know. I think they know what's going on, but they aren't really saying. But I think they know I was directly involved."

Steven attempted to calm Chris down and told him he was going to call Bart and see what he wanted to do. Bart told Steven to get Chris up to Sugar Land so the three of them could talk about what was going on, and how to deal with the police officers.

Steven called Chris back, and after much cajoling, he convinced Chris to get out of his parents' house and come visit them. Chris attempted to beg off because he claimed he did not have enough money for gas to make the jaunt, but eventually he relented and drove to Sugar Land. Once he arrived, Bart suggested that they go to the movie theater and talk during a screening of the three-and-a-half-hour fantasy epic *Lord of the Rings: The Return of the King*. Bart figured the length of the film would give them plenty of time to deal with their current problem of the police.

Bart made sure both Steven and Chris made it to the movie theater to discuss what had transpired between the cops and Chris. He told Steven that they were there to "support" Chris through the difficult time. Of course, Bart was mainly concerned that Chris would crack and let loose the truth as to all of their involvement in the double murder. Bart could sense that Chris was "getting weak," and he wanted to put an end to it immediately.

The three young men bought their tickets and took their places near the back of the large screening room. As the first reel of the film began to unspool, Bart scooted Chris over a couple of seats away from Steven so they could be closer to the corner. Bart did not notice the man sitting directly behind them, an undercover police officer.

Steven turned his attention to the Peter Jackson–directed spectacle of Hobbits, Orcs, and Mordor as Bart attempted to calm Chris down. Steven felt secluded away from his friends, plus he had a nagging suspicion about the man sitting behind them. He believed they had been followed through Sugar Land and into the theater. He was starting to get nervous, as he believed the so-called filmgoer was actually an undercover police officer. He hoped to God that Bart and Chris were not talking about the actual murders.

After the movie ended, the three friends took off from the theater. Steven checked out Chris to see if he was cool. Apparently, whatever Bart said to him did the trick; he no longer seemed freaked out. Furthermore, the man sitting behind them did not follow them outside the building, so Steven could breathe a bit easier.

January 21, 2004
Harbour Town
Willis, Texas

Two weeks after their first encounter, Sugar Land detectives Marshall Slot and Glen White paid Steven Champagne a second visit, again at Bart's townhome. Unlike the previous visit, the detectives arrived in the evening, and they did not appear to be as nice as they had been the first time around.

The detectives began to go through the same set of questions they had asked Steven previously: Where did he work? How did he know Bart? What was he doing on the night of the murders? Steven answered the questions exactly the same way he had two weeks prior, including the information about going out to a bar the night of the murders with his friend Patrick.

"We spoke with Patrick," Detective Slot informed Steven. The young man worried that his Adam's apple might come bursting through his throat, he gulped so hard. "He said that the two of you did not go out together on December tenth."

Steven did not respond.

"Why would he say that to us, if it weren't true, Steven?" Slot asked.

"I have no idea why he would lie to you," Steven calmly replied. "Maybe he just got the days confused."

"No, Steven. He seemed very adamant that the two of you did not go out together that night."

"I don't know what to tell you, Detective," Steven replied, seemingly nonplussed.

"Steven, is there something you want to tell us? I'm sure it will make you feel a lot better to get this off your chest."

"I have no idea what you're talking about, Detective." Steven remained calm and did not crack under pressure.

Detective White leaned in toward the young man. "C'mon, Steven. We know what happened that night. Bart put you up to it, didn't he?"

"What are you guys talking about?" Steven continued to play ignorant.

"The murders, Steven. Tricia Whitaker. Kevin Whitaker. Bart's family. He put you up to this, didn't he?" Detective Slot continued the interrogation.

"Wait a second." Steven acted stunned at their insinuations. "You guys think I was involved in killing Bart's mom and brother. That's insane."

"Is it?" Detective White countered.

"Of course, it's insane. I cannot believe you guys would try to pin something like that on me."

"C'mon, Steven. I know you want to confess and get it off your chest. It's got to be eating at you every day," Detective Slot persisted.

"I'm sorry, Detectives, but I am going to have to ask you to leave my house," Steven boldly commanded.

"I had absolutely nothing to do with the Whitaker murders, and I want you off the property now."

"Okay, Steven," Detective Slot responded. "But you think about it and give us a call if you decide to change your mind." The detectives nodded, turned around, and exited the premises.

Steven closed the door behind the men. He could not let out a yelp of anxiety that he so desperately needed to release.

31

February 2004
T.G.I. Friday's
Lake Woodlands Drive
The Woodlands, Texas

Bart invited Steven out to dinner at a nearby T.G.I. Friday's. Steven correctly assumed Bart was checking up on him to make sure he would not spill the beans. He was right.

"So, how are you doing?" Bart asked with a sly smile.

"I'm doing all right. How 'bout you, Bart?"

"All things considered, I'm doing pretty good." Bart took a menu from between the salt and pepper shakers on the table and began to peruse it. Once he knew what he wanted for dinner, and confirmed that Steven was ready, he motioned to the waitress to come take their order. After she left, Bart started in with a little chitchat.

It was not long before the conversation turned to the overriding issue in both men's lives: the murders.

"I can't believe Chris didn't take out my dad," Bart bemoaned.

Steven simply nodded. He did not want to have this conversation in a restaurant, but he could tell Bart was determined to do so.

"He was at point-blank range. How do you *not* kill somebody who's standing directly in front of you, and you shoot them?" he asked incredulously.

"I don't know," Steven quietly answered.

"I don't know, either." Bart chuckled at the thought. "Less than a foot away from him, and he doesn't die. Unbelievable."

Bart took a sip from the water that the waitress had brought to their table. "Of course, Chris's failure to complete the job pretty much screws everything up. You understand that, don't you?"

"I figured as much," Steven responded.

"There's no way we can collect on the life insurance money, since my dad didn't die."

"Yep," Steven muttered.

"We are going to have to do something about that," Bart reasoned in his head and spoke out loud.

"What are you talking about, Bart?" Steven wanted to know.

"I think you know."

"What?"

"We've got to finish what Chris couldn't," Bart stated emphatically.

Steven began to get paranoid again. He just knew Bart was going to say something about the murders (or even more murders) loud enough to where some of the other customers in the restaurant could overhear them. "Bart, keep your voice down, man. I don't want anyone to know what the hell happened."

Bart smiled at him. A mischievous grin flashed as he lowered his voice, only slightly. "I need to make a plan so we can deal with my dad."

"Bart, you're fucking crazy," Steven scolded his friend. "There is no way you can make a foolproof plan to kill your dad. And even if you were able to pull it off, everyone would suspect you. I mean, c'mon, man, it would be too damn obvious. To everyone."

"I know it would look fishy, but I feel like I could pull it off again, and be sure that he dies this time," Bart answered.

"No, man. No. No, I don't want anything to do with this anymore, Bart," Steven pleaded.

"What do you mean?" Bart seemed genuinely surprised, if not a bit hurt by Steven's reaction.

"I don't want any part in killing your dad," Steven declared.

Bart paused momentarily and looked Steven directly in the eyes, as if to size him up, right then and there, to determine if his friend still had his manhood intact. Steven shifted in his seat, visibly uncomfortable. Bart nodded and said to Steven, "We've got more work to do."

It was work that was never completed. Bart did not pursue the follow-up murder of his father.

32

Adam Hipp knew he needed to do something to rectify his situation. A big part of him felt horrible for what had happened to Tricia and Kevin Whitaker. He felt that if only he had spoken up years ago, their deaths might have been prevented. He also felt horrible that his previous actions and omissions might leave him in a major bind, and he could possibly face some serious jail time of his own for acting as an accomplice in a conspiracy to commit murder. He was not sure where he stood legally, but he knew, morally, he was nearly bankrupt. He wanted to make amends in some way, shape, or form.

Hipp believed the only way he could make a difference now was to help the Sugar Land Police Department catch their man. As a result, he approached Detective Marshall Slot with the idea of wearing a wire and engaging Bart in conversation about their murder plans, and to nail Bart somehow for the actual murders of his family members. It would be a

risky and tricky proposition. Hipp feared for his own
life and for those of his family members, but he realized he could no longer sit by idly. He later admitted,
"It was worth it to me . . . [because] I know nothing
would ever justify what I did or had listened to, instead of trying to convince him otherwise."

Hipp and Detective Slot spoke extensively and
specifically as to how they planned on setting up Bart.
Slot told Hipp that he was only to contact Bart in the
detective's presence. The reason being, so Slot could
properly set up the recording equipment to capture
the conversations between the two young men. Slot
also provided a cheap Motorola cell phone to Hipp to
use for the recorded conversations. The only people
who knew about the phone were Hipp and Slot. Bart
would be the only other person with that phone's
actual phone number.

In addition to the technical aspects of the setup,
Slot and Hipp worked on exactly what Hipp would say
to Bart to get him to admit to the previous conspiracy
to murder his family, but *also* to the actual killings
themselves. Slot intended for Hipp to script out his
various conversations, and he expected the young
man to practically know the scripts by heart. Slot
made sure to have several key bullet points emphasized, in case Hipp screwed it up, so he could still
manage to hit the high points in their conversations.
The plan was for Adam to reestablish his friendship
with Bart. It was also the intention to make Bart
uneasy, as he would know Hipp probably knew what
had happened to his mother and brother based on
their original plans.

The first two calls between Hipp and Bart occurred
on January 10, 2004. Hipp called Bart, who returned

his call. The initial conversation was simply for Adam to let Bart know that the detectives had contacted him, and they wanted to know what he knew about Bart.

The squeeze was on.

The third phone call took place one month later, on February 10, 2004. This call entailed Adam telling Bart that the Sugar Land Police Department detectives contacted him again and that they now wanted to meet with Hipp in person to discuss the murders and learn everything they could about what he knew.

The goal was to get Bart to admit that he had employed Hipp years earlier in a failed attempt to murder his family. Hipp would talk about certain aspects of the actual murders and then try to relate them to what they tried to do on the earlier failed attempts.

While Bart never overtly admitted to killing his parents, or of devising a plan to do so, he did ask Adam to lie for him to the police, to discredit their earlier accomplice, Justin Peters.

During the third phone call, Adam informed Bart that he wanted some money for his compliance. This was at the behest of Detective Slot, who instructed Adam that "the tone of the conversations needed to be a little bit more aggressive and demanding." By the end of the third phone call, Adam convinced Bart to pay him $20,000. Bart agreed, but he informed his old friend that he would have some difficulty gathering the money on such short notice. Bart told Adam that he would send him what he could, and that the amount would only be $200.

Ironically, during this third phone call, Bart asked Adam if he would be willing to wear a wire when he had a conversation with the detectives. Bart wanted to hear firsthand what the detectives knew about him.

Adam agreed to do it for Bart. "It was to establish my credibility with Bart that I was doing what I could for him, and to show that I had done exactly as he'd asked." Hipp and Detectives Slot and Billy Baugh would actually, later on, set up a fake interview in Adam's living room so he could take the recorded conversation back to Bart.

During the third phone call, Adam noted Bart's controlling behavior: "He was always interested in trying to manipulate whatever he could to serve his personal interests above anybody else's. I take that as, 'You know what you need to do, and you know that you don't need to say anything.' He would consistently speak within layers. It was never just a surface type of suggestion with him."

33

March 10, 2004
The UPS Store
Preston Road
Dallas, Texas

Detective Marshall Slot had every intention of using Adam Hipp as much as he could against Bart Whitaker. One more avenue came in the guise of attempting to frame Bart by using a post office box (POB) in Dallas. As Adam began to let Bart know that he was onto him and that he wanted a little hush money, Slot felt as if he had Bart right where he wanted him. He figured the next logical step would be to set up a POB so he could catch Bart making physical transactions with Hipp in order to pay for his silence.

Adam agreed to the scheme and set the plan in motion by acquiring a box at The UPS Store in Dallas, in the general vicinity of Chase Bank, where Hipp worked. Slot contacted Detective Marshall Bearor, of the Highland Park Police Department, who would oversee any transactions that took place at the POB inside The UPS Store.

Hipp told Bart about the POB and said that he should send the money to Hipp as quickly as possible. Thus, the "blackmailing" of Bart Whitaker had begun.

Detective Slot explained to Hipp the necessity behind the transaction. If Hipp was to receive a payment from Bart, it would show "further acknowledgment or admission from Bart that he had previously tried to do this (conspire to murder his family) and that he knew that the 2003 murders had particular coincidences with the previous conspiracies."

Once Hipp made the call to Bart to set the transaction in motion, all he could do was sit back and hope that something would arrive.

It did.

Just a few days later, Detective Bearor visited The UPS Store to check on the post office box. Sure enough, there was a package sitting inside. It was addressed to Adam Hipp. It was a standard white bubble mailer envelope. Inside the envelope was $200, in cash.

Upon closer inspection, Detective Bearor spotted the unusual return address on the upper left-hand side of the envelope. On it was written the following:

K. Soze
Windlass Ln
Willis, TX 74358

Bart was fully aware that Hipp knew of his affection for the film *The Usual Suspects*. The basic premise of the movie is that five well-known criminals are brought in for a police lineup following a carjacking incident.

While in a holding cell, they conspire to plan a heist together.

The film, however, is far from simple to digest. Its non-linear storytelling structure is narrated by a supposed physically challenged man named Verbal Kint, who retells the story to a corrupt police officer. As Kint, the only other survivor of a ship explosion, unravels his tale, it becomes clear that a criminal mastermind has been playing puppeteer to the assembled criminals who have all allegedly wronged one individual—Keyser Soze.

At the end of the film, it is revealed that the narrator, Kint, is more than just a crippled sidekick. As he escapes the clutches of the police, it becomes evident that he is the one and only Keyser Soze, the criminal whom the other usual suspects feared, and whose name is on everyone's lips from the bad guys to the good guys alike.

The Usual Suspects went on to receive much praise for its intelligent script and its laudatory references to the 1940s film noir style of moviemaking. The film was also nominated in numerous categories for a slew of awards, including a Golden Globe nomination for Best Supporting Actor for Kevin Spacey (who played Verbal Kint), and two Academy Award wins, for Spacey and for screenwriter Christopher McQuarrie.

The film was also seen as a hipster cool flick that the smart college-aged kids would dig; so naturally, it was right up Bart's alley.

Hipp later mentioned that Bart had "a great affection for the movie, as well as for the way he identified himself with Keyser Soze, because he was able to get away with whatever he wanted to."

Hipp believed that Bart's admiration for the film went beyond a casual filmgoer's appreciation, and even beyond the love of it from a devoted film fanatic. "I think there was a disconnect between reality and fiction," Hipp noted. "I think he truly believed he could be like Keyser Soze."

Hipp had a real concern about Bart's obsessive nature with the film. At the end of *The Usual Suspects*, every one of Soze's co-conspirators, who helped him pull off the caper and commit numerous murders, all end up dead. Hipp believed he would end up just like them in Bart's world of crime and retribution. "It definitely led me to believe that if he really thought he could be Keyser Soze, then what would prevent him from trying to demonstrate that." He noted with a chill, "Because in the movie, essentially he (Soze) goes back to kill the people that were going to testify against him."

Hipp's fear of Bart's retribution also inspired him to try to communicate from beyond the grave, if necessary. "I had torn a couple of pages out of a journal," the young man recalled, "and expressly written out that if anything was to happen to me or my family, that I had places underneath my bed that had other pieces of paper that said if something happened, or if I died, or if any member of my family was injured, that Bart was the one to be held responsible."

Additional phone calls were made between Adam Hipp and Bart Whitaker in an effort to secure a meeting between the two men in person. The plan was for the two men to meet at Sam's Boat restaurant on March 19 and to get Bart to admit, on tape, that he was directly involved in the murders of his mother and little brother. Bart agreed, and the Sugar Land Police Department set their surveillance team into motion.

On the day of the scheduled meeting, Adam was wired up, undercover police officers were stationed at the restaurant, and even more officers with cameras were in tow. The extra personnel were brought on board because of Hipp's fear that Bart would retaliate and possibly attempt to murder him.

A nervous Hipp entered the restaurant and took a seat and waited.

And waited.

And waited.

Bart was nowhere to be seen; he failed to appear. Adam placed a call to him on his cell phone and wanted to know where he was. Bart informed him that he had left his house to come visit Adam; however, he believed he spotted police officers outside the restaurant and decided not to enter. Hipp then suggested they meet at The Ginger Man, the same bar where Steven Champagne and Chris Brashear decompressed after the murders. Bart nixed that idea, so Adam suggested they meet in a nearby park. Again, Bart said no, then suggested that Adam come visit him at his house.

When Adam Hipp informed Detective Slot of Bart's desire, the officer told Hipp they would arrest Adam if he went to Bart's. The reason given was that he feared for his safety and could not guarantee they would be able to protect him. As a result, Adam had to call Bart back and make up an excuse as to why he could not come over to talk with him.

34

March 19, 2004
Houston Livestock Show and Rodeo
Reliant Stadium
One Reliant Park
Houston, Texas

Before the murders took place, Kent Whitaker remembered, there was one afternoon when his youngest son, Kevin, was exhilarated to the point of giddiness. Kevin had found out that his favorite musician, country singer Pat Green, known for such songs as "Wave on Wave" and "Carry On," and such well-received albums as *Here We Go* and *Three Days*, would be performing at the Houston Livestock Show and Rodeo the following March 19, 2004, which just happened to be the same day as Kevin's twentieth birthday.

Kent remembered the day vividly. He remembered how Kevin had bolted down the stairs, yelling at his father with joy, "Dad, guess who's going to be playing at the rodeo on my birthday? Pat Green!"

"That's your favorite guy, right, Kevin?"

"Yeah, Dad. Can we get the skybox for the birthday party?" Kevin queried his father rather exuberantly. The skybox he was referring to was the one owned by the Acme Brick company, located in Reliant Stadium.

Several months later, Kent Whitaker, with more than twenty complimentary tickets in hand, made his way over to the home of the Houston Texans National Football League team to celebrate his youngest son's twentieth birthday, as a way to honor something important to his murdered son. Among those in attendance that night was one of Kevin's best friends, Brittany Barnhill, the daughter of one of Kent's best friends, Matt Barnhill, a pastor, from the River Pointe Community Church, in nearby Richmond.

When Matt heard that Kent was taking the young adults to see Pat Green to celebrate Kevin's birthday, he decided to help Kent out with something a little extra special. Barnhill knew a parishioner at his church who just happened to be a former FarmHouse Fraternity brother of Green's at Texas Tech University, in Lubbock. He still kept in touch with the now-famous country singer/guitarist. Barnhill was able to score six backstage passes for a meet-and-greet with Green before the concert at the rodeo. He gladly handed them over to Kent.

On the evening of the rodeo and concert, Kent and his twenty-two-person entourage made its way to their perfect-view box seats provided by the Acme Brick people. The rodeo began in 1932, and features the usual events, such as barrel racing, lassoing calves, wrestling calves, and a whole slew of rodeo clowns to provide some laughs. Musical acts were added in 1942, with country legend Gene Autry as the so-called halftime entertainment. By the 2000s, the entertainers took the stage after

the rodeo events. Many top country artists, such as Garth
Brooks, Charley Pride, and Mickey Gilley, have performed there, as well as several pop artists, including
KC & The Sunshine Band, Styx, and 98 Degrees. The
2004 edition featured, among many others, John Mayer,
George Strait, Beyoncé, and, of course, Pat Green.
Though seeing Green perform later that evening as part
of the Spring Break Stampede would seem bittersweet
without his youngest son by his side, Kent could see
how excited all of Kevin's friends were to be able to
celebrate his life with his favorite musician.

While the rodeo activities kicked off, Kent and five
friends of Kevin, including Brittany Barnhill, were
promptly escorted to the backstage area inside Reliant
Stadium to have a personal meeting with Pat Green.

The musician could not have been more accommodating. He took time with each person backstage to
make sure to shake a hand, say a quick hello, or auto-
graph a CD or a photograph. Kent was duly impressed
as he realized this young man would soon be out there
performing in front of more than fifty thousand people.

When Green made his way over to Kent and the
others, he was quick with a smile and handshake for
the father. Kent informed the friendly musician that his
song "Poetry" sounded as if it had almost been written
specifically for Kevin. He mentioned that Kevin had recently been murdered and that they were all at the concert to celebrate his birthday with his favorite singer.

Brittany suddenly spoke up, "So, are you going to
play it?"

Green actually hesitated, then stated, "We actually
don't play that song in concert anymore."

"Aw, c'mon, you have to!" Brittany retorted pleasantly.

Green hemmed and hawed for a brief moment,

looked at the young lady and the father, then said, "Well, sure! Yeah! We're gonna play it!" He started laughing, then took out a Magic Marker and wrote down Kevin's name in the palm of his hand. He then asked if the crew would like to take a picture with him, which they all eagerly agreed to; then they were off to their box seats.

Not long thereafter, Green kicked off his performance. After three songs into the set, Green stepped up to the microphone and said, "We weren't going to do this song, but I met some folks backstage who asked me to." Kent could not believe his ears as he heard Green say, "So, Kevin," he declared, then pointed up through the hole in the roof of Reliant Stadium as if pointing up to Heaven, "this one's for you." He then performed "Poetry." There wasn't a dry eye in the Whitaker skybox section. Kent said, "It was all I could do from losing it." Kent had even purchased a package of disposable lighters for the kids to fire up during the emotional song and described their skybox as looking like "a seventies rock show."

Even Bart seemed to sense the enormity of the moment as he feigned as much sorrow as he could muster.

The following morning, Kent fetched the local newspaper, the *Houston Chronicle,* from his driveway, brought it inside, and opened up to the Star section, where he read a review of the Pat Green concert. The reviewer made special mention of the song dedication by Green and also of the lit-up skybox. Kent later asked, "I wonder if he had any idea how much that meant to us?"

35

Whitaker Residence
Heron Way
Sugar Land, Texas

Kent wanted Bart to know how much it meant to
have his son live in his childhood home. In addition
to a core group of male friends, known as the FAT-
men, who stuck around with Kent to help him deal
with the grief of losing Tricia and Kevin, Bart provided Kent with a sense of belonging he was sure
would not exist without his son's presence.

The two men would arise in the morning, chat quietly over breakfast, then go about their separate ways
during the day. They would both return home in the
evening and spend time reading inspirational books
together, such as *The Purpose Driven Life* by Rick Warren
and *If You Want to Walk on Water, You've Got to Get Out
of the Boat* by John Ortberg. They would read pas-
sages aloud to one another and then spend time discussing the meanings behind the works and how they

pertained, not only to their grief-stricken situations, but to their roles as men of God.

Lynne Sorsby noticed the positive change in Bart after the murders of his brother and mother. Bart furthered that belief by delving deeper into church and reading religious tomes as well. He also decided to add to the attitude adjustment by asking Lynne to marry him. She eagerly agreed, and the couple set a date for July 24, 2005. Kent Whitaker was ecstatic for the young couple. He believed their union was further proof of God's will in attempting to allow him to heal over the losses of Tricia and Kevin. Though life ends, there are always new beginnings around the corner. He looked forward to having Lynne as his daughter-in-law, and the prospect of becoming a grandfather appealed to him beyond anything else in his life.

36

Bart began to feel claustrophobic. He knew that Detective Marshall Slot was going to be coming after him any day, and he had to be prepared. Of course, he was ready.

One week, he spoke with Rogelio "Rudy" Rios, a busboy at the Bank Downtown restaurant. The two men had been workplace acquaintances ever since Bart took a job there in late January. Over the next few months, Bart began to open up to Rios and tell him about what had happened to his mother and brother. The media's version of the events, that is. He told Rudy that he believed he was the main suspect, and that the police would be after him any day.

For his part, Rios did not want to hear what Bart was telling him. He believed Bart to be a good kid, and thought he was nice, but Rios simply wanted to keep his nose clean. According to Rios, he had a bit of a criminal history—two theft convictions and another for drugs, which led to time in prison, back in

1982. Now he was merely trying everything in his power to stay out of trouble.

Bart would constantly complain to Rios that the police were out to get him, and that they wanted to prosecute him for the murders. Rios politely nodded and feigned interest, but he mainly wanted to be far away from Bart's potential criminal issues.

Over time, however, Rios began to learn more about Bart. The main thing that piqued his interest was the younger man's access to money. Bart never shied away from talking about his family's economic status. Rios also noticed Bart usually dressed well, drove a nice vehicle, and never seemed to want for the finer things in life. One day, after hearing Bart's repeated fears of being arrested, Rios decided to get involved.

"You know," Rios addressed his coworker, "I go to Mexico all the time. I've got family down there. If you ever want to go there, I can take you."

Bart seemed to perk up. "I appreciate your offer, Rudy. I may just have to take you up on that one."

"Just let me know," Rios replied.

On, or around, June 21, Bart let Rios know. "So, remember your offer to take me to Mexico?" he mentioned.

"Sure," Rios replied.

"Can you do it soon?"

"No problem," Rios answered. "Just give me a few hours so I can get some things in line and we will head out right away."

"Sounds good. But let's wait until Monday to take off," Bart replied. He seemed distant and concerned.

"Of course, you'll need to give me some money," Rios stated.

"Of course, I will. How much do you need?"

"Three thousand," Rios confidently asserted.

"I'll have it before we take off," Bart replied, with nary a flinch. Rios wondered if he should have asked for more money.

The following Monday, Bart did not go to work. Neither did Rudy Rios. Instead, both men were on a decidedly more adventurous trek. They met at a pre-determined locale, picked by Bart, in a mini–strip mall parking lot, in front of an A-1 Dry Cleaners located on South Braeswood Boulevard and Fondren Road, near the BraeBurn Country Club. Bart suggested the spot because it was located in what he believed to be a higher-crime-risk section of Houston. Rios assumed it was so someone would steal Bart's Yukon and draw attention away from Bart. Bart stayed inside his vehicle and told Rios, who was driving his mother's car, to follow him to the Wesley Gardens apartment complex, on the southwest side of Houston, so he could drop off the car. Once they arrived at the complex, Bart parked the truck and left the engine running, plus the front door unlocked and open. Then he ducked inside Rios's mother's vehicle.

Minutes later, Bart Whitaker was on his way to being escorted across the border of the United States into Mexico. They were headed for the tiny town of Cerralvo, where some of Rios's family still lived.

According to Rios, the eight-plus-hour drive was quiet and uneventful. Neither he nor Bart uttered a single word during the entire excursion. Instead, it was more of a silent send-off for the lonely gringo desperado.

Bart, the man who once had everything of material possession—a nice home, an expensive rugged truck, the finest clothes that an aspiring clotheshorse could desire—now was stripped down to the bare essence. He had given Rios a mountain-climbing backpack a week earlier and began to rifle through its contents. He had very little in way of creature comforts—a pair of jeans, a T-shirt, a nice button-down long-sleeved shirt, shoes, socks, some clean underwear, and his toiletries. That was it—except for a large stack of currency, $7,000, to be exact.

As the two men drove onward toward the Texas-Mexico border, Rios nodded toward Bart's backpack and said, "If you have anything illegal in the backpack, get it out."

Bart did not even rifle through the contents of the backpack. He merely removed the wad of cash and stuck them in his pants pockets. Rios noticed the money but did not say anything about it. Besides, he already had his money. Of course, the excessive amount that Bart flashed, intentionally or not, reminded Rios that he should have learned to perfect his negotiating skills.

Rios continued to drive in silence toward the small town of Roma, less than fifteen miles west of Rio Grande City, which is located near the border. It was a familiar route for Rios, who would usually travel to Cerralvo, just forty miles, or a forty-five-minute drive, south of the border, to visit his rather large family, which included eighteen brothers and his father. This was the route that Rios always traveled each time he returned home.

When Rios and Bart finally arrived at the border, they were greeted by Rios's father. Rios had arranged it so that Bart would drive with his father to Cerralvo, where he would be welcomed by the Rios family and allowed to live with them. Rios claimed his brothers were much lighter-skinned than he was, and that Bart, due to the fact that there were so many Rios brothers, would easily blend in as one of the Rios clan. Bart would also adopt Rogelio's Americanized name of "Rudy Rios." Rogelio hadn't even asked his father if this would be an acceptable arrangement, but his father would have no qualms about welcoming Bart into his home.

After saying his good-byes and expressing his gratitude to his coworker, Bart made his way to Rogelio's father's vehicle. Rios turned his mother's vehicle around and headed back to Houston. Bart and Rios's father, who spoke very little English, drove off in silence as well. They went only a few miles before encountering the Mexican version of border patrol. Rogelio Rios had made it a point that Bart would have the necessary papers to allow him to continue on into Cerralvo. As a result, the checkpoint diversion went without a hitch.

Bart Whitaker was finally headed toward his new home. He had little in way of clothes and personal items. He did, however, have cash and a place to stay.

Bart Whitaker also had an entirely new identity. He was no longer Bart Whitaker. Nor was he the criminal mastermind Keyser Soze. He was now, simply, Rudy Rios. A gringo desperado on the lam in a small, run-down hovel of a town in Nowhere, Mexico. It was exactly where he never wanted to be at any stage in his life; however, as far as he was concerned, he had no other choice.

37

After Bart Whitaker split for Mexico, three letters arrived in various mailboxes across the Houston/Sugar Land area. Lynne Sorsby, Kent Whitaker, and Dan Cogdell were all surprised to find correspondence from Bart Whitaker.

Bart's letter to Lynne was a paean to bad choices, forgiveness, and running away. He told his fiancée that he could not face her, because he knew any emotional display she put on would make him reconsider fleeing, and he had to escape the people coming after him. He pretended he was doing her a favor, by selflessly sparing her the misery of a trial. He pledged his love to her, but ended by asking her not to inform anyone of the contents of his letter, to better facilitate his escape.

The letter to Kent Whitaker said:

Father,
  So many things to say, and yet I cannot seem to find my words. I am leaving, despite the advice I have been given. The reasons are many, and I am not going to

*waste the time writing them all. Just know that I
cannot, <u>will</u> <u>not</u> allow anyone else to pass through the
fire of the coming weeks with me. I must do this with
God, and no one else. If the sins of my life must go, then
I must start anew, completely anew. Know that I love
you, and that I go with God because of what <u>you</u> have
taught me the last few months. I am sorry. I love you.*

Bart

    *The longer you can give me before you release this
information the better for me. Please help Lynne. She
will need it.*

The letter to Dan Cogdell, the Whitaker family friend
and attorney, said:

Dan,
    *I am sorry. But I'll take my chances against what
they will bring after me, vs. the chance at a trial.*

Bart

38

While Kent Whitaker spent his days fretting about the whereabouts of his only remaining immediate loved one, Bart had somehow managed to infiltrate himself into the Cerralvo lifestyle. He was instantly accepted by Rogelio Rios's family, who welcomed an additional potential wage earner.

Surprisingly, this came rather easily for Bart. He was able to procure employment from a friendly Hispanic gentleman, Omero Salinas, who owned and operated a sizable furniture warehouse and store. Salinas also happened to be the father of a nice young lady, Cindy Lou Salinas, whom Bart began dating soon after his arrival in town.

Bart made quite an impression on the people of Cerralvo. The young ladies took an instant shine to the handsome, gregarious, easygoing, and gringo-looking newcomer they knew as Rudy Rios. They were smit-

ten with his charm and his less-than-stellar command
of the Spanish language.

According to an interview that aired on *48 Hours
Mystery,* one of the women, Gabriella Gutierrez, spoke
very highly of Bart, or Rudy as she knew him. "He was
a friendly person," she recalled, a huge grin on her
face. "He liked to drink. He liked to go with the girls.
He was very charming." She stopped and smiled from
ear to ear. "He had a way with the ladies," she stated,
giggling slightly.

It wasn't only the ladies who warmed up to the
newest person in their tiny town. Bart wasted no time
befriending as many of the young men as possible as
well. Bart would invite many of the young men over to
his new apartment, which he had purchased after just
a few months of work. In many ways, the gatherings
resembled Bart's townhome get-togethers in Willis,
with Steven Champagne, Chris Brashear, and his employees from The Dining Room. Bart was the quiet,
yet cool, ringleader who loved to open his doors and
share his generosity with those around him.

As a result, a cliché was born: The guys wanted to
be him. The girls wanted to be with him.

But only one girl would catch his full attention.
Cindy Lou Salinas was instantly attracted to the sweet-
looking young man who seemingly appeared in a
magical puff of smoke. Cindy Lou and Bart (or Rudy)
met in church. Cindy Lou was overwhelmed by Bart's
physical features and softened up by his seemingly
softer side, as evidenced by his attentiveness during
church services.

"I saw him," she recalled, "and I said, 'Wow! He's
gorgeous.'" She had never been around someone so
handsome and sophisticated. He seemed so worldly to

her that she was determined to get to know him better. "I found him very interesting," Cindy Lou fondly remembered. "The guys that I've known, I don't know . . ." She trailed off at the memories of previous paramours. "He just had something no one else had," she said, sounding like a schoolgirl.

Bart and Cindy Lou seemed like a mismatched pair. She was one of those rare individuals whose name perfectly represents her true essence: sweet, innocent, and starry-eyed. Bart, or Rudy, seemed more serious and steely-eyed, like a person who had seen things he wanted permanently erased from his memory bank. Theirs was a simple courtship with little to no fanfare.

It was an added bonus when Omero Salinas welcomed Bart not only as a suitor for his daughter, but as an employee in the family business. Salinas thought very highly of Rudy, as he knew Bart. "He was a very good worker. Very obedient," he recalled admiringly. "I really liked him and held him in high esteem. I ended up loving him like a son. Very, very much."

Bart's ability to woo the members of the Salinas family even extended to Uvaldo, her brother. Like the rest of the Salinas family, Cindy Lou's brother was also entranced by Rudy. Unlike most brothers of a sister who meets a new guy, Uvaldo was not interested in keeping a watchful eye over her new boyfriend. He was more interested in getting to know him even better. Uvaldo enjoyed being regaled by Rudy's fanciful tales of serving in the United States Marines in Afghanistan after the terrorist attacks of September 11, 2001, in the War on Terror. Uvaldo was fascinated by the many tales of adventure and bravery spun by Rudy. One epic stood out in the young Hispanic's mind. It involved Rudy's explanation for the bullet wound in his left arm.

"He said he got it in the Afghanistan War," a wide-eyed Uvaldo Salinas passed along the story. "He said there was a surprise attack on his group (of fellow Marines) by the Afghans. Most of those in his group were killed."

Bart, of course, was the most heroic soldier. Uvaldo continued in reference to him, "He said he shot at one with his rifle, but there was another Afghani soldier who got him in the shoulder." It is not clear how Bart escaped the clutches of the evil Afghans. Nonetheless, Uvaldo was duly impressed with his sister's new boyfriend. He graciously welcomed him into the folds of the Salinas clan, as did Omero and, of course, Cindy Lou.

Over time, Rudy allegedly began to open up to Cindy Lou and the Salinas family. When it came to his personal background, though, Bart never mentioned the murders of his mother and brother, for obvious reasons. Instead, he began to spin another familiar tale, just like he had with his college buddies, Will Anthony and Justin Peters. He told his new girlfriend that he had a horrible relationship with his family.

"He used to tell me he was an only child," Cindy Lou recalled. Rudy also told her that "he never loved his mother, because his mother never loved him, either. He also said that his mother was a prostitute, and that his family never gave him the love that he wanted." She added in a morose manner that "Instead, they gave him money, and they just ignored him."

According to an interview with *20/20,* Cindy Lou recalled an argument she had with her mother. The young girl, an avid guitarist, became so upset that she smashed her guitar in front of Bart. He consoled her by saying, "No, relax. Let's fix things. Don't be angry at your parents anymore. If you want, we can kill them." She was a bit freaked out by his suggestion, but she decided he must have been joking. She believed she knew Rudy was not capable of such behavior and simply blew it off.

The poor, pitiful background of Bart Whitaker once again had been securely cemented in the minds of those he needed to manipulate. He further endeared himself to the Salinas family members and Cindy Lou when he informed them that "they were the family he never had."

Not only did Bart endear himself to the Salinases, he also won over the entire town of Cerralvo during a true act of heroism. According to Rogelio Rios and members of his family, the tiny village was hit by a severe flash flood that nearly devastated it. Apparently, Bart helped the local authorities save some people, including a little girl who nearly drowned. He was hailed as a hero by practically everyone in town, including the Rios and Salinas families. As far as they were concerned, Bart was one of them.

Other times, however, Bart tended to keep a low profile while in town, mainly during various holidays. Rogelio Rios believed it was because there were many people from Cerralvo who lived in Houston and would often come back to celebrate the holidays with their families. He believed that Bart did not want any of these returning Cerralvo residents to spot him and return to Houston and report him to the authorities.

Bart did have an idea as per the status of his disappearance. He had access to an Internet café and was able to keep track of any news updates on the Web. It wasn't like having an inside man at the police station, but he could at least take some solace in knowing that they had no idea where he was, nor were they any closer to proving he was guilty of murdering his mother and brother.

39

Kent Whitaker had not heard from Bart since he disappeared. For the first time, he began to have doubts as to whether or not Bart was involved in the murders of Tricia and Kevin. Covering for his son, Kent called Bart's place of employment and told them Bart had to leave town unexpectedly and would not return for at least a week.

According to Kent, he met with his own family members to discuss Bart's actions. Kent's sister simply would not believe Bart had been involved. She dismissed Bart's behavior as being under a ton of stress due to being considered a suspect. Kent stated, however, "By the end of the evening, everyone had accepted the truth. Bart had fled and this gave credence to the possibility that he had been involved in the slaying of his own family."

The Monday following July 4, Lynne Sorsby's mother

sent out wedding cancelation notices. Lynne had not heard from Bart, so the family made the call to pull the plug on the impending nuptials.

Kent then spoke with Dan Cogdell and informed him that there was still no word from Bart. His good friend and attorney suggested that a press conference be held to announce that Bart had gone missing, to which Kent agreed. Cogdell held the media event on Wednesday, July 7. The hope was that Bart would somehow see the report and turn himself in.

According to Kent, he also began to receive Bart's many unpaid utility bills in the mail. Surprisingly, the man who admitted total forgiveness for the shooter of his wife and of his youngest son was infuriated at having to cover Bart's debts. In his words, "I grew very angry at Bart for deserting me like this. Commitments are serious things to me, and I couldn't understand how he could be so cavalier about them. His lack of regard for others cast doubt on his sincerity and innocence, making it a lot harder for me to continue giving him the benefit of the doubt." He added, "It was becoming clear that my son had a side that none of our family had seen, and I was furious, hurt, and worried about how far the deception had gone."

40

October 2004
Camp Pendleton
Between Oceanside and San Clemente, California

After the murders, Steven Champagne decided he needed to make something of his life. He opted for the U.S. Marines. Soon after he joined, he was shipped out to California, where he was stationed at Camp Pendleton. While there, he received a visit from two detectives from Sugar Land. He could not recall who the officers were, but he knew that they were not Detectives Slot and White. Steven claimed that the two new detectives offered him a plea bargain: if he confessed and told them that Bart Whitaker had set the murder plot of his family into motion, they would grant him immunity for his participation in the conspiracy. If such an offer had been accepted, it would have been a sweet deal for the young Marine.

Steven, however, feigned ignorance and subsequently ruined his chance at any type of sweetheart deal. He claimed he lied to the officers because he thought it was a trick. He remembered an earlier conversation with Bart where his friend told him that there were no deals made between cops and suspects in cases of capital murder. Bart had apparently convinced him that the police would attempt to offer some type of deal so Steven would rat Bart and Chris out, and then they would rescind their offer and he would spend the rest of his life in prison—if not face the needle as part of a death sentence.

Bart was right that they did eventually question Steven and made some type of offer—thus, the reason for the lies.

According to Steven, when the detectives did not get what they wanted from him, they decided to exact revenge. Steven claimed the detectives made a point to speak with the Camp Pendleton military police investigative unit about some of his past behavior. Allegedly, Steven lied on his application form for the U.S. Marines and failed to mention that he was the subject of a pending criminal investigation. He also alleged that the detectives informed the military that he had used several drugs in the past, such as cocaine, marijuana, and Ecstasy, and failed to mention that on his application form as well.

"They threw a few kinks in my training," Steven recalled.

The biggest kink came with his participation in Intelligence School training. Steven was being conditioned to become an "intelligence analyst." His job would be to gather information for use on battlefields by high-ranking officers. With the position, he also received a security clearance. At the behest of the Sugar

Land detectives, however, Steven's security clearance was pulled.

Steven Champagne realized that the house of cards was ready to collapse. It would take several months before he truly realized what he had gotten himself into.

41

Steven Champagne was somewhat surprised, though he probably shouldn't have been, when he received a grand jury summons from Fort Bend County. His presence was demanded back in Texas the following month. Later that same day, he found out that his mother and his girlfriend had also received subpoenas to appear before the grand jury.

Steven did not want his mother or girlfriend to be put through the paces. He also came to the realization that he "could not go before a grand jury and lie," so he picked up the phone and contacted Detective Marshall Slot. His reasoning for not being able to lie before a grand jury, when he had no problem whatsoever lying to police before, was because he was "going to be under oath." Slot agreed and suggested Steven come see him.

Steven made the trip by the end of the month and met up with Detective Slot in a Starbucks coffee shop, in Conroe, Texas. Steven claimed that he agreed to sit and cough up the details of the murder with Detective Slot in return for immunity. He claimed that Slot agreed to proffer up immunity; however, he still elected to lie to the detective.

Steven began to give details to Detective Slot, but with one major omission: he had no idea what Bart had planned, and afterward, he had no idea that Bart had his family killed. "I kept pulling myself out of the situation," Steven later recalled about lying to the police officer. As with the officers who had visited him at Camp Pendleton, Steven recalled Bart's advice. Don't trust anyone. Thus, he had no idea if Marshall Slot was telling him the truth when he claimed he could give him immunity for his participation in a double capital murder.

Soon thereafter, Steven and Slot met a second time in Conroe to talk about Steven's knowledge of any evidence being tossed into Lake Conroe. Again, he failed to own up to his role in the murder plot.

Detective Slot kept up the pressure on the young man. After the meetings, he would contact Steven and keep asking him about his role in the plot. As usual, Steven would parse out a little bit more information as to what happened, yet continue to deny direct knowledge of the plot to kill the Whitakers, or of any actual participation. He eventually had to return to California, but Slot stayed on his back.

Steven came back to Texas on August 28, 2005, again at Slot's request, and met with the detective in The Woodlands. He again minimized his role and denied direct involvement.

The following day, Steven was still scheduled to attend the grand jury hearing at the old courthouse in nearby Richmond. Before going into the grand

jury, Steven met, once again, with Slot, as well as with
First Assistant District Attorney (ADA) Fred Felcman
and an FBI agent. Felcman informed Steven that he
had "blown his chance at immunity" by continuously
lying to Officer Slot. Once Steven realized he had
screwed up, he finally agreed to tell the truth. Detective Slot set up a meeting time for the following morning for him, Steven, and the FBI agent to meet to
discuss what really happened on December 10, 2003.

While in the courthouse, however, Steven happened upon Karen Montana, Chris Brashear's
mother. He spoke with her briefly and was able to get
Chris's phone number.

Steven was excused from his grand jury appearance. As he exited the courthouse, he spotted the
other person who was supposed to have been murdered that night, Kent Whitaker. Bart's father attempted to smile at the young man, but it came across
more like a wince of pain.

The following morning, Steven met with Detective
Slot and the FBI agent and gave a full confession on
videotape to everything that had happened in regard
to the murders of Tricia and Kevin Whitaker, and the
attempted murder of Kent Whitaker.

During their meeting, Detective Slot spoke with
Steven about setting up a meeting with Chris Brashear, who was now working in a bar/restaurant in Rice
Village called Two Rows. Slot wanted Steven to wear a
wire on his body and tape-record his conversation
with Chris in hopes of getting an admission of guilt
from Brashear. Steven agreed, and the plan was
placed into motion.

A couple of days later, Steven contacted Chris and
told him he wanted to meet to talk about the latest

goings-on with the police. Chris agreed and told Steven to meet him at Two Rows. Steven informed Detective Slot of the rendezvous place and time.

On the day Steven was to meet Chris, Detective Slot set Steven up with a wire hidden underneath his shirt. The plan was to get the two men close enough so that the wire Steven wore would pick up any bits of information from Chris, with the main goal to get a confession or, at the least, an admission of participation in the conspiracy plan.

Steven made his way up to Two Rows to chat with Chris. The two young men had not seen each other in ages. Their meeting was awkward, especially when Steven attempted to engage him in conversation about the murders.

"I don't want to talk about that, Steven," Chris stated firmly.

"I know, I know." Steven nodded empathetically.

"At least, not here. We can talk about it later," Chris added.

Steven made a few more attempts, but Chris continued to beg off. Finally the two young men agreed to meet at a later time to talk about the crimes.

That meeting never materialized.

42

August 29, 2005
FM 1097 Road Bridge
Conroe, Texas

Steven Champagne's conversation with Detective
Marshall Slot made him feel better about his potential sentencing for involvement in the murders. His
belief that he would receive immunity for ratting out
Bart and Chris was acceptable to him. To solidify the
detective's confidence in him further, Steven agreed
to lead him to where he and Chris had tossed the two
duffel bags that contained evidence from the scene of
the crime.

Steven and Detective Slot drove out together to the
bridge at FM 1097 Road that crossed over Lake Conroe.
Steven remembered it as if he had just driven there
yesterday. All of the memories of that dreadful night
came soaring back as he pulled up to the hazard lane
in the general direction of where he remembered the
drop-off spot to be located.

43

September 12, 2005
Sugar Land Police Department
Sugar Land, Texas

Sugar Land police chief Steve Griffith stepped before the phalanx of microphones. "We have made an arrest in the murders of Patricia Whitaker and Kevin Whitaker. The young man's name is Chris A. Brashear."

Griffith indicated that "there are some other individuals that we are looking at within the realm of the investigation. These are individuals that were known to the Whitaker family or portions of the family. This is not a roving band of criminals that perpetrated this crime. Having said that, I have to stress that the investigation is not complete."

Griffith was joined by Fort Bend County district attorney (DA) John Healey. The prosecutor spoke about the efforts of the Sugar Land Police Department: "They've been frustrated, the police department's been frustrated, and we've been frustrated." He bemoaned the long time it took to finally make an arrest in the highest-profile case in Sugar Land's history.

After the briefing, Griffith took questions from reporters, who mainly wanted to know the status of Bart Whitaker. "We are still interested in talking to him." When asked if Bart should be considered a threat, Griffith responded, "Do I think that he is an ongoing threat to public safety? I can't draw that conclusion, at this point and time."

Griffith attempted to assure the public that the case was about to wrap up any day. "I honestly believe the remaining pieces of this case are going to fall into place fairly quickly."

Healey was asked why Bart and Steven Champagne had not been arrested or charged yet in the murders. "Strategically, it is not in the best interest of the case to charge them at this particular time."

Griffith concluded the short press conference with a warning for Bart and Steven: "There will be more arrests in the coming weeks."

September 14, 2005
Sugar Land Police Department
Sugar Land, Texas

Detective Marshall Slot picked up his telephone. On the other line was Rogelio Rios, the man who drove Bart to Mexico and set him up with living accommodations. Only he did not give out his real name. Instead, he said he was "Mike Jones," named after the Houston rap artist.

Rios heard about the arrest of Chris Brashear for the murder of Tricia and Kevin Whitaker. When he realized they were Bart Whitaker's family members, he "felt pretty bad." Rios admitted, "I just give everyone the benefit of the doubt." He justified his aid of Bart because he "wasn't wanted then." He added, "When I heard the other dude got busted, then I figured that it was probably true" that Bart was also involved in the murders.

Rios eventually gave Detective Slot his real name and, more important, information as to Bart's whereabouts. Specifically, at his father's home in Cerralvo.

Rios's tip also garnered him $10,000 from Crime Stoppers. Combined with the $3,000 he received from Bart to transport him to Mexico, Rogelio Rios pocketed $13,000 off the murders of Tricia and Kevin Whitaker.

September 14, 2005
Camp Pendleton
Between Oceanside and San Clemente, California

For Steven Champagne, the jig was finally up. Authorities came onto base to arrest the twenty-three-year-old U.S. Marine for participating in the murders of Tricia and Kevin Whitaker. He was taken into custody and placed in the San Diego County Jail without bail. Sugar Land police spokeswoman Pat Whitty informed the press that they expected Champagne "to be brought back to Texas in the next few weeks."

Later that same day, the Sugar Land authorities filed an arrest warrant for Bart Whitaker for the murders of his mother and brother. The motive listed was for "financial gain," as Bart allegedly stood to inherit more than $1 million.

44

September 22, 2005, 4:00 P.M.
Laredo, Texas

One week after Detective Slot received the phone call from Rogelio Rios, and after an arrest warrant was filed for Bart Whitaker, he finally found his man. Based on Rios's tip, Mexican authorities were able to locate and arrest Bart in Monterrey, Mexico. They, in turn, contacted the FBI and turned him over in the border town of Laredo, Texas, where he was arrested and cuffed. Bart had a "thumb drive" computer memory stick in his pocket "with all the media information about him and the case" on it.

After Bart's arrest, Sugar Land police chief Steve Griffith and Fort Bend County district attorney John Healey held another press conference to announce his capture. "Hopefully, the recent arrests will bring closure to our community for this heinous crime." Griffith added, "Our work in this case will continue until convictions have been obtained for all three participants in the murders of Patricia and Kevin Whitaker."

District Attorney Healey added, "The possibility of the death penalty is definitely in play in this case."

Sugar Land police captain Gary Cox expected Bart to be brought back to Sugar Land by the following Sunday night. He added that Bart was forced to leave Mexico "for violation of Mexican immigration laws." Normally, Mexican authorities do not cooperate with United States officials when it comes to extraditing potential death penalty suspects, as the country's policy is to oppose execution. In this particular case, however, the Mexican police apparently decided to go against that country's established belief. Cox added, "They basically handled it as if it was an immigration violation," as opposed to a possible capital murder.

Bart's arrest warrant also revealed, for the first time, the alleged motive behind the slayings: "Financial analysis [by the FBI] shows that Bart Whitaker stood to inherit in excess of one million dollars in assets with the death of his parents and his brother."

Cox added, "We probably could've gotten an arrest warrant earlier, but we couldn't prove the capital case."

Tuesday, October 4, 2005
Fort Bend County Courthouse
Jackson Street
Richmond, Texas

A Fort Bend County grand jury returned indictments on capital murder against all three young men: Thomas "Bart" Whitaker, twenty-five; Chris A. Brashear, twenty-three; and Steven Champagne, twenty-three.

Saturday, October 8, 2005
Fort Bend County Jail
Richmond, Texas

Steven Champagne was finally transferred from the San Diego County Jail to the Fort Bend County Jail by officials from Fort Bend County Sherriff's Office and the Sugar Land Police Department, bringing all three co-conspirators back together under one roof.

45

November 1, 2005
FM 1097 Road Bridge
Lake Conroe
Conroe, Texas

Steven Champagne's excursion to Lake Conroe with Detective Marshall Slot had failed to reap any rewards, not because there was nothing to be discovered, but rather because Mother Nature stepped in the way. The Gulf Coast region was beset with two monstrous hurricanes in the form of Katrina, which came ashore near New Orleans, Louisiana, on August 29, 2005, and Hurricane Rita, which was projected to come ashore near Galveston, Texas, and make its way to nearby Houston.

Hurricane Katrina proved to be an untenable nightmare, with the storm causing the levees to burst, subsequently dumping millions of tons of water into the below-sea-level city of New Orleans. The nightmarish imagery—people stranded on top of two-story rooftops, with water lapping away near their feet;

rescue helicopters cherry picking stragglers from
treetops during monstrous winds; and, worst of all, the
sight of bloated corpses floating down main streets—
was enough to send chills down many Houstonians'
fragile spines.

The result was made relevant three weeks later when
the majority of meteorologists predicted that Hurricane Rita, a Category 5 storm, would hit Galveston and
march a treacherous path directly for Houston.

To avoid the mistakes of the citizens of New Orleans, the overwhelming majority of inhabitants, from
Galveston to Houston to Sugar Land, were determined to get the heck out of Dodge. The mass
exodus, however, was horribly coordinated by city and
highway patrol, and massive traffic jams plugged up
the main freeways from Interstate 10 to Highway 183.
Normal drive times were magnified nearly ten times
with the wait. A simple three-and-a-half-hour drive
from Houston to San Antonio, approximately two
hundred miles, was stretched out to an interminable
thirty hours of bumper-to-bumper hell.

As a result of all the chaos on the freeways, and the
need for diving crews to help fish out survivors, along
with those who were not so lucky, official police diving
teams were redirected either to New Orleans, Galveston, or the eastern portion of Texas, including the
Beaumont/Orange area of Texas, where Hurricane
Rita actually came ashore. Subsequently the need for
a dive team to fish out two duffel bags from a possible
crime scene that occurred more than a year and a half
earlier was way down on the priority list.

More than two months after Steven Champagne
clued Detective Slot in as to the whereabouts of the
bags, dive crews finally became available for a search.

The weather in south Texas was, once again, on the cusp of turning frigid. Diving into Lake Conroe at this time of year was not going to be a quick, brisk dip into soothing warm water. The team was prepared for some miserable, murky, near-freezing waters, with practically no visibility whatsoever.

The lead person on the dive team was Texas Department of Public Safety (DPS) state trooper Brandon Curlee, who was stationed in Edna, Texas, nearly 140 miles from Conroe. Curlee's main beat was working the highways of Texas for speeders and accidents. The dive team was something he did on the side.

Curlee was one of fourteen dive team members statewide whose job it was to recover evidence and/or human bodies from the water. According to the trooper, "We've recovered bodies that are found in the water in homicides—where bodies were weighted down and placed in the water—evidence recoveries, as far as weapons and guns, knives, and any other evidence involved in any type of crime."

Curlee and eight other divers arrived in Conroe on November 1. He received the call just the day before. Upon Curlee's arrival, he was briefed by two Sugar Land detectives that he would be searching for two canvas bags located on the north or northeast side of the FM 1097 Bridge.

Curlee's description of the team's diving methodology was that they were "kind of like commercial divers." He added, "We don't use normal scuba-diving equipment." They used "a Superlight 17 helmet with surface-supplied air" so they could stay underwater as long as necessary. Basically, the men would dive in their gear and have a giant hose attached to the top of the helmet, called an umbilical line, which would

pump air from above the water down into their suits
The helmets were extremely bulky, weighing almost
thirty pounds. The suits were even heavier at nearly
fifty pounds apiece. In addition, they would be sporting a twenty-pound backup tank on their backs.
Going into the water, they were already lugging
almost one hundred pounds of equipment.

The dives were to take place in water approximately
twenty to thirty feet deep. Curlee estimated their time
of underwater availability would be ninety minutes to
two hours apiece. They would be down on their hands
and knees, in the dark, murky waters, so, despite un-
limited air, the men were destined to become fatigued
just from the sheer weight of their gear and the
amount of exercise they would undergo. There would
always be two divers in the water at the same time. Ro-
tation shifts were implemented to keep the divers
fresh and safe.

Curlee and the dive team have a predetermined
method of searching underwater, using what they call
a "grid pattern." Once the diver jumps into the water,
fully weighted down, they immediately sink to the
bottom. At that point, in the pitch-black water, a diver
would have to rely on the dive tender, who stays in the
boat with radar. The dive tender then guides the diver
either left or right, backward or forward, so that the
diver can search the bottom. The diver then takes the
umbilical line, lays it underneath his stomach, and
lays flat on the ground on his stomach. Then he
begins a sweeping motion, from right to left and back
again, sifting through the mud, silt, rocks, whatever
lies at the bottom. The dive tender is then able to
follow the diver's motions by observing the air bub-
bles that rise from the diver's helmet to the surface.

This method is used to track the diver's position along the grid. This routine is repeated over and over until the body or items in question are discovered.

According to Curlee, Lake Conroe's bottom was filled with debris. He encountered all sorts of trash, including concrete, rebar, fishing rods, beer bottles, and beer cans. He even discovered a motorcycle at the bottom of the lake.

After almost three days of searching the black waters, at a quarter to noon, the Department of Public Safety dive team found what they were looking for—by using the sweeping motion, Curlee discovered one of the large canvas bags. He realized it was one of the bags because he could tell "it was lengthy and kind of bulky with different items inside it." Using an underwater verbal communications system, he was able to contact the dive tender about the presence of the bag.

Curlee attempted to wrap the bag as close to his body as possible. As he snuggled it next to his diving suit, he waited as the men on the boat hoisted him to the surface. He had no idea if, after nearly two years at the bottom of a lake, the bag would still hold together. It did, however, and he was able to bring it to the surface. He then laid it down gently on the diving platform attached to the boat. He was then lowered back down to begin looking for bag number two.

As Trooper Curlee searched underwater, Sugar Land detective Tracy Taylor commandeered the duffel bag that had been safely recovered. Detective Taylor and Sergeant Yolanda Davis were responsible for maintaining the integrity of the duffel bag. Davis placed a call to Sugar Land crime scene investigator (CSI) Max Hunter, who retrieved the evidence the following day and took it back to his lab in the Sugar Land Police Department.

Meanwhile, back in the water, Curlee and another diver, who had joined in on the search, gave up on looking for the second duffel bag. They called it a day.

The following day, CSI Max Hunter picked up the duffel bag and its contents and shuttled them off to Sugar Land. He arrived at the police station and combed his way through the contents of the large canvas bag. The list of items discovered in the bag included:

- one Black & Decker DustBuster
- one can of KILZ latex primer
- one plastic grocery bag
- one baseball cap
- one Sony Walkman, with headphones
- one athletic shoe, size 9½
- six latex gloves
- one rubber mallet
- one roll of clear plastic sheeting
- one Mini Maglite
- two Motorola Talkabout handheld radios
- two Virgin cell phones
- one metal chisel
- one Smith & Wesson Lockback pocketknife, with a blade on each end
- one cigarette pack cellophane wrapper
- five rounds of Cor-Bon nine-millimeter ammunition
- four Texas license plates

- one expandable ASP tactical baton, similar to what police officers use
- one Leatherman tool
- five additional rounds of loose Cor-Bon ammunition
- black nylon cord
- one deteriorated shirt
- nylon straps with metal buckles
- nylon rope
- clear plastic sheeting
- one clear plastic water bottle
- an undetermined amount of United States currency, which was severely deteriorated

The items discovered in the duffel bag were covered in a strange milky white substance that had since dried up. It was later determined that the substance was primer from the primer paint can.

As Hunter sifted through the items, he began to make sense of what was used in the commission of the murders. He assumed the chisel had been used to pry open Kevin Whitaker's gun lockbox. The lab had already run tests on the lockbox and determined that a flat-head pry tool had been used. He was even able to run transfer paint tests taken from the safe to determine what brand of tool was used—it was a Dasco. When he looked at the tool from the bag, he noted that it was indeed a Dasco pry tool.

One cell phone that had been recovered was a Nokia, the same brand as Bart Whitaker's, which was not found at the scene of the crime. The cell phone was later submitted to a company called Forensic Telecommunications Services to see if they could actually retrieve any phone call data from the microchip inside, even though it had been submerged in lake water for nearly two years.

The plastic water bottle still contained water inside and was sealed by a plastic twist cap. Hunter determined he would be able to send out the bottle for possible DNA analysis. They might be able to find out who drank from the bottle.

Hunter also made sure to submit the Black & Decker DustBuster hand vacuum to the Texas Department of Public Safety Lab for fiber analysis. The goal would be to locate various carpet fibers, possibly from the crime scene or the killer's vehicle. Oftentimes murderers will vacuum out their car in hopes of getting rid of any evidence. Usually, trace amounts of fibers will remain. Hunter was also able to directly inspect Steven Champagne's mother's Camry, which had been delivered to the Sugar Land PD. Champagne's mother had been asked to remove any personal items from the vehicle, to which she readily complied.

Hunter also processed the rubber mallet. It was a safe bet that the mallet was used, along with the chisel, to open up Kevin Whitaker's gun lockbox.

Hunter also submitted the shirt to the lab for testing. Unfortunately, the clothing was too severely deteriorated to be of any use. He also submitted the shoe for DNA analysis, but it, too, had been underwater for too long, and was not useful for tracing any DNA.

Hunter's focus of the examination centered on the backseat of the car. His belief was that some of the blood from any of the Whitakers might have ended up on the shooter, and subsequently had been transferred to the backseat. The first step in the process was to videotape the backseat by using a camera and an alternate light source, which allowed the investigator to scan visually for any potential clues. According to Hunter, the alternate light source was "a wavelength that allows you to see things that wouldn't be readily available to the naked eye." He also used a barrier filter, or colored blue light, to assist in the examination. While searching the backseat with the alternate light source, Hunter also employed a chemical agent known as fluorescein, which allowed him to check for finite and infinite traces of blood. He was able to discover traces of blood in the back of the Camry, on the floor carpet, as well as on the upholstery of the backseat. The samples were bagged and tagged and sent off to the lab for testing.

Hunter also took a control sample from Champagne's mother's Camry that consisted of a portion of the floor carpet from the car's back. He wanted to check the carpet samples with the fiber samples located inside the DustBuster that had been recovered from the bottom of Lake Conroe. He removed carpet from one area where he expected to find evidence and another area where he did not expect to get anything. The samples were bagged and tagged and shipped off to the DPS lab for further inspection. The tests would reap huge rewards, as the DNA from the water bottle matched Chris Brashear's, and the fiber matched the carpet in Bart's Yukon, among other findings that would provide enough evidence for the prosecution of Bart Whitaker.

46

Another behind-the-scenes figure played an important part in helping to shape the case of the Whitaker murders—and he did it with several bloodhounds.

Fort Bend County sheriff's deputy Keith Pikett and his three scent-smelling bloodhounds—Quincy, Columbo, and Jag—appeared at the Whitaker murder scene that night.

It was apparent that the dogs had hit on a scent. Now, with the confession of Steven Champagne and the arrest of Chris Brashear, Pikett's dogs would be put to the test to determine if the scent they discovered that night would match either one of the two young men.

In 1989, Pikett began working in the K-9 division with the bloodhounds. His job was to help train them to follow invisible scents not discernible to the human olfactory senses. Pikett's involvement in dog searches began at home with his own personal pet, Samantha, a bloodhound. As he recalled, he and his wife "were just playing with the dogs. We had no intention of doing anything like looking for lost people or doing police work." Over time, however, Pikett could discern that Samantha was not your average scent hound. She became so good that Pikett developed "a guilt complex and figured we had to work the dog to find lost kids or Alzheimer's patients." Pikett decided to take Samantha to the American Kennel Club (AKC) so she would receive the proper training to become a bloodhound scent dog. According to their website, the American Kennel Club is dedicated to upholding the integrity of its Registry, promoting the sport of purebred dogs and breeding for type and function. Founded in 1884, the AKC and its affiliated organizations advocate for the purebred dog as a family companion, advance canine health and well-being, work to protect the rights of all dog owners and promote responsible dog ownership. The objective of the organization is to "advance the study, breeding, exhibiting, running and maintenance of pure-bred dogs."

Pikett entered Samantha in a training competition and she bested the other dogs. After her training was complete, Pikett and his wife decided they needed to volunteer her services to help find lost people.

The Piketts were able to find a group of trainers known as The Old Timers, which specialized in bloodhounds. Apparently, these groups were difficult to locate because bloodhounds are not commonly used in law enforcement. Samantha spent over 175 hours in training to perfect her skills as a search dog. Eventually she became schooled well enough to go out and help locate missing persons. She was the first of many dogs that Pikett had trained. He would eventually go on to train them himself, as well as teach others how to train dogs. His services were used statewide, and he was also called up by the FBI to help in training their scent dogs.

Pikett is very fond of his bloodhounds. "They have the best nose of any breed of dog," he has bragged about his canine companions. "Their olfactory sensing mechanism is twenty-six times that of a human." He added that the bloodhounds are able to follow a scent trail even when no fingerprint evidence or DNA has been located.

Pikett talked about training new bloodhounds to follow a scent trail. "I get them at eight weeks old, and it takes about seven to eight months to train one to start to go out in the street, work real cases, and verify him with another dog that's already working well." He offered up an explanation as to how the dog training works. "If we were to trail to a house, with a young, inexperienced dog, I would run the trail again with an experienced dog, just to verify that the new dog is doing things right. I want them to just be trailing scents and nothing else, that way they gain more experience."

Once a bloodhound is trained on trailing scents, the dog graduates to more complex levels of scent detection, which include scent pad lineups and human being lineups.

Pikett and his pooches' services have been widely used across Texas, from Colorado County to Liberty County to Montgomery County, to cities such as Austin, San Antonio, Fort Worth, and Dallas, to towns such as Wharton and Denton. His services have also been used as far as North Carolina, Alabama, Mississippi, Virginia, Kansas, and Montana.

Pikett's pups have been involved in some of the country's highest-profile cases including the Texas Railroad Killer, serial murders committed by Angel Maturino Resendiz, aka Rafael Resendez-Ramirez, between 1997 and 1999. They also worked the Atlanta Olympic site bombing, which later was determined to be caused by an abortion-clinic-bombing domestic terrorist, Eric Rudolph. There were several other important cases in which the dogs played a major role in discovering the perpetrators.

The night of the Whitaker massacre, Pikett was called out to the scene. Upon arrival, he sussed out the situation and immediately set his dogs on to any scents they could find. They received a walk-through of the crime scene by one of the deputies. One of the first pieces of evidence Pikett spotted was the Glock 17 pistol, near the back door of the Whitaker house. Pikett halted his dogs, took out a two-by-two-inch sterile gauze pad from his evidence kit, removed it from its individual wrapping, and then placed it on the can. He purposefully did not wipe the gun down with the gauze pad, in case there were any fingerprints on the weapon. Instead, he merely laid the pad on the gun for ten seconds, removed it, and placed it in a plastic Ziploc bag. He then labeled the bag and stowed it away for safekeeping.

Pikett next went into the master bedroom on the first floor, where he proceeded to take samples from the open dresser drawers, closet drawers, and from the pillowcase that lay on the floor. He then made his way over to Kevin's room, where he took samples from some more open drawers, as well as a gun lockbox.

In addition to the samples Pikett gathered, Max Hunter also secured a gauze swab of the black glove found in the front yard next to Bart's SUV.

Once the scent samples were collected, Pikett went outside to begin his work with Quincy, Columbo, and Jag. Realistically, only one dog would be necessary at a crime scene. Pikett, however, liked to be extra cautious, so he brought three dogs to have backups. Pikett liked to be "very sure of what my dog is saying. I use another dog as backup to ensure that the first dog is doing what he's supposed to do."

The first dog up was Quincy. Pikett had the dog smell the scent pad used for the Glock. The sheriff started off near the back door of the Whitakers' home, because it was readily apparent that the attacker had fled through the back door and through the backyard. Once Quincy sniffed the scented gauze pad, he immediately went through the back door, turned left, and then made his way over to the driveway. The dog then made a beeline for Bart's Yukon, which was parked out in the street in front of the home.

Next up was Columbo. This time, Pikett used a scent pad that had been taken from the pillow and pillowcase found in Kent and Tricia Whitaker's bedroom. Columbo took off on almost the exact same scent trail as Quincy—directly toward Bart's Yukon.

Pikett later described this type of behavior as very unusual. He also said of his own dogs that they were very "arrogant" and that "the last thing they would do is something the other dog did." In other words, for both Quincy and Columbo to scent their respective trails back to Bart's Yukon made it very clear that whoever had touched the Glock and/or the pillow and pillowcase went back to Bart's vehicle.

The third dog up was Jag. He received the scent pad from the drawers in the master bedroom. Pikett had swabbed the gauze pad on as many as ten open drawers, making sure to wipe the corners and underneath the handles to ensure scents were taken from the person or persons who had opened the drawers. Once Jag got a whiff of the pad, he took off on the trail. Not surprisingly, Jag also ended up at Bart's Yukon.

Pikett's immediate conclusion from the dogs was that whoever had touched the various items had been inside the Yukon parked in the street in front of the Whitaker home. At the time, he had no idea who that might be, much less who even owned the vehicle.

Less than one month later, on January 9, 2004, Pikett brought his dogs in for a "scent pad lineup," which involved the animals getting a scent from a scent pad and then attempting to sniff out the potential perpetrator. Scents are taken from individuals—whether they be suspects or decoys not associated with the crime in any way—and placed on one of six pylons, which are spread out, about twenty feet apart from one another. In this particular case, scent pads were taken from Chris Brashear and Steven Champagne, and were placed on pylons labeled #4 and #5, respectively.

The first dog up was Columbo, who was then given the scent pad from the Glock. After swiftly getting a whiff, the bloodhound took off and headed directly toward pylon #4, which had Chris Brashear's scent pad on it.

The second lineup involved Quincy, who was given the scent pad from the pillow and pillowcase found in the Whitakers' master bedroom. Again, Brashear and

Champagne's scents were included in the lineup. As with Columbo on the first lineup, Quincy also hit on pylon #4, which again contained Chris Brashear's scent pad.

The third lineup involved Quincy, and was from the bedroom drawers. Once again, the dog hit on Chris Brashear's scent pad. Quincy also handled a fourth scent that covered another drawer and also the gun lockbox. Again, Chris Brashear.

The fifth scent was done by Columbo for the black glove. It also matched Chris Brashear's scent pad. Another glove scent was tested for Quincy, and he, too, hit on Brashear.

Sum total: five scents, two dogs, all Chris Brashear matches. It would become apparent to Pikett, based on the work of his bloodhounds, that "Chris Brashear touched the items in that house" and that "his scent was on the gun, the drawers, the pillowcase, the lockbox drawers upstairs, and the black glove."

47

January 30, 2006
Fort Bend County Courthouse
Richmond, Texas

Fort Bend County DA John Healey announced to the press that his office would seek the death penalty for Bart Whitaker for the murders of his mother and brother. "The facts and the circumstances surrounding the murder of two members of the Whitaker family merit the citizenry of Fort Bend County having the opportunity to consider exacting the most severe penalty." It would be the first death penalty case to pass through the Fort Bend County Courthouse doors since April 2003, when Steve Charles McKinney was convicted of killing three people, including a five-year-old girl. McKinney did not receive a death sentence, however, but rather a life sentence.

First Assistant District Attorney Fred Felcman, a boisterous sort, with a shock of white hair and a corresponding walrus moustache to boot, informed the

court of the district attorney's decision. Felcman
would be the lead prosecutor against Bart Whitaker.

Kent Whitaker, on the other hand, was mortified by
the announcement. He was furious because he and
his family had practically begged and pleaded with
the prosecution not to sentence Bart to the execution
chamber. "A little over two years ago, I lost my wife
and my son, and today I found out the state is going
to try and take the life of my only other son," Kent
spoke before a throng of reporters outside the courthouse. "Tricia would not want this. Neither would
Kevin, and those of us who are closest to them don't
want it, either." Kent concluded his public statement
by saying, "If the state is successful, the last living
member of my family will be put to death by the
state."

It was a conundrum for the prosecution: how to get
the death penalty for a man whose only surviving
victim did not want him to be executed. The prosecution team knew they would be walking a precarious
tightrope before a jury potentially sympathetic to the
defendant.

As a result of Felcman and Healey's announcement
that they would seek the death penalty, Bart Whitaker
refused to make a plea of not guilty before Judge Clifford J. Vacek. Bart's attorneys blamed the state for not
agreeing to a plea bargain as the reason why Bart did
not take responsibility for the murders. Judge Vacek
entered a plea of not guilty on Bart's behalf.

It would be several months before talks of trial
dates would surface. In April 2006, the first dates were
penciled in for January 2007. By May, Bart Whitaker's

trial was solidified for January 16, 2007. No trial dates were secured for Steven Champagne and Chris Brashear. Felcman, however, was in negotiations with attorneys for both men. The prosecution did not inform the press as to whether or not they would seek the death penalty for Bart's two accomplices.

By December 2007, the first talks of legal ramifications for Steven Champagne cropped up. Only, it wasn't for an actual trial, but, rather, for a plea bargain. Champagne declared that he would "testify truthfully" against both Bart Whitaker and Chris Brashear in their respective trials in exchange for a fifteen-year prison term for his participation in the murders. The announcement was made by Fort Bend County ADA Jeff Strange, who stated, "This agreement was appropriate after examining the evidence in this case and the roles each party's played in the murders."

Gordon Dees, Steven Champagne's attorney, seemed pleased with the result of the plea deal for his client. "We feel like what we are doing is right. The agreement speaks for itself."

Champagne's willing participation would come soon enough. Bart Whitaker's trial date had been pushed back slightly, to January 22. It would be less than a week before a jury would be chosen, and Bart Whitaker would finally face a jury of his peers for masterminding the murders of his mother and brother.

48

December 29, 2006
Richmond, Texas

A few weeks before Bart Whitaker's trial was scheduled to commence, First ADA Fred Felcman received something very unusual in his work's mail pile. It was a Christmas card from Bart Whitaker.

The card was postmarked December 27, 2006. Inside was a note from Bart that wished the ADA happy holidays. However, Bart also made a reference to how ADA Felcman should pay special attention to his family: *I hope you are able to compartmentalize all of the nastiness you are made to see on a daily basis, and concentrate on your family.* Felcman thought this could potentially be viewed as a threat to his loved ones.

At the bottom of the card was a quote from the Bible: *For God so loved the world, that He gave His only begotten Son.*—John 3:16

49

January 22 to March 5, 2007
Fort Bend County Courthouse
Richmond, Texas

The jury selection for Bart Whitaker's trial would take six weeks. The guilt or innocence phase of the trial—truly an afterthought due to the testimony of Steven Champagne, Adam Hipp, Justin Peters, and Jennifer Japhet, and a sizable amount of evidence against Bart—was a mere formality.

Bart was ably represented by Randy McDonald, and the state of Texas was represented by Fred Felcman and Jeff Strange. While there was much Sturm und Drang during the trial, the reality was that Bart Whitaker would be convicted for the murders of his mother, Tricia Whitaker, and his younger brother, Kevin Whitaker.

Sure enough, on March 5, 2007, the jury took only two and a half hours to declare Bart Whitaker guilty of both murders. The real issue, however, lay in the sentencing phase. The state of Texas sought to make Bart pay the ultimate price for his transgressions—his death. The defense, joined by Bart's father and most of the rest of the surviving family, would argue to spare his life.

50

One of the key people to step up and defend Bart was his uncle, William "Bo" Bartlett Jr., Tricia's brother. He was at the trial to represent the Bartlett family, which consisted of "an eighty-three-year-old mother, myself, my wife, and two college-age kids."

Bo Bartlett was led through his testimony by Bart Whitaker's defense attorney, Randy McDonald. The veteran attorney asked Bartlett to express himself in regard to how Bart's actions made him feel.

"It's all pretty devastating," the still young-at-heart man spoke quietly. "There's no doubt about that. It's just hard to imagine that this happened to our family." Bartlett described how "blessed" they had been up until that time. "We never expected to be here at this point in our life. It is something we will never, ever get over. As you go on, you learn to manage the pain. You never get over something like this. You just learn to manage the pain that has come about."

Bartlett shifted about in his chair, trying to find just the right spot to feel comfortable. He added that the murder of his sister had been devastating for his and Tricia's mother as well.

McDonald wasted no time in getting down to the business at hand: sparing his client the needle. His tactic was to point out the prosecution's inability, specifically that of Assistant District Attorney Fred Felcman, to settle the case before a trial and to avoid a death sentence for Bart Whitaker. "Did you ever learn of . . . the communication between Dan Cogdell"—Bart's first attorney before he was even charged with anything—"and Mr. Felcman?"

Bartlett responded, "In the beginning, we kept trying to work something out where we did not have to drag our family through this, and where the communication broke down, or if either side did not agree to it, it was our whole intent not to be drug up here and be put in this situation we're in. That was the last thing we wanted to do. We're a very private family, and to be in this scenario, it's devastating."

"Were you concerned with what you had heard as to what you wanted to happen in this case?" McDonald asked.

"What we wanted," Bartlett replied, "was to accept a life sentence as a plea bargain and to leave us out of this situation."

McDonald asked about a meeting between himself, Bartlett, John Healey, and Jeff Strange. "Do you know what the purpose of that meeting was?"

"It was just a continuation of the family efforts to meet with the Fort Bend people to try to convince them—actually, I begged them so that we could accept some type of bargain for Bart going to prison for the rest of his life."

McDonald continued on in the same vein of questioning: mainly trying to decipher why the prosecution was unwilling to accede to the victims' family members' wishes. "Did you know at the time that we had offered Mr. Healey anything at all to reassure that Bart would be in the penitentiary for the rest of his life, and that we were willing to do that at that time?"

Bartlett nodded in the affirmative. "We were willing to do that at that time," he agreed with Bart's defense attorney, "or what our family's beliefs were. That's what we had concluded—as a family, that is what we wanted. We tried to convince them that we did not want to be here."

"And you were telling them, that was acceptable to you?" McDonald continued.

"That was acceptable to us."

"In fact, as you said, you were actually begging him to do it?"

"Yes, I actually begged," Bartlett stated. He then chuckled and added, "I'm not a very good beggar, either."

The defense attorney awkwardly attempted to switch gears. "Now, obviously, you're close, or were close, to your sister, Tricia Whitaker?" McDonald frittered horribly.

"Correct," Bartlett replied rather curtly.

"And how would she feel in this situation?"

"I can tell you exactly how she would feel," Bartlett responded. "She would not want her son to go to death row, no matter what he's done. She loved him more than anything else in the whole world. She loved both those boys. Their whole life revolved around family."

McDonald then asked Bartlett about some of Bart's codefendants. "Did the situation come up as to what was happening to the shooter, Chris Brashear, in this case?"

"Yes, it did."

"Did you become upset when you learned that the state was seeking the death penalty against Bart Whitaker, but not seeking the death penalty against the shooter?"

"Very much so," Bartlett replied adamantly. He also had no desire for Brashear to receive the death sentence, either. "I think justice needs to be done, but if I don't want it for the shooter, I surely wouldn't want it for Bart. That still holds true." In reference to Brashear, Bartlett added, "I think he needs to go to prison for a long, long time for what he's done, but, definitely, we don't want the death penalty for the shooter as well."

"Did it bother you at the time that they were considering a lesser sentence for the shooter, as opposed to Bart?" McDonald continued the particular line of questioning.

"It still bothers us, because we understand that Bart was the conspirator in this, but still, somebody had to pull the trigger, and in my viewpoint, he's worse than Bart," Bartlett responded.

"Do you think it takes a different type of person to be there and actually pull the trigger?" McDonald queried.

"To put a gun to a nineteen-year-old kid's chest and pull a trigger after he smiled at you"—Bartlett shook his head at the thought of his other nephew, Kevin—"that is one horrible person."

"Would you agree that Bart Whitaker is a horrible person for being involved in this, causing it to happen, carrying out his part of the conspiracy—would you not?"

"I would feel that he's a pretty bad person," Bartlett intoned.

"How do you feel about Bart Whitaker at this time?"

"He's in trouble. He needs to go to prison for just as long as he can possibly go. We don't ever expect to see Bart Whitaker out of prison."

Bartlett continued on about the health of his mother and how an execution of her grandson would have an adverse effect on it. "The death sentence is not only for Bart, it's for the rest of us. It's my mother. It's our family. The stress level that is brought unto us by this is a sentence as well."

McDonald circled around the witness-box and looked at the jury as he spoke to Bartlett. "So you're saying that, in spite of all the horrible things that he's done, that that's your position? That's what you want this jury to do?"

Bartlett nodded. "That is our final position."

McDonald asked Bartlett about Bart's desire for money. "Did money ever seem like an important thing to Bart?"

"Not any more than any other twenty-, nineteen-, twenty-one-year-old kid."

Bartlett talked about some of the mistakes his sister may have made in raising the son that eventually had her killed. "When you love your kids, like my sister loved those two boys, we do some stupid things. And we've all done that. A lot of parents will stick their head in the ground and think, 'Well, that's just part of growing up.'"

The uncle also spoke about the pressure Bart must have felt growing up. "There is a tremendous amount of pressure for kids that grow up with successful parents. My dad was very successful, and it's hard to follow in a successful parent's footsteps. It really is. You just have to learn that, sooner or later, you're going to make your own footsteps and try not to follow in your dad's footsteps." He added, "All parents want their kids to do great things, but you have to realize that not all kids are destined to do great things, and the best you can hope for them is to make sure they are happy."

Bartlett admitted to the court that all of the success in the world could not change his family's current tragic situation. "There's so much pressure on making money, so much pressure on having to succeed in business. But it's just not that important. You can see here that the money that we have successfully worked for, [for] two generations, got us to this point. Let me tell you what—the money is not worth it."

McDonald asked Bartlett how his sister responded to Bart's arrest in high school for stealing computers. "She was the ultimate mother and she was so embarrassed. But she brushed herself off, got up, and started all over again. It was devastating for her, but she was not ever going to give up on Bart."

"Would it be safe to say," McDonald continued, "that, frankly, she smothered Bart with her love?"

"She was, you know, a mother. All mothers smother their kids. It was always 'He's so handsome, he's so smart, he's so wonderful' when she spoke about Bart. Yes, you could say she smothered him."

McDonald asked about Bartlett's brother-in-law. "How about your relationship with Kent Whitaker?"

"Poor Kent. You have to feel incredibly sorry for what's happened to him. I mean, for a year after it happened, he was in total denial. He came to work probably five or six weeks because he had to get his mind on something else. You can't imagine how it has devastated him and his friends and my sister's friends. It took Kent a year just to kind of realize what had happened. It probably took him two years to admit to what had happened."

Bartlett continued to speak highly of his brother-in-law. "The Kent you see now is just an incredibly strong person. I can't imagine being Kent and having to live the lifestyle that he's living now, for the amount of pain that he has gone through. I mean, my gosh, how does he get up every day? How has this affected him? You can't judge Kent until you imagine being in his shoes. I mean, there's just no way."

Bartlett admired how Kent treated his sister. "He was a loving husband, he was a loving father. Their lives centered around those two boys. He was excellent in business, and to think how this has devastated him, and where does his life continue after all this? It's just hard to imagine how he gets up every day and puts his shoes on. He's a much stronger person than I am."

The discussion turned toward blame. "There's no blame that can be placed on any of y'all for this happening," McDonald posited.

"There's no blame you can place anywhere," Bartlett surmised.

"Except at the foot of Bart Whitaker?"

"Knowing Bart my whole life," Bartlett contemplated aloud, "there were certain signs that now, in hindsight, we could recognize. But let me tell you—

growing up—we never saw anything that would lead us to this point. You can ask Tricia's friends. There was never anything we saw that would lead Bart to this point. Absolutely nothing." Bartlett shook his head as if stunned. "We knew of some things, but all parents think it's just a part of growing up, that they'll simply look the other way this time. But all parents need to think about the bigger picture if something like stealing computers happens."

"Could it be a cry for help?" McDonald managed to fire off.

"I definitely think—" Bartlett was cut off by Jeff Strange before he could respond.

"Objection. I'm going to object to that as leading and self-serving hearsay."

"Sustained," Judge Vacek declared.

McDonald decided it was as good a time as any to wrap things up with Bo Bartlett. He asked if there was anything the grieving brother-in-law wanted to share with the jury.

"I can go back to the same point," Bartlett reiterated, "that it is important for us to have closure. Closure for us would be a life sentence. Let him go off to prison," he pleaded, acknowledging Bart's presence. "Let him be able to think every day, every minute of every day, 'What a mess I've made of my life. What a mess I've made of my family's life.' That is much more of a closure for us than a death sentence."

The prosecution knew they needed to navigate a delicate balance between being guardians of the people of the state of Texas and seeking punishment for Bart Whitaker's actions, while also functioning as decent human beings in regard to Bart's living relatives. The state wanted Bart dead, while his family, obviously, wanted him alive. It proved to be a difficult moment for the prosecution.

Assistant District Attorney Jeff Strange approached Bo Bartlett. The two had met previously to discuss the case and Bart's potential plight.

"Good afternoon, Mr. Bartlett. How are you doing today?" Strange asked in a cordial, easygoing manner.

"Pretty good, Jeff," Bartlett replied.

"We know each other, and you've been kind enough in the past to let me call you Bo, but I've got to be a little more formal in court," he said as he smiled. Bartlett returned it in kind.

Strange then jumped right into the fray. "You've known our position for some time now—is that fair to say?"

"Correct," Bartlett answered.

"And you expressed your concerns, and what your family's position was, to us sometime ago?"

"Correct."

"We have continued to visit with you anytime you've asked us to, true?"

"Correct."

"And we've also continued to provide appropriate victim-type services to your family, as much as our office could?"

"Very much so."

"This is not a situation where your family is adversarial. We just disagree on the appropriate outcome of this case?"

"We're just looking for justice," Bartlett solemnly replied.

"We just have a different sense of what justice may

be in the case," Strange nodded. He then switched topics. "Let's talk about something else before we start talking about this defendant. Nobody has really let us get to know your nephew Kevin and your sister, Patricia, so I think it's going to fall on you, if that's okay. It's my understanding that you and Kevin were particularly close, because you're both outdoorsmen. Tell us a little bit about your relationship with Kevin."

Bartlett straightened up in the witness stand's chair. "I had a great relationship with Kevin." He smiled slightly. "He liked to hunt, liked to fish. We had a place up in the country, and Kevin would come up there and stay with us. He just enjoyed being outdoors."

He paused momentarily and then began to speak of Kevin's older brother. "I would have had a similar relationship with Bart, but Bart did not enjoy those type of activities."

Bartlett stated that he and Kevin, along with his own son and daughter, would go out hunting or fishing at least once or twice a year. Bartlett described his nephew as only an "average" hunter, but he said it with a sense of wistful remorse. He then added that he himself was a "below average" hunter. The people in the gallery, many of them family friends, released a collective chuckle at Bartlett's self-deprecating sense of humor.

Bartlett then spoke of Kevin and his attachment to Texas A&M University, and how his nephew had dreamed of becoming an Aggie.

Strange mentioned that Kevin struggled a bit his first year at Texas A&M. "Had a little bit of trouble with grades—and was looking forward to going back—when he was killed?"

"That's what makes a great Aggie." Bartlett nodded.

"Perseverance?" Strange wondered.

"Yep," he answered succinctly.

Bartlett then spoke about how he and Kevin had gotten closer in the last year of his nephew's life, mainly while up in their place in the country. "I don't think at that time he knew what he wanted to do, like most any eighteen- or nineteen-year-old. He was just a typical kid."

Bart's uncle then talked about how his kids got along with Kevin, and Bart as well. "There were many times where we gathered as a family at the lake house and had great times together as a family."

"How often would y'all get together at the lake house?" Strange asked.

"Before we got the ranch, we used to spend all the holidays at the lake house—Labor Day, July Fourth—or, at least, all of the summer holidays."

Strange wanted to know about Kevin's relationship with his mother. He merely reiterated that the boys were her life, and that she would have done anything for them. He also spoke of how she had spent extra time with Kevin, because he had struggled in grade school.

"He inherited that from the Bartlett side of the family." Bo chuckled.

Strange wanted to know how Tricia's relationship with Bart compared to her relationship with Kevin. "Tricia and Bart and Kevin," Bartlett recalled, "they all had the same relationship. I don't think there was the golden child. Neither Kevin nor Bart was the golden child in her eyes. They were both equal, as far as Tricia was concerned. I think she equally loved those boys." He added, "She took care of those boys, and she took care of them equally. There was no animosity among the boys. They had a great childhood."

Bo Bartlett believed his brother-in-law could not have been a better parent. "Kent is a role-model parent. He's a role-model husband. He's a role-model citizen."

"So you agree that the defendant grew up in a good home, and that he had good parents?" Strange continued.

"He had great parents," Bartlett willingly conceded.

Strange wanted to know what Bart's parents had purchased for their oldest son: things such as his tuitions for Baylor University and Sam Houston State University, every car he had ever owned, including a Ford Explorer, a Contour, and his Yukon, his townhome in Willis, and an extensive, expensive wardrobe.

Bartlett also answered Strange's questions in regard to possible abuse in the Whitaker household, which Bart's uncle vehemently denied. Indeed, Bartlett insisted, Tricia tended to coddle her boys. "She could smother them pretty good." He laughed.

"With love?" Strange asked the obvious question.

"Oh yes, with love."

"Did Tricia show Bart the type of love that would enhance someone's self-esteem?"

"It should have," Bartlett reasoned.

Strange wanted to talk about Bart. "You indicated that you were a private family, and I understand and respect that. Would you agree with me, though, that the murders of Kevin and your sister are a community concern?"

"Oh, very much so," Bartlett responded while nodding.

"You understand that when the district attorney's

office has to make some of the decisions that we make, we have to also address the concerns of the community?"

"I understand the concerns of the community," Bartlett agreed, "but I also would like to think that the victims' concerns are just as equally or more important than the community's."

"You also understand that the criminal justice system has to have a deterrent effect on crime, and it has nothing to do with your family, correct?"

"Correct."

"And you also understand that the criminal justice system also has a responsibility to make the public have confidence in it, and that has nothing to do with your family, correct?"

Bartlett paused for a long duration before he resumed speaking. "Let me tell you what, Jeff. This is such a unique case that I doubt you've seen many similar to it. You know, where the family members are the victims here, and it's been self-inflicted." Despite decades of research that indicate most murders are committed by either loved ones or friends, Strange let the grieving brother/brother-in-law/uncle continue. "I'm sure y'all don't have cases like this coming through all the time. I don't know how in the world you can figure what the community of Sugar Land needs, or what deterrent to crime there might be. I feel sorry for the community of Sugar Land, but I feel sorrier for my family and for the Whitakers."

"Without a doubt, Mr. Bartlett," Strange calmly responded, "everybody does. You also understand, though, that if we, as prosecutors, are going to make a decision on whether or not to seek the death penalty, it is vitally important that we be absolutely consistent."

"I don't know how you can use this case as being consistent," Bartlett countered, "because it is such an unusual case. There are no other cases that you can compare this one to."

"You still don't know all the facts to this case, do you?" Strange asked.

"And you don't know how I feel as a family for being brought into this situation," an apparently miffed Bartlett responded.

"Would you agree with me that when the decision was made to seek the death penalty, we knew more about this case than you did?"

"Well, you probably did."

"You would agree with me that absolutely no parent would want their son on death row?"

"Absolutely, no parent," Bartlett replied.

"You've said to me, 'Give me fifteen minutes alone with him and I'll save you the trouble.'"

"I have gone through all different emotions for the past three-plus years, and you can't imagine the things that have gone through my mind," Bartlett agreed. "But I can tell you, as of today, I am steadfast, no matter what statement I made prior to this one, that what I'm telling you today is three years of being able to process all this information, to talk and discuss with family members, to tell you that what I'm telling you today is exactly how our family feels."

"The point I'm making," Strange continued, "is that you don't care about Bart Whitaker. That's not why you're down here."

"I *do* care about Bart Whitaker," Bartlett disagreed with the prosecutor. "I *do* feel sorry for Bart Whitaker. I know that he's done something incomprehensible.

He's wasted his life from the chance that he could have had. I don't forgive him, but I do feel sorry for him."

"And you would agree with me that this is all his fault. One hundred percent of it?"

"I don't know if I would say it's all his fault," Bartlett answered to the surprise of many in the gallery. "Somewhere along the road, if we could have seen something as a parent, as an uncle . . ." His voice trailed off. "If we'd have seen something a long time ago that would have helped us out, hopefully, we would have said, 'Let's stop here and do something different.'"

"But you just saw the face that he wanted to show you, didn't you?"

"Yes." Bartlett nodded.

"You have expressed concern about future murder plots, haven't you?" Strange queried.

"Yes, we have."

Strange then began to read from an earlier victim impact statement made by Bartlett. "Let me just read it," the attorney stated as he pulled out the document. "You wrote, *We do not ever want our children to have to worry about whether or not they are safe in their own home and safe from future murder plots again, even if it's 40 years from now, and they have children and grandchildren of their own.* You, at least, expressed that concern to us?"

"Correct," Bartlett assented.

"Mr. Bartlett, I thank you. I'm not going to ask you any more questions."

Despite the seeming end of the questioning, Bartlett was determined to make his family's point heard, loud and clear. "Do we feel threatened once Bart gets to prison for the rest of his life?" Bartlett asked Strange, but he also seemed to be pleading with the judge and jury. "No, we don't feel threatened anymore."

Strange decided he was not done, after all. "You understand that if he gets a life sentence, he goes in general population?" Strange was referring to Bart being among hardened criminals, including murderers and rapists while inside prison. The prosecutor was hoping to appeal to Bartlett's strong sense of family, assuming the uncle would not want his nephew raped, assaulted, or murdered while behind bars.

"You know, Jeff, our family feels that if he goes into the general population, we feel comfortable with that. And we feel like there's not a problem with the safety of our family. We know what general population is about, and he has a chance to interact with other people. We're very, very comfortable with that."

"Thank you, sir," Strange was definitely done this time.

Bartlett did not respond.

Randy McDonald, however, was not finished. The defense attorney approached the witness stand one more time. He wanted to make sure the jurors were aware that the prosecution was open to deal making, if necessary. "Did you know the prosecution made the decision not to seek the death penalty for the shooter?" he asked in regard to Chris Brashear.

"Correct," Bartlett replied.

"Do you think someone has to be a little bit different to actually pull a trigger on somebody?"

"What I understand is that the shooter knew my nephew." He pondered and shook his head in disbelief.

"And to take a nine-millimeter Glock, with hollow-point shells, that is one horrible person."

"And in your opinion, the DA's office should give the same consideration to Bart that they've given to that person?"

"Absolutely." Bartlett nodded.

McDonald switched gears to Bart's rearing. "Do you think that your sister and Kent, in providing all those things like the cars and the townhome, were expecting Bart to be successful and step up to the plate?"

"I don't think they were expecting him to be successful," Bartlett disagreed. "I think they were just expecting him to have things so that he could go to college and not have to worry about that. It's a lot of pressure. When we give them all that, you expect something in return. It's an investment."

"If they're not able to pay back the investment," McDonald proffered, "that's a problem, isn't it?"

"It's a problem," Bartlett replied in a quiet voice.

"Thank you," McDonald stated in closing.

Judge Vacek excused the witness.

51

March 6, 2007
Fort Bend County Courthouse
Richmond, Texas

The members of the gallery had invested much emotional capital during the testimony of Bo Bartlett. They seemed slightly drained by the heart-wrenching declarations made by Bart Whitaker's uncle. They would not get a reprieve, though. The next person up to the witness stand was none other than Bart's father, Kent Whitaker.

For the penalty phase, Kent's return to the stand was a bit muted. His demeanor was noticeably downcast. The guilty verdict for his son seemed to drain the father of what little hope he still might cling to. He was, however, determined to salvage what was left of his family by making the case that Bart should not be executed.

Randy McDonald respectfully approached the father, who appeared smaller on the stand than he had during the trial phase. "Would you reintroduce yourself to the ladies and gentlemen of the jury?"

"I'm Kent Whitaker," he declared. Some of the jury members nodded back toward the witness, as if they had become friends with the grieving family man during this torturous ordeal.

"Mr. Whitaker," McDonald asked as he moved toward the witness, "this trial is about your son Bart Whitaker, and you know that the jury has found him guilty of capital murder?"

"Yes, sir." Kent nodded, not in anger, but almost with pity for the jury members. He knew that theirs was not an easy decision to make, and he almost felt sorry that they were forced to be put in such a position by his son's actions.

"And you are, of course, a victim in this case?"

Kent merely nodded again.

"I think you should be allowed to tell the ladies and gentlemen of the jury how devastating this has been to your life."

Kent paused momentarily. Some members of the jury appeared to lean forward to hear the quiet voice coming from the somber man. The entire gallery held its breath, almost as if the spectators were one collective entity.

"Thank you," he stated, easing into the conversation. "Everything in my life has changed, as you can imagine. My wife, and best friend, is gone. My son is dead. My other son is charged with murder." He shook his head as if the absurdity of the entire matter had hit him square in the face for the very first time.

Kent then began to tick off the numerous ways the murders forever altered his life. "Tricia was our family historian," he said, slightly smiling. "There are parts of

my life that I'll never even remember. I can be looking
at pictures and I won't recall who people are. I will not
have grandchildren of my own. My career has changed.
I no longer am employed where I was for thirty-one
years. My home is still my home, but it's not the place
it was before December 10, 2003."

Kent went on to talk about the manifestations of his
anguish, both physical and mental. "It has affected me
medically. My mental recall of things has deteriorated
as a result of the trauma and the grief. I have trouble
remembering friends' names." Apparently, his doctors assured him that he would recapture his memory
when the traumatic events had run their course. "Unfortunately, that has not been the case for me, because we've had these criminal proceedings hanging
over my head for so long."

He next spoke of how the events had affected his
other surviving family members. "It has affected my
family. It has aged my parents considerably. I fear that
it has affected Tricia's mom's health as well. All of our
families—everything—everything has changed."

McDonald attempted to console the grief-stricken
father. "You recognize that this is not your fault?"

"I agree," Kent responded.

"And the only one who can be blamed for this, and
punished for it, of course, is Bart Whitaker?"

"Yes, that's true."

"Mr. Whitaker, you're a very religious man, are
you not?"

"I do have faith in my Lord," he replied.

"And has that been of some comfort to you during
these trying times?"

"I honestly cannot imagine trying to go through a

major loss without the Lord giving me strength to get through this. I just can't imagine this."

"And as part of your religious beliefs, do they have anything to do with forgiveness?"

"They're centered around it. There's no way you can view my actions without filtering it through my Christian faith. The underlying tenet of the entire Christian faith is that everyone sins. Everyone does things that are wrong, and that affects our immortal soul, the part of us that will live on when our bodies die. There's going to be a part of us that lives on forever and ever and ever. There's only two places where that soul can be—with God in Heaven or away from God for eternity, by themselves, with their thoughts in a place we call Hell."

Bart Whitaker shifted uncomfortably in his chair.

"And the problem," Kent asserted, continuing the theology lesson, "is that we all have this sin in us, and the Christian faith tells us there is a way, and only one way, to get that sin out of us. And that is to rely on the work of God's son, Jesus Christ. To wash that sin off, so that in his eyes, we'd be viewed as clean."

McDonald stepped in. "You're speaking of the New Testament, as opposed to the Old Testament, where we have the 'eye for an eye,' 'you reap what you sow,' and things like that?"

In regard to the New Testament, Kent explained, "You might look at it like the caterpillar who spins a cocoon, and the butterfly that emerges. The seeds of God's forgiveness and his plan were what the Old Testament is all about, and God chose to hide it in several ways, but it's there. Christ came into the world to not remove all the Old Testament, but to prove to everyone that the Old Testament laws are not a way to achieve salvation. You actually have to have those sins removed by someone who is perfect. So, in one respect, the Old Testament was an improvement over the then-current conditions, was much better than what it used to be, which was 'Somebody faults you, you kill them if you got a chance.' But the New Testament is a completion of what the Old Testament was hinting at."

McDonald steered Kent out of the religious discussion and back to the actual crime. "Of all the people that are the victims of this, you are the greatest victim, because you lost, not only your wife and your son, but it was your other son that caused all the problems?"

"Yeah. I think everyone will agree that I was the center."

"And the bottom line is that you are here today to talk to this jury about justice for this situation?"

"Absolutely." Kent perked up. "Justice is important. I don't think anyone could have misunderstood us from the start, thinking that we were trying to go through some legal proceedings that would absolve Bart of his responsibilities for this, or him to have to pay a debt to society for this."

"Would Tricia feel the same way?" McDonald wondered aloud.

"I promise you, yes," Kent offered. "She would have been appalled at that"—he was referring to Bart's potential punishment—"that the state chose to pursue the death penalty in this case."

"Now, you understand that the state, in their discretion, can choose [in] which cases to seek the death penalty?"

"I do, yes."

"You don't actually fault Mr. Felcman or Mr. Strange

for doing their job that Mr. Healey decided was the proper way to go about this?"

"I do not," Kent firmly replied. "Someone asked me if I felt like I was the victim of the fact that the state has chosen to pursue the death penalty, and I told them no, I don't feel like a victim at all. The state is given the responsibility of protecting society, and there are laws on the books that they operate from, and they made this decision. I think it is the *wrong* decision," he added, "I think there's a lot of collateral damage to the family as a result of having to go through this trial.

"It's been a long time since Bart was arrested," Kent continued. "I would like to have an opportunity to have resumed our relationship through the court systems, with him being remanded to the state for the rest of his life."

"You agree that that would be an appropriate sentence for Bart? That he be sentenced to life in the penitentiary?"

"I agree, yes. I believe that would be an appropriate answer."

McDonald again steered the conversation into a different direction, focusing on the night of the murder, and Kent's hospital night of forgiveness. "As you were laying there in that hospital room, you didn't know what had happened, or who had done this to your family—is that correct?"

"That's correct. We had no idea."

"What was your reaction in the hospital with regard to the person, unknown to you at the time, that actually did the shooting?"

"The night of the shootings, after the nurses had left from hooking me up to some IVs, and cleaning

me up the best they could, after they left—and I was
there by myself for the first time—I tried to wrap my
mind around all the changes that I knew had happened to me." Kent began to describe the painful, immediate aftereffects of the worst night in his entire
life. "I was having a hard time with all of it, but one
thing that kept coming into my mind was that I had
told many people, for many years, that faith was an act
of willpower. That faith wasn't, or isn't, a feeling. Because your feelings will lie to you, and if you rely on
your judgments, on just emotions, then you will make
mistakes. But if you have faith in the word of God, and
you read in the Bible that it tells you to do something,
even though it doesn't feel like it makes much sense
to you, the Bible tells you what faith is. And I realized
that this was the granddaddy of all situations." Kent
faintly smiled at the absurdity of the situation.

"I was faced with a situation that changed my life,"
he continued as the audience sat, enraptured. "I had
spent the last two hours since the shooting bouncing
back and forth from being numb, from extreme
anger, from a desire for deep revenge—even revenge
with my own hands—to shock. There were all these
different feelings that I had been experiencing, and I
knew that if I chose one of them, my life would be different as a result of making that decision."

Kent Whitaker continued to talk about the internal
struggle that he was forced to confront. "I came to the
inescapable conclusion that, even though I could not
understand how it could possibly be true, I believed."
He paused. "There's one verse in the Bible that says
the Lord will take all things and work them for good
for those who love him and are called to his service. I
made the conscious willpower decision that 'all things'

included the murder of my wife and my son, and that I was going to trust him to work good from it." A few patrons in the courthouse nodded their heads silently. Others looked dumbfounded.

"At the moment that I made that decision, another question popped into my mind, and it was kind of a strange one, which was 'What about the shooter?' And immediately I knew what my response was going to be. I thought, 'I want whoever is responsible for this to stand next to Tricia, Kevin, and me in Paradise and sing the praises of the Lord.' And I haven't wavered from that. I looked in my heart, and that's what I really wanted."

The silence in the courtroom was marred only by the nearly imperceptible sound of someone crying.

Kent straightened up in his chair and continued. "I had no idea at the time that one of those I was praying for was my son," he stated as he looked up at Bart.

"I think what happened that night was that God knew what was coming, and he knew that people are redeemable, and he knew Bart was going to need someone to stand with him and show him what my faith was all about, so he could see, firsthand, the forgiveness of the Lord, who has forgiveness for all of us who repent. And he gave me the power, the strength beyond what is reasonable to expect, to forgive someone for an awful crime without knowing who they were, because he knew that only if I was able to get past that forgiveness, for real, when it didn't mean anything, when there was nothing I could gain from it, that I would be able to truly spend time with my son when he came under suspicion, and then later ran, and after he was arrested." Kent took a deep breath. "It was only by truly forgiving everyone involved, including the real shooter, that I would be able to stand up to what was coming."

Defense attorney McDonald stepped in. "Based on your beliefs, now that you know your son was involved in this, you haven't wavered in your position?"

"No, I have not," Kent responded. He also added that he came to the decision of his own accord—with God. "It was a decision between myself and the Lord. This was my heart speaking."

McDonald steered the questioning toward the conversation between Kent and Bart that occurred in prison, on the second anniversary of the murders of Tricia and Kevin. The men had spoken about Bart's potential sentencing, and how they both hoped he could serve a sentence of life in prison instead of facing execution.

"Have we ever proposed anything other than pleading to a life sentence for capital murder for Bart?" McDonald wondered aloud.

"No. That is the only thing we've ever sought. It is what I begged the district attorney's office to take when we met, before you came on the scene," Kent acknowledged.

"And we have even tried to do it in such a way that they could stack life sentences, if they wanted to?"

"Yes. As I understand it, that was really the first and only offer we've ever made. Bart was willing to accept stacked sentences, which, as I understand, means that the sentence for the first murder has to be completed in its entirety before the second one can even begin."

McDonald asked Kent about the jury members. "Is it your desire that they assess a life sentence in this case?"

"It has been from the start," Kent stated, then gave

a knowing glance toward the jury box "and it still is. I would ask that they would determine the appropriate punishment in this case is to give him life in prison, so that he would never be released to the public again, but that I would have the chance to rebuild the relationship he and I had before this, and allow everybody in the family to say, 'All right, this awful nightmare has passed from one stage to the next, and we don't have to go through the state of Texas–required series of appeals that will take years and years to play out,' which is going to happen if the death penalty is assessed."

"If it's a life sentence, there will be no appeal?" McDonald asked.

"No, no. That's what we've been pursuing ever since the day he was arrested."

McDonald wrapped up his initial round of questions for Kent Whitaker. "Pass the witness."

After a short break so the jurors could stretch their legs and attend to any bathroom needs, the court resumed with First ADA Fred Felcman taking over. He seemed to be in no mood to coddle Mr. Whitaker.

"Mr. Whitaker, I've listened very intently to your testimony, and also to the previous witness, Mr. Bo Bartlett. How does y'all's feelings about whether or not Bart deserves the death penalty aid the jury? The defendant is the one on trial. These people judge the defendant by his actions, okay? I have not heard from you or Mr. Bartlett talk about the defendant and his actions."

"I think I spoke directly to that," Kent Whitaker countered.

Felcman was not satisfied with the answer. "Let me talk about the actions of the defendant then," he declared, obviously miffed at Kent Whitaker's stance. "On the night that he had your wife and son killed, y'all went out to eat, right?"

"That's correct."

"He celebrated with you, broke bread with you, knowing that you were supposed to be dead, that your wife was supposed to be dead, that your son was supposed to be dead, in a matter of minutes. You understand that?"

Kent seemed flustered by Felcman's demeanor. He stumbled over his words in response. "I have . . . this is what I've been saying all along. I don't understand where we're getting off—"

"Because the testimony that you have just given to this jury," Felcman countered, "really had nothing to do with his actions. It had to do with the way you felt, and the way Mr. Bartlett felt, but it did not have anything to do with the defendant."

Kent attempted to defend himself. "Well, first of all, that was what I was asked to answer."

"I understand," the moustachioed Felcman responded.

"And secondly, I believed I answered that when I said that nobody was trying to absolve him of the responsibility of this crime. It wasn't a matter of guilt or innocence. It never has been." Kent continued in almost a defiant manner, though the timbre of his voice remained calm. "It has been a matter of what the appropriate response is for the state."

"Then you know what the defendant's plea was in this particular case?" Felcman prodded.

"I understood that the defendant did not plead at

all," Kent answered, using the same description of his son as the "defendant," as used by the prosecution.

"So, instead of the defendant pleading guilty to something you knew he did, that meant this jury had to wrestle with the decision of whether he was guilty or not?"

"I'm not an attorney, Mr. Felcman, but I have been told that there's a very good reason why a person chooses not to lie and say, 'I'm innocent,' but to stand silent and for the state to prove he's guilty."

Felcman decided to refocus the attention on Bart Whitaker. "The defendant, as he was growing up in your household with you and your wife and your other son, was never abused by you. You didn't physically abuse him, sexually abuse him, or anything else like that?"

"No, we did not," came Kent's terse reply.

"Fact is, as everybody said, he's lived a good life."

"Yes."

"Then, when he was seventeen years old, he started burglarizing the schools?"

"Yes."

"You didn't have any idea that he was doing that?"

"No, we did not."

"How did you find out, Mr. Whitaker, that your son had been burglarizing schools?" Felcman asked.

"We found out when he was arrested, and the school police called to say so," Kent admitted, still embarrassed to this day.

"Did you talk to the defendant about these burglaries at the school?"

"Of course, I did," Kent replied, annoyed. "At length, and many times. Tricia and I both did."

"What did the defendant tell you about the burglaries at the school?"

"It was more of a prank than anything else. He said that they figured a way how to do it, so they did it."

"It was a joke, or a prank?"

"Well, it was not a very smart prank, and it was a very stupid joke," Kent responded.

"Did he tell you how they went ahead and accomplished burglarizing these schools?"

"I heard they went on the roof and through a skylight."

Felcman pressed on. "Did he tell you he actually rented a storage room to store the items they stole?"

"Yes, I learned that after the fact."

"Would you say that it was well-planned, executed burglaries to gain property that he is not entitled to?"

"Yes, that's correct. You're right," Kent agreed with the prosecutor.

"After he's done these things, you then take him to see a counselor, to see if you can help him out?"

"Yes, we did. Tricia took him to Brendan O'Rourke."

"Was she a family friend?"

"Yes, we knew her before, or, at least, Tricia knew her."

"And this Dr. O'Rourke counseled the defendant about what, exactly?"

Kent looked down, shifted in the witness stand, and spoke. "This is going to sound awful, but the truth is, I don't know exactly what she talked to him about that. Tricia took him, and while Tricia and I talked, it was all thirdhand information to me."

"But did you ask Dr. O'Rourke to write a letter to try

to get the defendant back into Clements?" Felcman asked in regard to Bart's onetime high school.

"Yes, we did."

"Did the defendant tell you he was sorry for what he did with the burglaries?"

"Yes, he did."

"And do you know he [pleaded] nolo contendere?" per the burglaries.

"Probably on the advice of counsel," Kent surmised.

"Got placed on probation?"

"Correct."

"When he got arrested for that, do you remember how many days he spent in jail?"

"One," Kent answered.

"One day?"

"One night," Kent corrected the prosecutor.

"And y'all had to bond him out?"

"That's correct."

"Had your son ever been in jail before?"

"No."

"Did he appear to be or tell you that he was scared to have been in jail?"

"He did not say he was scared to be in jail." Kent seemed uncomfortable. "He said that he was apprehensive, but that it was just an experience he had."

"An experience," Felcman repeated.

"Yeah."

"You realize in his confession that he said he burglarized these schools because it was an adventure?" Felcman noted a recurring theme with Bart Whitaker and his need for excitement, adventure, and experience.

Kent merely nodded his head. "Probably, that's what it said."

"It was absolutely mortifying on y'all's part, wasn't it?"

"It affected Tricia greatly. There was a deep shame she felt, and it took a long time before she felt comfortable going out in public," Kent recalled.

"Did y'all forgive him at the time?"

"Yes, I did."

"You realize, Mr. Whitaker, that while he was on probation for the four years, he was plotting to kill your family?"

"I did not know that at the time," Kent responded.

"Did you know he actually plotted to kill the Bartletts at their lake house also?"

"I did not know that (at the time)."

"Nothing you did, nothing the court system did, prevented the defendant from continuing to try to kill you, correct?"

"I never knew he was trying to kill me," Kent simply answered.

"You found out in April of 2001 that there was a plot?"

"It was just an episode that was just beyond bizarre to Tricia and I." Kent shook his head at the memory. "We had seen absolutely no indication of any hatred on Bart's part, any interest in having us killed. And the results of the investigation by the Waco Police Department indicated there was nothing substantive to it, because there *was* nothing to it."

"That's after you talked to the defendant, who lied to you about what happened out there, correct?"

"Yes. Everybody talked to the defendant after this happened," Kent answered, unconsciously referring to his own son again as "the defendant."

"And he lied to everybody?"

"In retrospect, we see he did."

"Didn't it strike you as strange that your son had

been able to carry out burglaries on a sophisticated level, and how he had run after a plot that was exposed? Didn't that strike you as sort of strange? Maybe your son's not telling you the truth about things?"

"It struck me that three or four years earlier, when he had gotten in trouble in school, that he had changed," Kent answered. "That he had turned from the stupidity of something that was very foolish. Between that time and the night of the call from the police department saying that he was on his way down here to kill us, there were no indications that there was anything wrong. There were, quite the contrary, positives. And when the police department came to the conclusion that it was a misunderstanding between roommates, and that there was nothing substantive to it, there was no reason why I should have placed any particular value on it."

"That's because the defendant lied to you, right?"

"That's correct."

"Now, in August 2002"—Felcman shifted gears yet again—"the defendant was in some kind of psychotherapy, or something, where he talked to a Lynne Ayres. Do you know who she is?"

"Yes." Kent nodded. "Tricia arranged for that, too."

"Did you ever talk to Lynne Ayres?"

"I don't remember if I ever talked to her about Bart or not. We did visit with her about Kevin and testing for ADD, which I also tested positive for."

"Didn't she tell you that the interview she had with the defendant was very disturbing?"

"Yes, I guess she did. I'm sure your next question was that Bart said that he got angry at her for being so plodding, and in a perverse reason, [he] just answered the questions wrong."

"She told you that interviewing him was so disturbing that she labeled him narcissistic, didn't she?" Felcman pressed forward.

"I don't remember, but I'll take your word for it."

"He got irritated with her, correct?"

"Yes."

"Did she tell you how he thought his relationship with the family was like?"

"No," Kent answered brusquely.

"She didn't tell you that he found no use to have a relationship with friends or family?"

"I don't recall that."

"When she told you how disturbing the interview was, how did you react? What did you do about it?"

Kent scooted back in his chair. "Mr. Felcman, I don't remember. I promise you, if I could remember, I'd tell you the truth. I don't recall the details of that conversation."

"What happened, basically, is that you confronted the defendant, he gave you a reason, and you accepted it?"

"That's sounds about right."

"In other words"—Felcman paused dramatically—"he lied to you again?"

"Yes." Kent nodded.

"So, since the age of seventeen, this defendant has basically been lying to you about how his true personality is at this point in time, correct?"

"Correct."

"You told the jury earlier if you had found out that your son had not been going to school, you would have—what?—sought more counseling for him?"

"I would have done that and we would have pulled

him back from where he was and brought him back home."

"What was the reason the defendant gave you for not going to school?"

"He told me that the country club he worked at had gotten very busy, some people had left, and he spent a lot of extra time at work."

"You understand that would have been a good year and a half of extra work, and that he hadn't been going to school or doing anything during that period of time?"

"I did not know that," Kent responded, seemingly nonplussed by the assessment. "I thought it was just one semester."

Felcman decided to return to the night of December 10, 2003. "Let me get to the murders specifically. The defendant, in order to get into the house, had to step across your wife's body. You realize that?"

"Yes," Kent agreed. His demeanor never changed. "Yes."

"And to get farther into the house, he had to step across your other son, Kevin's body. You realize that?"

"I honestly don't know where he fell, but he either stepped over him or past him."

"Then, after that, he concocted a lie to you and to the police about what happened out there that night?"

"Yes, he did."

"Of course, you believed him?"

"I did. He was my son," he declared with a possible Freudian slip.

"You believed him in regard to the burglaries?"

"Yes."

"You had believed him in regard to the interview with Lynne Ayres, correct?"

"Correct."

"You had believed him in regard to his lie about why he was not working, correct?"

"Yes."

"And you believed him that, even before then, that he was going to school and graduating and going into the FBI, or having an internship in the FBI?"

"Correct."

"That this defendant was so good at lying, that he could fool the one person who should probably know him better than anybody else, right?"

Kent became defensive and responded, "At the time, I had no idea that any of these things had happened. My antennas were not up."

"That's not the question," Felcman countered. "It's not that your antennas are up—"

"Oh yes, it is," an adamant Kent butted in. "I think it is important. Because, after the fact, we can sit here in the courtroom and say these things happened in this sequence, and you did not recognize it here or there, and all the way down the line. There was no reason for me to have this expectation of guilt, and so I did tend to give him the benefit of the doubt. After the fact, after the shootings, after he became a suspect, it was totally different."

"That's not my question," a frustrated Felcman repeated. "You're not on trial here."

"Well, I feel like it," an exasperated Kent responded in kind.

"You're not on trial. The defendant is the one on trial."

"Yes, he is," Kent agreed.

"What I'm trying to get across is that the one person he should care the most about—his family, his father, and the people who should know him the best—[he] was able to lie to y'all and cover all these things up, correct?"

"That's correct."

"He even brought his dead mother into this and tried to use her to get out of it also, correct?"

Kent was taken aback. "In what way?"

"That she knew that he wasn't going to school."

"Oh yes, he told me that."

"You wanted to believe that—then you realized he was just lying to you?"

"Yes." Kent nodded again.

"You still wanted to believe that he had nothing to do with these murders, but did, at any point in time, the defendant come up to you and say, 'Dad, I got something to tell you. I had your wife and son killed,' at any time?"

"No, he did not."

"Fact is, he was so good at deceiving you, he actually went to the rodeo." Felcman recalled the Pat Green concert attended by Kent, Bart, and several of Kevin's friends.

"We did go to the rodeo and the song was sung in Kevin's honor, but it wasn't so much a matter of deception."

Kent then decided to talk, unprompted, about Bart prior to him skipping town and heading for Mexico. "Before I visited with him on his return from Mexico, I tried and tried and tried to believe the police or to believe Bart, and I was getting no details of the investigation. I got a lot of innuendos, a lot of saying that he's a horrible guy, but there is nothing I would have turned my back on my son for. I understand it was a criminal investigation and they probably couldn't have talked to me, but there should have been something that they could have said," Kent looked up at Felcman. "The point is, I was not believing Bart, nor was I believing the police."

"What was the defendant telling you while this investigation was going on? Before he fled to Mexico."

"That he was innocent," Kent said flatly.

"He also lied to you when you asked him about Adam Hipp and why the police were talking to him?"

"Yes."

"Of course, he never told you he was talking to Adam Hipp and was trying to get him to lie for him?"

"No, he did not."

"When the defendant would talk to you, did he just look you straight in the eye and say, 'No, Dad, I don't know what's going on'?"

"Yes, he did," Kent agreed.

"Looked you straight in the eye?"

"Straight in the eye."

"And you couldn't tell if he was lying or not?"

"I didn't know."

Felcman changed up the questioning by focusing on something Bo Bartlett brought up. "There's been some talk about pressure—that somehow he had pressure and he wasn't living up to expectations. What pressure were you putting on your son, if any?"

"To my knowledge, I wasn't."

Felcman spun around and almost smiled at the witness. "Mr. Whitaker, it sounds like you're one of the nicest men in the world. I can't imagine you putting any pressure on this defendant. Is that about right?"

"Not exactly, believe me." Kent shied away from the compliment.

"Well, you forgave him for the burglaries. You helped

him out afterward with that. You took him to a psychologist. You forgave him for not going to school and lying about that. I'm trying to figure out where in the world I'm getting this testimony that somehow Bart Whitaker is getting pressure to such an extent that he has to kill your son and wife. You didn't give him any type of pressure, did you?"

Kent simply replied, "No."

"Did Lynne Ayres ever tell you how the defendant viewed himself?"

"I don't believe so."

"That he viewed himself as an Atlas—that he could carry the world on his shoulders and do anything better than anyone else? Did she ever tell you that?"

Kent smiled and responded, "No, I don't think so." He began to chuckle. "That's ridiculous."

"She actually wrote that down," Felcman countered, a rather serious look on his face. "That's what the defendant told her. It's not ridiculous. It's what he told her.

"Did she ever tell you," Felcman continued, "that the defendant wanted to join the FBI because he thought like a criminal?"

"Mr. Felcman, I don't recall that conversation."

The prosecutor moved on. "The testimony that you have given to Mr. McDonald seems to be the defendant wants to ride on your shoulders and somehow let this jury panel answer those questions based upon your standing, and not what the defendant has done. Now, you've said that you only have one son left, and that's the reason you want this jury to spare the defendant. You realize you only have one son left because he's killed everybody else?"

Kent was nonplussed by the tone of the prosecutor's question. "I do realize that. Yes, I'm aware."

Felcman was ready to drive his point home one last time. "Can you give this jury anything"—he sounded almost as if he were pleading with Kent Whitaker— "*anything* at all in regard to the defendant's background, how he was raised, the way he was treated by you or your wife, that somehow lessens his moral blameworthiness in causing the death of your wife and son? I mean, anything at all?"

Kent did not hesitate to answer. "Regardless of what would have happened during his childhood, there is nothing that would reduce the horror of this act. I am aware of it."

"You just want this jury to say, 'No, we're going to give him life because it's going to hurt Kent Whitaker and Bo Bartlett,' right?"

"No," Kent responded emphatically. "No, that isn't it at all."

"Do you have any evidence to contradict that your son is not going to be a continuing threat to society?"

"I can't read his heart, Mr. Felcman. I don't think you understand the basis for my arguing against the death penalty in this case. I am a loving father and don't want my son to die. I admit it." Many observers in the gallery sat rapt in attention. Some were on the verge of tears. "I want a relationship with my son, even if it's in jail, where I can find out why this happened. But the majority of the reason for my objection to the death penalty is because I can't read his heart. While I believe that the person who came back from Mexico is different from the person who left, when he ran away, I don't know that for sure. But the single most important thing in my life right now is that my son go to Heaven, and if he has not accepted responsibility in his heart for this, if he has not asked the Lord for forgiveness . . ." Kent paused to compose his wits. "I have forgiven him. I forgave whoever was involved. But the important one is the Lord. If he has not done that, I want the jury to give him as much time as possible so that he can reach that conclusion."

Felcman interjected, "How would you . . . ?"

"Whoa, whoa, whoa!" Kent reacted quickly. "There's one more step. If he has reached that, I want the jury to give him as much time as possible so that he can speak to others about the way that the Lord has forgiven him. Redemption is something that everyone in this room has to have before they die. I want it for my son."

"You understand that you're not the only religious person in this courtroom," a piqued Felcman informed the father. "There are people on this jury panel that are deacons in the Baptist Church. You understand that?"

"I don't know the members of the jury."

"And here we don't look into a person's heart. God does. How would this jury have any indication as to whether or not the defendant has true remorse?"

"I will tell you some conversations that I've had with him. You want those," Kent asked, "or do you think that I'm so deluded that I'd be fooled by him?"

"Did he show true remorse? Did he ever say, 'I did it. I'll let the jury know I did it'? Did he ever accept responsibility? Anything like that?" Felcman shrugged his shoulders.

"In the legal system in which we are entangled, I do not know my way around. I have been told that it is imperative that you do not state specifics, because if it's recorded, that becomes the basis for shooting right through to the death penalty. And so Bart has been very careful not to say specifically, 'Dad, I did it.'" Kent paused briefly. "The first thing he told me when I saw him after returning from Mexico was 'Dad, I am so sorry. This is all my fault. I'm going to do everything I can to make this easy and painless and as quick as possible for everybody.' That was the first time I had any realization that there was a possibility that he could be guilty."

Kent was not yet finished.

"Ever since he was arrested," the father recalled, "he has tried to accept a penalty of life in prison. He would never, ever get back out on the streets, yet the state has chosen to pursue the death penalty." Kent looked more intently at Felcman. "Now, this is your choice, and I understand that you're good men and that this is a decision that y'all have made based on a lot of different factors, but I'm telling you it's wrong."

Felcman was not surprised at the answer. "He's always tried to negotiate. He has never put his neck on the line—"

"He tried," Kent interrupted emphatically. "I'm sorry, but that's just not true."

"Mr. Whitaker, do you see how this defendant has manipulated people time and time and time again?"

"I have. I see all of the lies that you're talking about. I recognize them." Kent's answer obviously did not seem to absolve him of any pain.

"Mr. Whitaker, I have one last question. Do you understand that the way you're testifying—how this is going to affect you—has nothing to do with what the defendant's going to do in the future?"

"I can't read his heart," Kent reiterated, "so I guess

I'd have to answer yes. I don't know what he's going to do in the future."

Felcman looked up at Kent and lowered his voice. "I'm sorry, Mr. Whitaker, that we got a little bit contentious. I did not plan on doing that."

"I believe you, and I never wanted to, either," responded the contrite father. "I think you guys are honorable men."

Randy McDonald returned for the final redirect examination of Kent. "There is no question in your mind that we have tried to plead guilty to this, for the life sentence?"

"We have tried mightily," Kent assented.

"And you have known for a very long time, as I have, that Bart Whitaker is going to testify here today, haven't you?"

"I thought there was a very good chance you might call him."

And call Bart Whitaker they would.

52

The moment everyone was looking forward to could not have been more of a letdown. The evil-genius mastermind Bart Whitaker had elected to take the stand in an attempt to humanize himself before the jury of his peers, who already had found him guilty of first-degree murder. Bart did very little in way of turning that impression around, based on his performance on the witness stand that day.

Bart took the stand, looking worse for wear. His close-cropped crew cut did him no favors in bolstering the innocent-looking portion of his redemption. Nor did his usual three-mile stare. A lack of emotion was not going to win him any brownie points with this crowd.

Bart sat across from his attorney, Randy McDonald, who asked his client to introduce himself to the courtroom.

"Thomas Bartlett Whitaker," Bart responded, using his entire given name.

"Mr. Whitaker," McDonald proceeded, "you are convicted of capital murder?"

"Yes, sir," Bart replied in a calm, even voice.

"Did that come as any surprise to you?"

"No, sir, not at all."

"In the entire time I've been representing you"—McDonald paused, then looked at the impaneled jury—"have we ever offered a defense?"

"No, sir, not on guilt or innocence," Bart responded, his gaze also drifted up from his attorney over toward the jury.

"Have you ever tried to—and before I knew any facts of this case—have me go to the district attorney's office and plead to any amount of time that they wanted to?"

"As many life sentences as they wanted to, sir," Bart responded in the most polite and obliging manner as was feasibly possible.

"Now, as far as you getting up here and pleading guilty," McDonald asked his client, "that was my call?"

"Yes, sir," Bart agreed.

District Attorney Felcman was annoyed by this entire sequence of events. He could make neither heads nor tails out of what McDonald and Bart were up to, so he asked for a conference with the judge. He was especially annoyed with McDonald because the defense attorney had insisted throughout the trial that he was not sure if he would ever call Bart up to the stand. Normal protocol is to provide the opposing side with a witness list, and Bart was never designated as definitive.

After some minor bickering between attorneys,

McDonald continued his questioning of his own client. "Let's get to the point," McDonald declared. "Bart, I know, because of the system and the way it works, the jury had to make the ultimate call to get to this stage," he stated in reference to their decision to render guilt after the guilt/innocence phase of the trial. "Do you understand that?"

"Yes, sir." Bart nodded.

"And had we known for a very long time that at this stage you were going to testify?"

"Yes, sir." This, of course, was news to Felcman, but he chose to ignore the defense attorney's machinations.

"In our discussions, have we ever talked about anything with regard to any defense?"

"No, sir." He repeated, "No, sir."

"Have we always—since I've been involved in this since last April—tried to conclude this matter in a way that you are confined for life and we didn't have to go through this? And we didn't have to have these citizens come up and make this call?" McDonald asked, referring to his and Bart's desire to forgo a trial, accept a sentence of life in prison, and avoid a lengthy and expensive capital murder trial.

"That's what I wanted more than anything else," Bart reassured his counsel, as well as anyone who might take pity on him in the jury box.

Many people in the gallery scoffed in hushed tones. Of course, Bart would want to avoid a capital murder trial at all costs—the young man wanted to live. He had no interest in setting a date with a needle in Huntsville.

"Now, one might say that you would be willing to do that to avoid the death penalty." McDonald acknowledged the psychedelic polka-dotted purple elephant in the room. "You understand why someone might think you'd do that instead of taking a chance with the death penalty?"

"Yes, sir." Bart nodded calmly.

McDonald mentioned the jury members again, and discussed with Bart the decision they were now going to have to make against him. "What I want to do right now, Bart, is I want you to tell them exactly what you did in this case, and why you are absolutely guilty."

McDonald was asking Bart Whitaker to throw himself upon the sword of mercy wielded by twelve Fort Bend County residents. His demeanor, his intentions, and his sincerity would all now come into play and be questioned thoroughly. His connection to the jurors would determine whether or not his life would be spared.

Bart paused before he answered his attorney. He briefly glanced up at the jury and declared, "I am one hundred percent guilty for this. I put the plan in motion. If I had not done so, it would not have happened."

The gallery was silent. It was a promising start for Bart's contrition.

"I know that my perception of my parents, everything that they were translating to me when I was younger was love, and that I was receiving the signals wrong. I know, over time, that converted into a severe disliking of them." Bart paused, had a sincere look on his face, along with a slightly arched eyebrow, and continued. "I tried to think about how I got from Step A to Point Z, and I don't know . . ." His voice trailed off.

Every member of the audience had all of their attention focused on Bart Whitaker as he attempted to explain what drove him to massacre his family.

"I've had about three years to think about this, and

I cannot imagine how I let myself get to that point where things got so out of control." Bart continued on while trying to convey empathy with the family members he left behind, and simultaneously attempting to persuade the jury to believe his position. "I was in such a dark place that I lied to everyone, and I thought it was absolutely necessary that I do so.

"This is all my fault," he added, "and whatever you decide . . . whatever you decide I deserve for this, I accept."

McDonald returned to questioning Bart. "Of course, you could deserve the death penalty for this, don't you think?"

"Yes, sir," Bart solemnly agreed.

McDonald asked Bart how it felt to hear his uncle and his father testify before him. "Do you realize, and have you recognized for a while, how devastating this crime is?"

"Yes, sir," Bart responded. The presence of his uncle Bo seemed to hit him especially hard. "I haven't seen Bo since 2004, and it touched me in a way that it had not done until today."

"And do you realize you robbed your mother of a full life?"

"Yes."

"You robbed Kevin of a full life?"

"Yes."

"You actually even robbed your father of a full life?" McDonald asked, and turned around to look at Kent Whitaker for added emphasis.

"Yes," Bart acknowledged; his head was facing down toward his clasped hands.

"And, of course, all of your other relatives?" McDonald continued the public flogging of his client.

"Yes, sir."

"And because of your involvement, you also recognize that you affected other people's lives that came into this courtroom?"

"Many, many lives," Bart responded.

"And it's all because you just developed this dislike for your parents and just lied about everything?"

"Yes, sir."

McDonald paused and perused the courtroom. Most people in the audience sat stone-faced, while others seemed skeptical of the defense's ploy. Others, such as Kent Whitaker, simply seemed sad.

"Did you know who you were then?" McDonald resumed the line of questioning.

"Absolutely not," Bart responded steadfastly.

"Did you even know what you wanted to be?"

"I had no clue."

McDonald began to paint the picture of Bart as an aimless drifter, searching the hinterland desperately for some guidance, some assurance, some pathway, that would steer him down the trail toward happiness and decency—a drifter who somehow managed to plunge completely over the edge into an abyss not of his own making.

"Now, that's no excuse, obviously." It was apparent, though, that was exactly what McDonald had hoped to conjure up in the minds of the jury members.

"No, there's no excuse for it," Bart agreed.

"And you understand that it is hard for someone like myself, as well as the ladies and gentlemen of the jury, to even understand this conduct?"

"Yes, sir."

The next question came as a shocker to most people in the gallery. "It wasn't motivated by money, was it?" McDonald asked in regard to the plot to kill his family.

"No, sir, not at all."

Several members of the courtroom shifted around uncomfortably in their seats.

"Was the money what motivated the other people to be involved?"

"Yes, sir."

"And it really didn't take much motivation or manipulation for those folks, did it?" McDonald asked in reference to Steven Champagne and Chris Brashear.

"No, sir."

McDonald conveniently passed over the reality that Bart tended to seek out people who were down on their luck, for whatever reason, and were potentially vulnerable to financial gain, group acceptance, and even something illegal to possibly reignite the fires that had been doused in their own lives.

"When did it dawn on you how horrific a crime it was that you committed?"

"It began to dawn on me almost instantaneously, as I was lying on the floor." Bart recalled having been shot and watching as Chris Brashear dashed out of the family's back door. "But I don't think it really hit me until the funeral."

McDonald continued the barrage of negativity toward his client with the ultimate goal of pity and, hopefully, forgiveness for Bart Whitaker. "There's evidence before the ladies and gentlemen of the jury that you continued to lie and deny culpability, and even plot with Adam Hipp to somehow get him to not testify," he stated in regard to the bribe he offered his former friend and onetime cohort in the intended crime. "What do you think your motive was there?"

"Yes, sir, I did continue to lie," Bart responded while looking down. He raised his eye forward to look at his attorney. "The inertia of the six years that I had been living—the way I had been living my life before that—just carried over."

Most of the spectators in the gallery looked puzzled. Again, the skeptics frowned. A few, on the other hand, looked concerned for the young man on the witness stand.

"It was shortly after the funeral that I started praying again for the first time in a long time," Bart continued. "I know that forgiveness, when you truly believe in Christ, is instantaneous. Spiritually, though, it's a very slow thing." Most of the words escaping Bart's lips sounded eerily similar to those of his father in the press and on the witness stand. Mentions of Christ, forgiveness, and redemption seemed to pour out of the young man.

Not so much when it came to Tricia and Kevin Whitaker.

"I was just very weak at the time," Bart continued. "I continued to lie, even though I knew it was wrong."

"Weren't you a little bit scared that you would go to the penitentiary?" McDonald, ever the sensor of skepticism, smartly asked.

"Yes, sir. I was also scared of looking at myself in the mirror and realizing that I had done this." Bart paused, wiped his brow, and continued on. "I knew I did it, but there was, on some level . . ." He sounded disjointed. "I just couldn't look at myself and say that to myself."

Having positioned his client to display full contriteness and acceptance of responsibility for his actions (though the words "murder," "Mom," or "Kevin" never entered the conversation at this juncture), McDonald was ready to attack the particular night in question.

"After this case, you did just like you did in April of 2001. You ran, didn't you?"

"Yes, sir," came Bart's response.

"Are you a coward?"

"Absolutely."

"Are you owning up to every responsible party in this?"

"Yes, sir. Yes, sir, I am."

"Is it your fault?"

"It's one hundred percent my fault," Bart owned up.

"And do you really want to give this jury any excuse for your conduct?"

"No, sir. I do not."

McDonald seemed to be heading toward the point that everyone in the courtroom wanted to know more than anything—why did he do it? "Can you actually explain your conduct to us? Can you answer the question 'Why?'"

Unfortunately, Bart's response was less than forthcoming, but not unexpected.

"No, sir," he replied simply. "I've come up with a lot of reasons for how I got to where I was going, but they do not explain it."

McDonald then wanted to make sure that Bart understood that his admissions of guilt basically eliminated any chance he might have had to appeal a sentence of the death penalty. This led to an objection by Fred Felcman, who insisted that a defendant cannot plead guilty during the punishment phase and have his attorney tell the jury that his client has no grounds for appeal.

McDonald moved on once again, trying to ascertain

the reason for the defendant's actions. "Bart, you had everything going for you—loving parents, a good possibility for an education. What was it that caused you to go into this abyss?"

Again, it seemed as if a collective motion forward was made by nearly everyone in the gallery so as to get closer or to more clearly hear this all-important answer.

Bart was calm. He seemed in his element, having people hang on his every word. "I know, looking back on it now, I always felt that, whatever love they [his family] sent me was conditional on a standard that I just never felt I could reach."

He was just getting warmed up.

"I know that's not the way it was. I don't put any responsibility on them for that," he declared in reference to his parents. "That was my misperception of the way things were, but that's really how I felt about everyone. My friends, my girlfriend, I just always felt like they loved the person that I could become if I tried really hard, and not the person I was."

"But who were you?" McDonald queried.

"I don't know," Bart answered, slowly shaking his head. "I tried to figure that out for a long time. The more I tried different things, the more lost I felt."

"Well, do you feel any remorse for this?"

"Yes, sir, I do," Bart replied with a respectable look of sincerity on his face.

"Who do you feel remorse for?"

Kent Whitaker's attention perked up at the question.

"I feel remorse for everyone involved," Bart responded. "Starting with my dad"—whom Bart acknowledged with a glance in his general direction— "my mom, and my brother. My whole . . ." Bart stopped momentarily and began to cry. He did not

cry long and loud sobs, simply brief gasps punctuated
with slightly damp eyes. A tear or two attached themselves to Bart's eyelash and flashed briefly.

". . . Everyone I ever met in my life," he soldiered
on. "I feel sorry for them having come in contact
with me."

"Bart, do you still feel this way?" McDonald wanted
to know. "Do you feel like you can't deal with it?"

"No, sir, I don't."

"What do you think the difference is now?"

"This whole experience has changed me in ways
that I can't even begin to express in words."

Some members of the gallery muttered, while
others actually rolled their eyes at Bart's response. He
was nonplussed, however, and continued on.

"I know that going to Mexico was a wrong decision.
It was wrong for me to run, to hide from my responsibility in this. But a lot of things happened down there
that made me a much stronger person than I've ever
been in my life, and that's continued through my experience in jail."

Kent Whitaker beamed at the revelation. Many in
the gallery, however, were steamed. Even some of the
courtroom staff members had to stifle a chuckle or
two. What had been a capital murder trial in the
brutal slayings of a mom and her youngest son had
now become the oldest son's psychotherapeutic release. Through the tragic mistakes, a better, stronger,
fully formed individual arose.

Bart's personal rising phoenix was in full display.

He would not have wanted it any other way.

"I have come into a relationship with God," Bart
proselytized. More eyes rolled as the story of Bart's
jailhouse conversion was about to begin. "I grew up in

the Church. I went to a Baptist high school and a Baptist college, but I always looked at Christianity through the eyes of people that I thought were Christians that knew me, and their hypocrisy just always turned me off. But I know, in the past year and a half especially, I have truly come to an understanding of the word of God, and I walk with him on a daily basis. That's really why I am able to be up here today."

"So, on that basis," McDonald resumed, "it doesn't really matter what verdict that they come up with?"

"No, it does not at all." Once again, Bart would float above the fray, regardless of the price he himself would ultimately have to pay.

Now McDonald was finally able to drive home the point he wanted to make with this jury by having Bart get on the witness stand. "They should simply do what the law says. Follow the law and make a determination of whether, in answering those questions, that you deserve the death penalty, or whether you should receive a life sentence?"

"Yes, sir."

McDonald and Bart spoke of his days at Baylor when he spent time with his friends Justin Peters and Will Anthony. McDonald wanted to know if Bart had even wanted to attend college in Waco.

"I didn't want to go there in the first place," Bart replied. "But I was too weak to do what I wanted, which was to join the navy. It's the only thing I knew I wanted to do in my life at that point, but I was under the impression that that was not what a son from First Colony was supposed to do with himself. They were supposed to go to college. All of that. So that's my fault. I should have done what I wanted to do. None of this would have happened, had I done what I wanted to do."

Bart also spoke about his weakness during college. "Nothing interested me. Nothing was going on there," he spoke, in reference to Baylor. "I tried so many different courses of study. When I went to class, I got decent grades. But the fact is that I stopped going to class because I couldn't find anything that interested me in the least. I started to withdraw from that." Bart's supposed intelligence seemed to be rearing its head once again. He believed he was too smart for his own good, and that he was well beyond what a piddly first-tier institution of higher learning could provide him. "That's when I started to grow close to Justin and Will, because they really felt the same way I did," Bart added.

"Did you have any confidence in yourself at all?" McDonald wanted to know.

All signs to the contrary, Bart responded, "No, not at all."

"And why is that?"

"I've never done anything as well as I wanted to. Not as well as I thought I was supposed to."

"Did you impose greater expectations on yourself than even your parents?"

"I know at the time I was thinking that these were their expectations. I know that I put them far higher than anything they put on me."

McDonald continued to humanize his client. "Obviously, you were failing in college?"

"Yes, sir. I was failing."

"Even if your parents had high expectations of you, they loved you very much," McDonald stated, sounding as though he was having a normal conversation with the young man. "What were you going to do one day when you had to tell them that you were a complete failure?"

"I don't know how I would have that conversation," Bart stated rather matter-of-factly.

"Then your lie was a complete lie for all those years?"

Bart repeated, "I don't know how I would have that conversation."

"That would be true, wouldn't it?" McDonald asked, almost as if he were playing the role of the prosecutor. "Your life was a lie?"

"Everything about it," Bart easily agreed.

"You didn't know who you were or any circumstances by which you could live?"

"I know I presented myself [differently] to different people, because I went different ways, trying to figure it out. But, no, I had no idea."

McDonald continued applying pity paints on Bart's canvas, explaining to the jury, in the form of a question, that it was very understandable how someone like him—in the sad, confused, emotional state he was in—could make such a horribly wrong choice.

"The deeper I sank into that," Bart stated, describing his own self-pity, "the further away I got from my morals."

McDonald pointed out that Bart did not care for himself during this time, but he managed to project an image of self-appreciation and confidence to those on the outside world. "So you were projecting a lot, but deep down inside, you knew you were nothing?"

"That was sort of my defense, I guess. If people thought I was one way, they wouldn't see how I really was."

"So you would hide the true you, which, in your own mind, was basically a worthless person?"

"Yes, sir."

McDonald paused; then he looked up at Bart. "And so if you're worthless, is anybody else meaningful?"

"No. No one else means anything," Bart described with a steely-eyed stare.

McDonald questioned Bart on how he could attempt to go through with the murders the first time, have the plan fail, and then still believe it was okay to try it again a second time.

"No," Bart answered, "I think I knew it was always wrong."

"But you went forward, anyway?"

"Yes, sir, I did."

"You couldn't face your parents with the truth of how miserable a person you were. Is that what you were saying?"

Prosecutor Fred Felcman had just about had enough of the self-flagellation that was taking place on the witness stand. Instead of making a scene, however, he simply objected to McDonald's leading question; to which, Judge Vacek agreed. Bart, nonetheless, still wanted to answer the question.

"Can I answer the question?" Bart asked, almost pleading with the judge.

Judge Vacek turned to face the young man. "You know Mr. Felcman is going to come up here and he's probably got lots of questions for you. You understand that?" he asked, almost as if he felt a bit sorry for the young man.

"Yes, sir, I do."

"And you understand that you've provided absolutely no defense for your conduct?" Judge Vacek continued.

"I don't believe there is a defense for my conduct," Bart assented.

The defense attorney was not done admonishing his young charge. "The jury's going to have to be answering questions about you in the future—what it might be like if you are in the penitentiary or whether you're a future threat. Do you have any designs on any conduct that would, in any way, shape, or form, [or] hurt another individual?"

"No," Bart responded calmly. "The only people I've ever hated—I know it's not for the right reasons—but the only people I ever hated were my parents and my brother."

"The irony of it all is that your dad is actually the one that's come to the rescue and put you back on track?"

"He's become my best friend in the last year," Bart replied, and looked out for his father. Kent saw the glance, yet remained stoic.

McDonald was ready to close. "Bart, I want to get back to it one more time." The attorney paused and looked at the jury before returning his attention to his client. "Tell the jurors how you really feel about yourself and what you've done."

Bart paused before answering. "I feel horrible about myself. About what I've done." Suddenly he began to cry again. It lasted only for a brief moment and was barely noticeable. He then regained his composure, but he did not speak anymore.

"Do you have anything to say to your dad, who's in the courtroom?" McDonald wondered.

Felcman again had enough of the grandstanding. "Judge, at this time, I'm going to object." It took every ounce of his being to restrain himself. "It's not evidence. It's a self-serving statement on the part of the defendant."

Judge Vacek sustained Felcman's objection.

McDonald continued by rephrasing his question. "Have you come clean about all this stuff?"

"Yes, sir."

"Think you're on a different path, a different direction?"

"I know I am, sir."

McDonald spent the next several minutes letting the jury know, via questions to Bart, that Bart manipulated several people to get what he wanted, but that he was only being charged for partaking in the murders, and not for his mastery of manipulation. McDonald wanted to make sure the jury's heads were not poisoned with images of cultlike leaders, such as Charles Manson, Jim Jones, or David Koresh.

"So, when Mr. Felcman asks these questions," McDonald warned, "with regard to manipulation and those things, you need to be honest with him."

"Yes, sir," Bart acquiesced.

"He's going to try to make it look like you're manipulating the jury right now," McDonald stated in regard to his adversary. "Are you?"

"No, sir," Bart declared.

"Pass the witness." Randy McDonald had ended the direct examination of his client.

53

Fred Felcman wasted no time in cross-examining Bart Whitaker. His patience had worn thin during Randy McDonald's direct examination of the convicted killer. Now he wanted to bring the jury back to his version of reality, which just so happened to coincide with most people's version of reality.

"Mr. Whitaker," Felcman broadcasted in a booming voice, punctuated by his unique physical appearance of a white, handlebar mustache and corresponding head of salty hair, "when did you decide you were going to testify in this case?"

"Many, many months ago," Bart answered, not intimidated in the slightest by the prosecutor's demeanor or question.

"Many months ago?" Felcman repeated. "Way before this jury was ever picked, you and Mr. McDonald decided you were going to testify in this case?"

"Yes, sir."

"Tell me something, Mr. Whitaker," Felcman stated as he sauntered up toward the bench directly in Bart's line of sight. "If this jury over here," he stated, motioning with his hand toward the twelve assembled citizens of Fort Bend County, "[if] these fine ladies and gentlemen over here had made a monumental mistake and found you *not guilty* of this after the argument by Mr. McDonald, how were you going to correct that?" He was insinuating that Bart should have testified during the guilt phase, if he truly believed he was guilty of the crimes committed.

"I didn't think there was any possibility that they would find me anything other than guilty," Bart responded.

"But you took the gamble that maybe they would make the mistake, didn't you?"

Randy McDonald was already getting hot under the collar based on Felcman's methods. "Calling for a legal conclusion, the way I'm trying this lawsuit," he objected.

"Overruled," Judge Vacek declared without a second's hesitation.

Bart went ahead and answered Felcman's question. "Do you mean by not pleading guilty?"

"Yeah," Felcman responded. "See, these people over here," the prosecutor motioned again toward the jury as he spoke, "listened to everything, okay? They had to go back, and they deliberated for a little bit over two hours. They got instructed from the judge that I was the one who had to prove everything and you didn't have to do anything."

Bart sat compliantly as Felcman continued.

"If somebody up there," Felcman referred to the jury members, "had come back with a not guilty [verdict], I want to know just what you would have done?"

"I don't know," Bart answered. "That never entered my mind, sir. I was always under the impression, from the very beginning, that there was no other outcome for this. That there would be no other outcome other than a guilty verdict."

"How could there not be another outcome from these ladies and gentlemen when they decide guilty or not guilty?"

"That was my feeling, and the impression that my attorney had given me," Bart answered without ever acknowledging the fact that if he truly believed he was guilty, then there should never have been a trial at all.

"Well, then, what was this, 'I refuse to plea,' and make the judge up there enter a plea of 'not guilty' if you didn't think maybe this jury panel may have found you not guilty?"

"I don't know. That was not what I wanted to do. This is all huge to somebody sitting in my chair." Bart reached out for more sympathy from the jury and the members of the gallery. "When you have an attorney that's been practicing law for thirty years tell you you're not going to do something one way—I listen to him. I didn't agree with it at the time, and I don't agree with it now, but that was the way it was done."

Felcman pounced on Bart's rising insolence. "You don't want to really drag Mr. McDonald into this, do you, that somehow he made you do this?"

"I took his advice, sir, so it was my decision. But it was his very strong decision," Bart mistakenly stated, when he probably meant to say "opinion" or "suggestion."

"You were in this courtroom when these jurors heard from Mr. McDonald that he's trying to seek justice on this case, were you not?"

"Yes, sir."

"And now, if this jury had made the mistake of finding you not guilty, I want to know what Bart Whitaker would have done."

"I don't know," Bart reiterated. "From the moment I was arrested, I knew from that moment on, I was going to spend my life, the rest of my life, in prison."

Felcman believed Bart was not answering his question. "I want to know what you would have done, had they done that. Would you have just walked out the door? Would you have called them up and said, 'Hey, you made a big mistake, I did this'?"

McDonald objected that Felcman was being argumentative, which Judge Vacek sustained, which meant he agreed with the defense attorney.

McDonald then asked for a sidebar to explain his position for having Bart on the stand to testify on his own behalf during the penalty phase. "The bottom line is, if he enters a plea of guilty, then the accomplice testimony is all that has to be offered. They are seeking the death penalty," he stated in reference to Felcman and the district attorney's office, "I am trying to get life. I am trying to actually get him to plead to life. He would have [pleaded] guilty if he'd have given him life." McDonald seemed exasperated by Felcman's actions. "But why are we going over this stuff, over and over?"

"Because he brought it up on the direct," Felcman answered. "That it was his idea to do not guilty."

After some bickering, the court resumed. Felcman grilled Bart on his desire to testify, after he had already been convicted. "Do you find it convenient?" he asked Bart. "You don't have anything to lose now by getting up here and telling them what happened, because they already know, see? Do you find that convenient on your part?"

"No, sir."

"You don't find that convenient at all?"

"Since Mr. McDonald got on the case, this is pretty much the way we had said it was always going to be," Bart countered. "I guess I didn't think about alternatives as to why it could be any different. Pretty much from the beginning, we knew it was going to be a guilty verdict, that it would be tried on punishment."

Felcman finally changed tactics and began to delve further into the territory that McDonald had dug for his client. "You said that you felt worthless."

"Yes, sir." Bart nodded obediently.

"When did this worthlessness that you felt come about?"

"Junior high." Bart nodded as he answered.

"So, how old were you when you started feeling worthless?"

"Sometime in junior high, elementary school."

"So you were thirteen, fourteen years old?"

"Earlier," Bart answered.

"You told Lynne Ayres," Felcman spoke of the educational diagnostician consultant/psychologist from the Tarnow Center for Self-Management, "that you were Atlas."

"Yes, sir, I did."

"And tell me something"—Felcman looked directly at Bart, who seemed to stare right through the attorney without even being aware of his presence—"were you trying to manipulate her, or were you telling her the truth?"

"It was a lie," Bart admitted. "A common lie that I told many people, not just Lynne Ayres."

"You actually told her you had no need for anybody else."

"Again, a common lie I told many people," replied the nonchalant Bart.

"Who were the 'lot of people' you would tell that you didn't have need for anybody?"

"I told that to a lot of people," Bart replied. "It made me feel stronger. If I thought that somebody thought that I was strong, I sort of became that strong."

"Why would you tell Lynne Ayres this lie?" Felcman wanted to know. "She didn't know you."

"She was trying to get to know me."

"And you lied to her for what reason?"

"Again, I could not show her the true me, probably the greatest fear I had at that time."

Felcman continued to suss out the truth from Bart, or at least when Bart believed he was telling the truth. "Which answers were the truth? That you felt like you were Atlas and could do better than anybody else?"

"That was absolutely *not* the truth," Bart declared emphatically.

"What about that you didn't need your girlfriend? That she had people she could pay to take care of her emotional needs?" Felcman asked in regard to Lynne Sorsby.

"That was not the truth."

"What about the fact that you said your brother was a lazy, good-for-nothing bum?" Felcman continued.

"I probably did believe that at the time."

"So that was the truth, as far as you were concerned?"

"As far as my perception of Kevin," Bart replied, "yes, during 2002."

"How did you draw that perception of Kevin?"

"During that time, he had discovered a video game

called EverQuest that he was spending eight or nine hours a day on the computer. I could see how I could draw—the person that I was in those days could draw that conclusion."

"Now, Lynne Sorsby," Felcman continued, "who was your fiancée, were you lying to her about whether you loved her or not?"

"No, I wasn't lying. I did love her. But I did lie to her also."

"But you told Dr. Lynne Ayres that you didn't have any need for her."

"That was a lie," Bart responded curtly.

"Tell me something," Felcman directly addressed Bart. Felcman seemed peeved. "Why would you tell the educational diagnostician that you didn't have a need for your girlfriend? What would be the purpose of lying to her about that?"

"That persona that I put on for her was a person that just didn't need anyone," Bart responded, discussing himself as if he were some other, outer-body composite of spiritual antimatter. "He was," he continued, referring to himself in the third person, "he was complete, in and of himself, and he didn't require other people, which was the total polar opposite of what I really felt. I was absolutely petrified of anybody knowing that."

"You mean you were the opposite way? You were the kind that needed people?" Felcman quizzed the defendant.

"Yes, sir."

"Needed people for what reason?"

"Very specific reasons, I imagine. Same as any other person needs someone else. I needed Lynne Sorsby more than anyone else, probably, in my whole life."

"What would you need people for?" Felcman asked again in a slightly altered manner.

"I got acceptance from her that I didn't feel I was getting from anyone else. I thought there were [fewer] requirements for that acceptance with her than anybody I ever met in my life," Bart admitted.

Incredulous, Felcman addressed Bart directly. "Mr. Whitaker, you were getting acceptance from everybody in your life."

"I know that now, sir. Yes, I was."

"I know you say that now," retorted the disbelieving assistant district attorney, "but that was true back then. You were getting acceptance from everybody in your life, right?"

"My perception," Bart replied, "was that there were always conditions attached to that."

Felcman became even more annoyed with the defendant. "Let's start over. Back to the basics. See if I can get you to admit to a few things. Everybody in your life was accepting of you, correct?"

"Yes, sir."

"Your mother, your brother, your father, your fiancée, everybody. Correct?"

"Yes, sir."

"That's the fact, correct?"

"Yes, sir."

"And now you want to tell the jury panel [that] somehow you perceived that in a different manner?"

"In those days, yes," Bart calmly answered. "I did perceive it in a different manner."

"When are we going to get this new perception?" Felcman wondered. "When is the next time somebody accepts you, like your father has again, and you now perceive it in a different manner? When is the next time you're going to come out with somebody, such as your father, who accepts you as you are."

"I don't believe I do that anymore."

"Are you manipulating this jury panel here today? Are you telling them what you think they want to hear?"

"No, sir. I'm telling the truth today."

"Of course, this was after my opening statement, right? About how you manipulate people and project as a chameleon what people want to see, correct?"

"Yes, sir."

"Do you have any remorse at all for these poor people up here, having to put them through this?"

"Yes, sir, I do." Bart turned and looked at the jury members and addressed them directly. "I'm very sorry y'all have to be here. I know y'all had better things to do with your time than to come here and deal with it."

Felcman's ire began to rise. "Had better things to do? Having to watch a video of a dead body. That's what you want to tell them? That they probably had something better to do?"

"I just meant that they had . . . ," a clearly disconcerted Bart explained, "this is a horrible thing they had to come here and see, and I'm sorry they had to do it."

Knowing he had burrowed deep into Bart's thick skin, Felcman switched gears. "Let's go over your background. When you burglarized all the schools, you wrote a confession. You said you did this as an adventure?"

"Yes, sir."

"Can you tell the jury panel what you meant as 'an adventure'?"

"I had lived pretty much an invisible life, up to that

point. I felt that I didn't really have any real identity I wasn't part of a sports team or a club, or anything like that, and I just felt extremely bored." Bart shifted in his chair on the witness stand. "I felt at that time— I know you don't like me to say this," Bart addressed Felcman, "but my perception from my parents was that I didn't require any help, that my brother required all the help, that I didn't need anything. So I felt what that meant was that I just wasn't worthy of the attention that my brother was getting, and I did these robberies, and I wanted to get caught for them."

"You did all these things because you wanted to get caught?"

"Yes. Also, the adventure, and then the idea that when it would go bad, because I think all three of us knew that it would go bad at some point," he stated in reference to his juvenile criminal cohorts, Peter Keller and David Price, "that it would be impossible to ignore." In other words, they were eventually going to get caught and suffer the consequences and potential punishment for their delinquent and criminal behavior.

Felcman referred to the report. "What kind of doublespeak is this?" he queried in regard to Bart's statement at the time. "*I'm hiding burglaries, but I want them to know about it*"?

"I didn't mean it to sound like doublespeak. I just meant that it was something that Peter, David, and I sort of discussed toward the end there, that we were going to get caught. I knew that couldn't be ignored by my parents. It would have to be something where they would look, and I would be able to say, like a big neon light, 'Hey, look, I'm here! I did this! I'm not invisible.'"

"You think your parents treated you as an invisible person."

"That's how I felt at the time."

"Well, they didn't, did they?"

"No, not at the time."

"Do you find anything dangerous about this? Do you have any perception [of] reality at all here, Mr. Whitaker?"

"Yes, sir, I do. I think my ability to look back and see these things as they truly were in those days, rather than how I perceived them, means I've grown some."

There were a few noticeable mutterings in the gallery.

Felcman returned the focus of his questions back to Bart's halcyon youthful days of indiscretion. "You actually rented a storage unit to keep this stuff in there," he asked in regard to the computers and other equipment Bart stole from his school.

"Yes, we did," Bart answered, making sure to include his companions in his response.

"What were y'all going to do with the stuff?"

"We had no intention of selling it. As far as I know, everything was returned."

"So, literally, you were taking taxpayers' money, stealing their computers, just because you thought it was fun."

"Yes, sir."

"So it was fun, not a cry for help?" Felcman tripped Bart up with his comeback.

"It was both, sir," Bart feebly responded.

"Fun, and a cry for help?"

"The adventure was the initial motive."

"So we have a double motive on this one—it was fun for Bart Whitaker, and it was also a cry for help?" Felcman was able to delineate the pattern between Bart as a juvenile delinquent and Bart as an adult delinquent.

"Yes, sir."

"So you cried out for help from your parents," Felcman stated, refreshing Bart's memory. "They sent you to the psychiatrist. Remember that?"

"Yes, sir, I do."

"Well, the cries for help, did they stop or did you continue to cry for help?"

"I felt at that time their sending me to a psychiatrist meant that they didn't want to deal with it themselves."

"Where did you get that idea from, Mr. Whitaker?"

"I don't know." Bart slightly shrugged his thin shoulders. "I'm not saying it was the right idea. I know it was not the right idea. It's just how I felt at the time."

"You were seventeen years old. You didn't think by sending you to a psychiatrist that they didn't want to help you?"

"I thought that they didn't want to discuss it with me themselves, [that] they wanted somebody else to do it."

"They were trying to get you back into Clements High School, right?"

"No, I believe the letter was actually to allow me to withdraw from the school rather than to be expelled. I was already going to Fort Bend Baptist by that time."

"They felt like you had gone off such a deep end that they needed to seek professional help for you?"

"Maybe, yes."

"Yes or no?"

"I believe that was so."

"But then you told the jury panel they wanted to wash their hands of you," Felcman declared in regard to Bart's parents.

"No. I know that that was how I felt at the time. That's not how they were actually, or how things actually were."

"You told Lynne Ayres one good thing about your education. You said you could charm the teachers into giving you A's. What did you mean by that?"

"At Fort Bend Baptist, there was a lot of subjective grading—tests, multiple choice. There were a lot of speeches and presentations. So I guess I could . . ." Bart's voice suddenly tapered off.

"Okay, go ahead," Felcman prodded. "You could manipulate people to get what you wanted?"

"Well, I guess, if you mean by presenting something to someone to try to persuade them to a viewpoint, yes," Bart responded in his most seemingly innocent voice.

"I'm sorry," Felcman countered. "Explain to this jury panel, when you say, *I could charm the teachers into giving me A's,* how that's not manipulating people into doing what you want?"

"It's sales, so I guess, yes, it's manipulation," Bart agreed.

"Sales?" Felcman asked, his eyebrow raised.

"I suppose, selling an idea."

Felcman shook his head and moved on. "The burglaries that you committed were quite sophisticated, were they not? I mean, you planned them out far in advance, right?"

"Not really." Bart shook his head.

"Well, you had pagers, you had ropes. I think you had crowbars. You had cars available, you had a place to store the items. Tell the jury how they could reach any other conclusion than that these were well-planned burglaries?"

"We had all that stuff available, incidentally. It

wasn't something that we planned out months or
even days ahead of time. But, yes, they were planned.
I don't mean to give the impression that we didn't go
over it. It just wasn't something that we hashed over."

"Mr. Whitaker, my question was, they were planned,
right?"

"Yes, sir, they were planned."

Felcman asked Bart about getting arrested and
spending a night in jail for the school burglaries.
"And your father had to bail you out?"

"Yes, he did."

"Anything about that jail time that changed your
mind about *Maybe this is not something I want to do with
the rest of my life?*"

"Yes, sir."

"Really?" Felcman feigned shock.

"For sure."

"It changed you?"

"No, not significantly, but it did affect me."

Felcman asked Bart to inform the jury how it had
changed him.

"Sometimes something has an effect on us and it
lasts for a while, but if you're not rooted in a moral
system that says that [the] thing was wrong, eventually
it just sort of fades away."

"It didn't change you?"

"For a period of time, it did. But, no, the overall
change was . . . no."

"I don't understand this doublespeak. Did it change
you or not?" Felcman wanted a clear answer.

"I'm trying to answer as best I can, sir," declared a
miffed, but still rather cool, Bart. "I believe, yes, it did.
For a period of time, it did change me."

"How did it change you?"

"I was very remorseful for what I had done. I tried to have a relationship with my parents, tried to get myself on a good track, but I think that lasted for a while. I think it lasted for a year, maybe two."

"A year or two?" Felcman looked at Bart like Bart was delusional.

Bart simply nodded his head.

"You certain you want to say a year or two?" Felcman gave Bart an opportunity to amend his statement.

"Somewhere in there. Yes, sir."

"Because within two years, you're plotting to kill your family!" Felcman exclaimed, and shook his head while looking toward the members of the jury.

"It was a little later than that," Bart began to correct the prosecutor, "but I'm not going to argue dates with you."

"There was nothing about jail, being put on probation, standing in front of a judge, where you could go to the penitentiary, that scared you, was there?"

"Absolutely, it scared me," Bart disagreed.

"How did it scare you?"

"I was seventeen," Bart answered, which confused Felcman. "I was seventeen," Bart repeated. "The idea of going to prison was pretty scary."

"If you kill your parents, you go to the penitentiary."

"By the time I had gotten to that place, I didn't care what happened to me afterward," Bart attempted to explain.

"Well, yes, you did care about what happened to you, right?" Felcman wanted to know.

"Not really."

"You're trying to get Adam Hipp to lie to these people."

"The momentum of all of that, yes, I did lie about that."

"And you also cared about yourself, because you sent the people you care most about letters when you ran. You told them in those letters, *Don't tell the police because then I can get away better.*"

"I shouldn't have put that in there."

"Can you tell me how anybody can misinterpret the statement *The longer you keep anyone from knowing I am gone, the better my chances are?*"

"The purpose of that comment shouldn't be misinterpreted."

"It shouldn't what?" Felcman was unclear as to what Bart meant by his answer.

"It can't be misinterpreted, that part of the comment," Bart insisted.

Felcman switched gears yet again, this time fast-forwarding to Bart's initial days in college in Waco. "You get put off of probation and then you go to Baylor. Now tell me something in here," the attorney said, referring to Bart's probation report. "It says, *I never felt loved by my parents while I was growing up.* Is that true?"

"No. I did [feel that way], but I always felt it was conditional on me being something," Bart replied.

"Mr. Whitaker, didn't you see your father testify in this case?"

"Yes, I did."

"How much more unconditional love could you possibly have from a man?"

"Couldn't," Bart replied succinctly.

"So, what you're telling them," Felcman directed Bart's attention back to the jury, "is that your touch with reality is not there, is it?"

"I know that my dad is a different man now than he was back then, but my touch with reality was, I don't want to say out of touch, but it was . . ." Bart could not complete his thoughts. "I really don't know how to look at those days. I wasn't seeing things as they were."

"You heard your uncle Bo Bartlett testify that your mother loved you, and that her whole life was you and Kevin. But then you tell me that you never felt loved by your parents?"

Bart nodded his head as he responded, "Yes, sir."

"Do you find anything scary about this, Mr. Whitaker?"

"There's something tragic about it."

"How do you jump [hypothetically] from 'I'm not living up to expectations' to 'I'm going to kill my mother and brother and father'?" Felcman theorized.

"It wasn't a gradual thing," Brad answered. "I know that after high school when I got to Baylor, I knew pretty early on that I was not happy there, and I tried to talk to them about that, and it just seemed like everything I was saying was going in one ear and out the other. And all the time, the hate grew, all of the disconnected feelings I had with them grew into hate."

Felcman countered, "Because you didn't want to go to Baylor, you decided, 'I'll kill my parents'?"

"I don't know, sir. It was more than that. It was about expectations and how I was supposed to be living my life. It was about everything that I was feeling at that time. It wasn't just one thing."

"What did you expect they wanted from you?" Felcman queried Bart in regard to his family.

"I don't know," Bart answered, shrugging his shoulders. "Everything. They wanted me to be perfect, [that] is the way I felt."

"You really thought your father wanted you to be perfect?"

"Yes, sir."

"You know that's not true, right?"

"Yes, sir. I know it's not true now, that that was not what he was sending me. That's how I was perceiving it."

"Therefore," Felcman's inquiry went unabated, "even if the person is not doing that, they just love you unconditionally, Bart Whitaker may interpret that [as] 'Huh-uh, that's not the way, and I need to kill them'?"

"That's how I saw it at the time."

"If somebody interacts with Bart Whitaker, it can be on a totally innocent basis and you decide to perceive it different, you could kill that person?"

"No, I could not."

"You killed your mother and brother on totally false circumstances, right?"

"Yes, sir. I was a different person then."

"I know," Felcman smirked. "So, at Baylor, how did you go about deciding you're going to kill your parents again?"

"I don't know exactly how the conversation came up," Bart attempted to describe how the genesis of the familicide came to fruition. "I believe that me and Adam had discussed, or began to discuss, things like that. But I don't honestly remember the first time or how. I can't even imagine how it was brought up initially." Bart shifted uncomfortably in his seat. "I know that once the ball got rolling, it was easier to talk about, and it got to the point where it was very easy to talk about."

"Did you have Adam Hipp or Justin Peters do anything so you could test their trustworthiness?"

"I believe by that time I pretty much trusted both of them."

Felcman skipped forward to the night of the massacre. "On the actual killings, you had Steven Champagne and Chris Brashear do things to confirm their trustworthiness, right?"

"I believe I trusted them from the experiences we had at work."

"You sent them out to do a few things, didn't you? Sent them out to see if they would steal stuff or follow certain instructions from you?"

"No, sir, I did not."

Reverting back to his previous attempts at killing his family, Felcman asked Bart, "So, what Adam Hipp testified to and what Justin Peters testified to was the absolute truth?"

"We remembered some things differently," Bart recalled.

"What parts do you remember differently?"

"Nothing that takes the blame off me in any way." Bart fell on his sword yet again.

"That's not what I asked you, Mr. Whitaker," Felcman pointed out to the defendant. "I just asked you, what was different?"

"There were just things that they said. I don't recall them all now, but I just remembered them a little differently."

Felcman again steered Bart back to the previous murder attempt, back in April 2001. "Where were you going to go that night?" the prosecutor asked in regard to Bart's fleeing Waco.

"The night when Justin left for Sugar Land, I was in Waco. I stayed in Waco," Bart clarified.

"Weren't you going somewhere else?"

"No, sir, I was not."

"Why did you run off, Mr. Whitaker?"

"Initially Justin called me and said that the car had run out of gas, and I said, 'All right, I'm going to bring you some gasoline.' And I drove down there to get a little two-gallon can filled. I filled it up and was taking it to him. Right before I got to him, I received calls from a number I didn't know. Then I got a call from my parents' number. I didn't answer either one, but thought there was no reason they would be calling me at two-thirty or three o'clock in the morning."

Felcman again seemed almost as bemused as he was annoyed. "I just asked you, why you ran off?"

Bart seemed flustered, but managed to corral his composure. "Okay, I just freaked out. I knew something had happened. I didn't know what, but I knew that there was no reason why my parents would be calling me at two-thirty in the morning. And then Justin told me he had gotten a call from someone— I think it was a police officer—and was asking if he was with me, did he know where I was, and I knew that something had happened. I didn't know what, but I just thought . . ." Bart stopped speaking.

Felcman interjected, "You ran off because the plot had gotten discovered?"

"Yes, sir."

"Why didn't you just tell the jury panel that?"

"I'm sorry," Bart feebly responded.

"Now, you stay hidden until you were able to talk to your father and convince him there was nothing to it, right?"

"I think by the time I came back, the police had already thought that it was nothing, but I know I talked to him about three days after I left, two or three days after I left, and Justin had already told them that it was a drunken comment that had been made while watching a program about the Menendez brothers, and that's what they believed." Bart was referring to the Beverly Hills brats/brothers who killed their parents with a shotgun. "I talked to Justin also, and he said that. So I did come back, and I spoke with somebody with the Waco Police Department."

"You convinced your father there was nothing to it?"

"Yes."

"I want to know something." Felcman addressed Bart as though they were two lifelong friends confiding deep, dark secrets that no one else was privy to. "You're caught red-handed trying to kill your parents, but that, in and of itself, didn't stop you from finally doing it, did it?"

"No, sir, it did not."

"Now, Will Anthony doesn't kill your family because the alarm goes off. What did you do, forget to turn the alarm off?"

"No, I couldn't turn the alarm off."

Bart's vague response raised Felcman's hackles. "You mean, physically you were unable to do it? Or for some reason, you developed a moral conscience and decided you just couldn't do it?"

"I just couldn't do it."

Felcman again began to get agitated with Bart's evasiveness. "I want to know," he said in slow, dulcet tones, "was it moral, or was it you physically couldn't do it?"

"It wasn't that I physically couldn't do it," assured a defensive Bart. "It was a moral/cowardice combination."

"This talk about you being a coward, that's not true, is it?" Felcman glared at Bart and did not give him time to respond. "You just didn't want to pull the trigger because then we'd have you in here as the shooter. The plan was to have somebody else as the shooter, so this jury over here would have to have evidence to show you're a party [to the actual shooting]. That's the whole plan, right?"

"No, sir. I couldn't pull the trigger myself." Bart again attempted to paint himself as a human being with moral choices and failures.

Felcman knew the door was now wide open. "Mr. Whitaker," he intoned with a slightly raised voice, "you stepped across your dead mother's body and stepped across your dead brother's body and then got shot in the arm. You want to tell me that now you're a coward?"

Bart began to fidget again. "No, I did all those things, yes, and I can only tell you that there's just no way that I could pull the trigger. I don't know where the difference is, or where the line is there. I just know I couldn't do it myself."

Felcman believed his sudden inability to directly kill his own flesh and blood was actually something much simpler. "You didn't pull the trigger because—the jury already knows—if you did that, then you wouldn't be a party to it, you'd be the shooter, right?"

"Well, that would be true, but I still couldn't do it myself. I know that I couldn't pull the trigger myself."

Felcman looked square into Bart's eyes as he said, "You understand they're about to go back and decide whether you're a continuing threat, and you want to give this jury panel the excuse that you're a coward and you couldn't pull the trigger?"

"I told the jury the truth, sir."

"But that you would plan the death of your family," Felcman continued, "get shot in the arm, and actually break bread with them, knowing they're going to be dead?"

Bart nodded. "Yes, sir."

Felcman was incensed. "Do you find this absolutely chilling, Mr. Whitaker?"

"Extremely chilling," Bart assented. There wasn't an iota of emotion written on his face.

"That there's absolutely no way anybody could ever find that you're not a continuing threat to society, no matter how long you live?"

"Sir, I have no intention of hurting anyone else. The only people in my life I ever wanted to hurt are the ones I did," Bart declared succinctly.

"These were the people that loved you the most, right? Right? Yes or no?"

"Yes, sir."

"So, why would a stranger like me mean anything to you, Mr. Whitaker?"

"I have no disliking of you, sir."

"You sent me a Christmas card asking me to focus on my family." Felcman referred to the unusual gift he received from the defendant.

"You took that in totally the wrong way. I must not have written it very well," declared the man who believed he was a superb writer.

Felcman stood close to Bart. "You killed your mother and your brother, and then tell me to set aside the nastiness, and [to] focus on my family. How am I supposed to take that, Mr. Whitaker?"

"How I meant it, sir, was in reference to something you said about that you were asking somebody if they had become a cynic because of what they do. You said you had become a cynic. That was really what I was going for with that message, was that I hoped that you could put all of that aside for the holidays." The kinder, more compassionate Bart was on display with his response.

"I can't," a furious Felcman declared, glaring at Bart. "It taints my soul! I look ten years older than what I am, Mr. Whitaker, because of people like you." The last phrase flicked off Felcman's tongue in disgust.

This, naturally, brought defense counsel's objection, but Felcman immediately apologized to the court for his sidebar remark.

"Was that an attempt by you, Mr. Whitaker, to somehow manipulate me into this somewhere along the line?"

"I only wanted to talk to you," replied a chastened Bart.

"All you had to do was call up your attorney and say, 'I want to talk.'"

"I had done that, sir." Bart then took the time to address his nemesis directly. "Mr. Felcman, it was my impression back when Dan Cogdell was my attorney that that was what I had relayed to him was what I wanted to do. I felt that if you and I could just sit down for a few minutes, an hour or two, that you would either decide I was lying or not, but if you decided I was lying, we wouldn't be anyplace other than where we are today. But if you decided I wasn't, that we could somehow save my family all of this. That's what I wanted with the letter, more than anything."

"You wanted to manipulate me through your family," Felcman tossed back, "so I wouldn't seek the death penalty."

"No, sir. You turned my words around."

"That was it, wasn't it?" Felcman's voice raised a pitch. "You used your father to get to me so you wouldn't get the death penalty?"

"No, sir," Bart flatly denied the accusation.

"You used your good father to get to me." Felcman's disgust was becoming more difficult to contain. "So I wouldn't seek the death penalty?"

"No, sir. That was not how I thought about it."

"That telephone call to your father on the anniversary of your mom and [brother]'s death, you used your father to get to me, so maybe I wouldn't seek the death penalty."

"No, sir. I was very confused. I guess by that point, it was in December. I had been locked up for about four months, and I was under the impression when I got back that I could just take care of it, and that we could put it behind us." Bart rolled his shoulders as if to exorcise some deep-rooted kinks. "It had taken so long up to that point, I was just really confused about the messages I was getting [from] the various people that Mr. Cogdell, my attorney, was sending to me. I was just upset. I needed somebody to talk to that day. I knew my dad was coming that afternoon, but I had just got my phone privileges that morning. I just wanted to talk to him."

"You know, we don't have a recording, we've got to take your word for that." Felcman chided Bart.

"You could take the word of my father," Bart retorted.

"Your father perceived that you didn't do anything for years. Understand?"

Bart did not answer; instead, he simply nodded his head.

Felcman informed Bart that the only recording he
had of Bart and Kent Whitaker was when Bart was
upset because he could not get Felcman to agree to a
life sentence.

"What I was really upset about," Bart retorted, "was
that we hadn't come to some sort of agreement. The
year count was, like, ninety years anyway. That really
didn't matter to me."

"Really?" asked a mockingly surprised Felcman.

"It could have been a thousand years," Bart declared.

Felcman knew better. "You just didn't want a jury
saying you should be subject to the death penalty."

"Sir, what I wanted was to put it behind everybody."

"A man who—several times multiplied—tries to kill
his family, never gives up, despite numerous setbacks,
and finally breaks bread with them before he actually
does kill them, and you don't think maybe you
shouldn't be subject to the death penalty?" Felcman
shook his head, almost as if he felt pity for the delusional young man seated before him.

"I didn't say that." Bart was attempting to backpedal.
"I just wanted it to be over for everybody."

After a quick glance at his notes, Felcman steered
the conversation back to the night of the murders.
"You leave at four o'clock from Willis on the way to
kill your family, right?"

"Yes, sir."

"Chris Brashear was in the back of the Yukon,
correct?"

"Yes, sir."

"So this jury knows that when Deputy Pikett did his
good job and tracked it back to Chris Brashear, he was
in the back of your Yukon, right?"

"Yes, sir."

"Marshall Slot, the guy who had no idea what he was doing," he stated sarcastically, "was also correct that Chris Brashear rode up there with you in the Yukon, right?"

"Yes, sir."

"The gloves he had"—Felcman noted in regard to Brashear—"did you give those to him?"

"He had some latex gloves that I had given him."

"What about the black gloves?"

"I don't recall ever giving him that glove, no."

"They were your gloves," Felcman stated.

"Yes, sir. They were my gloves."

"And what happened, then, is you went inside and celebrated your false graduation." Felcman was sneering.

"Yes, sir."

"That's absolutely correct?"

"Yes, that is correct."

"Is that why I've got these pictures of you with your brother, Kevin, real happy?"

Bart nodded in the affirmative.

"And then there are the pictures of you and your family at Pappadeaux, right? Of course, you know they're going to be dead in a matter of minutes."

Bart bent his head down, as if in shame.

"Fact is," Felcman continued, "your whole family is supposed to be dead, correct?"

"Yes, sir."

"I don't see any worthlessness here."

"Sir, I was always very good at covering that up," Bart insisted.

"You could present a real good image, right?"

"Of that, yes," Bart conceded.

"That's why you told the jury you were always able to hide the true you," Felcman wanted to know.

Bart nodded silently.

"Which begs the question that probably every one of these jurors wants to know"—the assistant district attorney lined up his prey—"is this the true you now?"

"Yes, sir." Bart paused before continuing on. "I tried to figure out how to answer that, but there's just no way to answer that. I have to rely on the experiences you've had in your life."

Bart's comment drew puzzled glances from nearly everyone in the courtroom. No one was exactly sure what he meant, or toward whom it was even directed.

Felcman spun around and addressed his opponent forthrightly: "Do you understand that you have now created such a web of deceit, lies, and manipulation that there is no way of ever knowing the true you?"

Bart agreed with Felcman. "I believe it's very difficult, under the circumstances, yes."

Felcman paused again, before charging in. "Except for one thing—that you're a pure sociopath that just uses people as tools."

"No, sir. I disagree with that." Bart denied the accusation quietly.

"That's why Lynne Ayres said she had a very disturbing interview with you on August 20 of 2002, isn't it?"

"I don't know."

"That's the true you, isn't it?"

"No, it's not true." Bart's smooth veneer began to show infinitesimal cracks.

"You don't need anybody." Felcman's voice began to boom throughout the courtroom. "You can do everything better than anybody else! That's the true you—isn't it, Mr. Whitaker?"

"Absolutely not, sir." Bart continued on with his demure façade.

"Now you go inside your house and your mother's there. She's all excited and she gives you a Rolex for your graduation. I mean, did you cry? Did you get happy? Did you say, 'Thanks, Mom, I'm really looking forward to this?'"

"I suppose I was happy," came the nonchalant response.

"Did they say they were proud of you?"

"Yes, they did."

Felcman focused on the killings again. "Did you tell Chris Brashear where to stand to kill your family?"

"I told him the layout of the house, and we discussed it. So, yes, I did tell him."

"My question was really simple . . . ," responded Felcman.

"Yes, I did." Bart would try to answer definitively.

"Did you tell him where to stand?"

"Yes, I did," Bart repeated.

"Where did you tell Chris Brashear to stand?"

"In the foyer."

"And to shoot your family as they came in, correct?"

"Yes."

"This was not a random burglary. This was an execution of your family, correct?"

"Yes."

"Did you know Steven Champagne was following you over to Pappadeaux?"

"Yes, I did."

"That was part of the plan?"

"Yes, it was."

"So, Steven Champagne was telling the absolute truth when he came in here?"

"About that part, yes."

"You told Officer Prevost the guy sounded black," Felcman stated.

"Yes, I did."

"Why?"

"That was something we had come up with before, that I was supposed to say."

"Do you know how dangerous that makes you, and how offensive that is?" Felcman decried. This confrontation recalled the Susan Smith child-drowning case and the Charles Stuart Boston wife-killing case, when both perpetrators calculatingly blamed unknown, fictional black males for committing the murders.

"Yes, sir, I absolutely do."

"Why couldn't you have just said, 'I don't know'?"

"I'm not sure."

"You know exactly why you told Phillip Prevost that the guy sounded black."

"That, I do," answered Bart. "I thought you were asking why I couldn't just say he was white. That, I don't know. I know I said that he was black, because it would take the blame off Chris."

Fred Felcman wanted to paint an even more devastating picture of Bart Whitaker for the jury. He turned his focus to how Bart allowed himself to be shot. "What kind of man are we dealing with here, Mr. Whitaker, that you would actually have that done to yourself to throw off suspicion?"

"It's just part of the plan," Bart replied nonchalantly.

"This is such evil that it's hard to even imagine, correct?" Felcman asked, nearly hissing his words.

"Yes, sir."

"I told the jury that you rushed in there quickly because you had to get shot by Chris Brashear, and he had to get out of there. Was I correct on that?"

"Yes, sir, you were."

"Why did Chris Brashear leave the Glock there?"

"I'm not sure."

"What was the plan? Was he supposed to take it with him?"

"[He was supposed to] leave it in the backyard, yes, sir. It was not supposed to be in the house."

Felcman backed up just a few steps to paint an even more vivid picture of the death scene. "You see your brother when you ran in, right?"

"Yes, I did."

"He was gurgling in his own blood, wasn't he?"

At the mention of Kevin's death rattle, Bart began to cry soft tears. Not many in the gallery were buying it. Bart was unable to answer the question.

Felcman looked astonished. He turned directly toward Bart and, in a state of bemusement combined with seething hatred, said to the defendant, "I've watched this whole trial." He paused, looked over at the jury panel, and continued on: "You've never cried until now."

"I did earlier," Bart answered, weeping with barely audible sobs.

"Why are you crying now?"

"Horrible memory."

"Well, you heard it for the past five days with this jury."

"And when you showed the video, I cried also." Bart recalled the videotaped crime scene footage of the Whitaker home, with Kevin, dead, sprawled out in the foyer.

"You know this jury was watching you?"

"Yes, sir, I do."

Felcman quickly diverted the jury members' attention away from Bart's tears, in the event that they were persuaded by his alleged trauma. He began talking about Bart's false graduation celebration. "Tell me something, I'm curious. How were you going to handle the fact that Marshall [Slot] and Billy Baugh were going to eventually find out that you hadn't graduated from Sam Houston?"

"I was in such a dark place," Bart responded. "Locked into the plan, I don't think I thought about it after that."

"Is that the answer you want to give me? That you didn't think this through?"

"As to what happened afterward, I didn't give it much thought, no."

"All you were going to have to do was tell the police that you had told your mother that you weren't graduating, and that you were going through this because you didn't want to upset your father, who was dead, right?"

"I thought about that in the hospital," Bart admitted, "to my shame. Yes, I did."

"How in the world do you convince Lynne Sorsby to still want to be married to you, after all this?"

"I hadn't actually proposed to her until after December tenth, but I know that when I was with the police, I lied to them every time I talked to them. And when Adam called, I sort of slipped back into the person I was when I knew him."

"What kind of person is that?"

"Well, the tapes show I was conniving and—"

"Manipulative," Felcman interjected, "talking in

cryptic terms, using people? Is that what we're talking about?"

"Yes."

"So, when I told this jury in my opening statement that's what kind of person we're dealing with here, I was absolutely correct, right?"

"Yes, I think you blew it out of proportion, but, yes, you are correct."

"How can I take it to any higher proportion?" a befuddled Felcman demanded. "You killed your mother and your brother."

"Yes, but I . . . You're right."

"So, when I told the jury what we're dealing with is a person who's purely manipulative, I was absolutely correct about it, right?"

"Sir, that's such a loaded word"—the comment elicited several sighs from some of the participants in the gallery—"and I know that I did offer these people money. But if you're talking about . . . I'm not really sure what you mean by manipulative. I did offer them money, but I think you mean something above and beyond that."

"You have a tendency, Mr. Whitaker, to talk in cryptic terms. You don't come out and say what you really mean. You don't speak forward with people and tell them how you really think. You use manipulative terms, correct?"

"I know I did some of that in those days, yes."

"You did that throughout the case."

"Yes, in regard to the police."

"Even the letters you wrote when you fled were still in manipulative terms," Felcman added.

"The last section, yes."

"The only time you actually told them the truth in

the letters is when you said, *Hey, the longer you keep anyone from knowing I am gone, the better the chances are.* That's the only time you actually talked about the truth. Everything else, you talk about, *I'll be the only one that has to go through the fire,* and so forth like that."

"I believe that was the truth, sir."

"You're not the only one who has to go through the fire. I do, these people do"—Felcman gestured toward the jury members—"a whole community does."

"I know that now."

"Did you ever make a comment to anybody, Mr. Whitaker, that the way you manipulate people is you give them what they want?"

"Well, that's what I did in this case, yes."

"Lynne Sorsby wanted to believe you, that you didn't do this. Lynne Sorsby loved you and wanted to marry you, and that's the reason you were able to get her to say, 'Yes, I will marry you,' despite everything here, correct?"

"There was much more to it than that, but that was a part of it."

"Really? What else?" Felcman wanted more information.

"After all this happened, I think the six months after this all happened was the best time in our relationship. I think the shock of this hit me in a way, like Will Anthony said, it didn't become real until it actually happened. It was sort of that way with me." Bart paused to let that bit of information sink in. "I knew it was going to happen, and I wanted it to happen, but on a level, I didn't understand it, like I did afterward. I tried to distance the person that I had been by becoming someone else, by being better than I had been before that. I did love her, and that's why I proposed to her, more than anything else."

"You love Lynne Sorsby?" Felcman asked.

"To this day, I do," declared Bart.

"Was she in any type of danger from you, Mr. Whitaker?"

"Certainly, she's not."

"Your mother loved you."

"Yeah," he answered unenthusiastically.

Felcman continued to hammer away at the phony exterior he believed comprised Bart. "You actually went to the rodeo with your father and held up one of those lighters when Pat Green played the song for Kevin?"

"I don't remember that, but I might have done so."

"All this emotion, of course, never once broke down your façade that you had about killing him, did it?"

"It broke me down, but not in a public place."

"Really?" declared Felcman. "Tell the jury. I'm just dying to know how this broke you down."

"It broke me down a lot afterward."

"Tell us."

"I remember the first time we got back from the hospital. I was in the shower, and it just hit me in a way I just couldn't believe that it happened, that I had done this. I don't think I had cried for maybe fifteen years to that point."

"You actually talked to Steven Champagne that you were upset that he didn't kill your father. Remember that?"

"I did not say that."

"So he wasn't telling the truth on that?"

"No, he was not."

"But you weren't upset with anybody that they didn't finish the job with your father?"

"No, sir, I never said that."

"So Steven Champagne, who has no reason to lie about that particular thing, was lying about that?"

"There were other people at that lunch where that comment was supposedly said. If I had said it, they would have testified here."

"Really?"

"Yes, sir, they would have."

"How do we know you just didn't talk to them on a private basis?"

"Because they were not involved in this in any way and wouldn't have been involved in it in any way."

"We didn't know you were talking to Adam Hipp, unless we tape-recorded it."

"Yes, sir."

"If Marshall Slot hadn't tape-recorded Adam Hipp's conversation with you, what would have been your response to that? That you never talked to Adam Hipp?"

"Testifying today, no. I would admit it today. Back at the beginning, when the police were talking to me, I would have lied about it, yes."

"But you told your father you didn't know anything about it."

"Yes, I did."

"So, once we catch you at it, then you come in and admit to it. But before then, no, right?"

"That's something that's happened over the last year and a half, sir, two and a half years."

"Well, you act like this is some minor thing. You're being investigated for killing your mother and your brother, and your father's asking you about Adam Hipp, and you say, 'I don't know what they're talking about, and I still don't know,' right?"

"Yes, I did say that, but it wasn't a minor thing. It was fear."

"The fear was that Adam Hipp was going to come forward and tell them about you," Felcman emphasized.

"Yes, sir." Bart admitted to the only thing that truly worried him: getting caught.

"You also thought maybe he was talking to the police, because you thought, 'I hope we're on the same page here.'"

"I don't know that I thought that at the time. I just thought that Adam would have gotten a better deal from them fiscally, financially. That meant he would have told them anything, yes."

Felcman moved on to the money Bart was able to take with him and use to escape to Cerralvo, Mexico. "Ten thousand dollars from your father's home. He said that you took it. He was right, correct?"

"Yes, I did."

"Where was that money at?"

"It was taped behind a drawer."

"Why couldn't you just have left? Why did you have to take the man's money, too, after killing his wife and son? Why couldn't you have just left?"

"I didn't have any money of my own."

"You had eighty thousand dollars, according to the trust fund."

"I didn't know I could access that."

"Everybody said you can access it," Felcman reminded the defendant.

"I know that's what they say. I didn't know I could access it. I would have wanted it, if I could have."

"Marshall Slot is able to track you down to the Lancaster Hotel. You had to spend four hundred dollars [on a hotel room] before you left. Tell the jury why?"

"I got really drunk and I wanted a last night out."

"One last time after killing your mother and brother, huh?"

"One last time in America was what I was thinking."

Felcman spun around and cornered the defendant. "Do you remember your attorney Dan Cogdell saying you ran away in fear?"

Bart nodded his head in his version of shame.

"You weren't running in fear," Felcman declared. "You actually had it planned for a while to spend a night at a nice hotel. You had it all planned. Then you skedaddled to Mexico, right?"

"Something I came up with that night, actually." Bart again downplayed his planning skills.

Fred Felcman was just about finished with Bart Whitaker. "Is there any way you want to change your plea to guilty from not guilty now?"

"If I could go back and do this over, I would have insisted on that, yes," Bart admitted.

Felcman, however, was not ready to stop painting Bart in the most negative light possible. "Why did you put 'K. Soze' on the letter," he asked in regard to the letter Bart mailed to Adam Hipp, along with bribe money.

"It was something that me and Adam had joked about in the past, that we both enjoyed that movie *The Usual Suspects*."

"You're sending him bribe money to cover up you killing your brother and mother, and you have time to write something you think is a joke?"

"I meant sort of as an inside, not an inside joke,

but . . ." His voice trailed off before he could complete his thought.

"It was a joke, right?" Felcman baited.

"No, sir. It was not a funny joke." Bart shook his head, "No, it was not."

"Why did you put it in there?"

"As something he would identify with, without putting my own name on it."

"You were stupid enough to put your own address on it," Felcman spat out, all sense of decorum evaporated. "Did you see that?"

"I had to," Bart claimed.

"This is not the first time you've told people in this legal system how sorry you were for all the pain and trouble you've caused, is it?"

"No, it's not."

"Remember me showing the confession you gave after burglarizing all these schools? Remember that," Felcman chided.

"Yes, sir."

Felcman read from Bart's confession: *"I am sorry for all the pain and trouble I have caused and will seek to amend the wrongs as soon as possible.* That's exactly what you're saying today, right?"

Bart replied, "You don't believe a person can be sorry for the things they did?"

Even more eyes rolled in the gallery as many in attendance could not believe what they were hearing from this young man.

"No, I think they can be, Mr. Whitaker." Felcman seemed to grow six inches taller as the opportunity of a lifetime presented itself to him. "But I don't think *you* are." He paused. "I think you're sorry you got caught, and now you're trying to figure out how to get out of the death penalty." More than a few heads nodded in unison from the crowd. "Tell me something, Mr. Whitaker, do you have anything in your background, for this jury, to somehow lessen your moral blameworthiness in this case?"

"I leave those decisions up to them," Bart answered, still attempting to gain control.

"Do you have any evidence they can listen to?"

"I believed they listened to me today."

"Do you have any evidence to show any lessening of moral blameworthiness on this case?"

Bart was unable to answer the question.

"The answer is no." Felcman decided to answer the question for him. "You haven't been mistreated, you haven't been abused. You haven't had anything like that happen in your life, have you?"

"I've never been abused, no."

"And the moral blameworthiness on this? The simple fact is this—without you, Mr. Whitaker, your mom and brother would still be alive today."

"Yes, they would be," Bart agreed.

"So your moral blameworthiness exceeds everybody else's, correct?" Felcman placed the final nail in Bart's coffin.

"I can see how it can be looked at that way, yes, sir."

"How could it not be looked at that way, Mr. Whitaker?"

"We were all in this together, but, yes, it was my plan. I started it. Yes, it was my responsibility."

"The second issue—you knew your family was going to be killed. You anticipated that human life would be taken that night?"

"Yes, I did."

"And finally, the continuing threat. I've got a person

who manipulates people, manipulated the court system, has been in trouble before with the court, correct?"

"I have been in trouble with the court, yes."

"And kills the people he loves the most," Felcman summarized.

"Yes, I did that."

"And then you had one last question. You say you don't have an ax to grind with me?"

"No," Bart quietly answered.

"If you should have an ax to grind with me, Mr. Whitaker, should I be scared?"

"Sir, I don't have an ax to grind with anyone."

"I could treat you nice and fine and love you as much as your mother and brother loved you, and you could make up some reason to kill me. Is that about right?"

"Not anymore."

"How many more years do you think you're going to live, Mr. Whitaker? Fifty?" Felcman queried.

"I don't know, sir."

"It only took five years from getting off probation for you to kill your parents. That's all it took. You're twenty-seven."

"Yes, sir."

"You've got a good number of years, don't you?"

"I do."

"And you didn't have to pull the trigger. You got somebody else to do it for you, right?" Felcman asked his final question.

"Yes, sir" was all Bart could muster.

"Thank you, Judge." Felcman nodded toward Judge Vacek, acknowledged the members of the jury, and refused to look at Bart Whitaker again. He was done.

* * *

Randy McDonald, Bart's attorney, had no further questions for his client. Bart was also the final defense witness.

Time had run out for the day, so Judge Vacek informed the jurors that attorneys from both sides would make their final arguments the following morning.

54

March 7, 2007
Fort Bend County Courthouse
Richmond, Texas

Nearly two months after jury selection began in the case against Bart Whitaker, attorneys for both sides were prepared to wrap up the trial. A bleary-eyed bunch of jurors shuffled into their familiar seats and listened, one last time, to each attorney argue why Bart Whitaker deserved to live or deserved to die.

First up was Assistant District Attorney Jeff Strange for the state. The forty-five-year-old prosecutor would eventually get to the defendant; however, he wanted to remind the jury members of what kind of people Tricia and Kevin Whitaker were.

"Kevin was a child. He was nineteen when he was killed. Kevin Whitaker could have become a doctor, or maybe some type of researcher that would find the cure for some disease. Or maybe a teacher or a police officer. He had a right to become whatever his talent and hard work would let him become, and this defendant has denied us all that."

Strange continued, "He was an Aggie. He liked to hunt, he liked to fish, he liked sports, he wore boots. He liked country music." He added, "There's nothing wrong with that. He was a good kid, and he had a right to grow up. When that Cor-Bon bullet hit him in the chest, that child spent the rest of his life with his hand over his chest trying to stem the flow of blood, staggering around the lobby of his house. What could that baby have been thinking? How scared must he have been? How much did that hurt?"

Strange then continued to address the jury panel about Bart's mother. "It would have been nice if she would have been able to help him. They died about ten feet apart. Patricia Whitaker's last words alive were to express concern over Clifton Stanley's health. I mean that literally. She said, 'No, Clifton. He could still be in here.' He's not even her child," Strange remarked, reminding jurors of the helpful, concerned neighbor, and how Tricia was selfless to the end.

The prosecutor spoke more of Tricia Whitaker. "She was a teacher. She spent her entire professional career educating the children of this community. She was a woman of great faith. I've been told she'd give you the shirt off her back. She deserved better than this. She had a right to become a grandmother. She had a right to grow old with Kent," he stated, and looked up at the grieving widower.

"Make no mistake about it, that's why we're here. This is as bad as it gets. This is absolutely as bad as it gets," Strange noted, and turned his gaze toward Bart. He turned the conversation to focus on Bart's murder plotting, failed murder attempts, and, ultimately, brutal double murder. "On April 5, 2001, it's the big day," he declared facetiously. "The Whitakers are supposed to die that day, but Jennifer Japhet has a conscience. She calls the police. The Waco police call the Sugar Land police. Mr. Whitaker's contacted, and—fortunately—nothing happened that day. [Bart] goes off and runs and hides. If he had any type of conscience, he would have fallen on his knees before God and prayed for forgiveness. He would have come back to Sugar Land and got down before each member of his family, one by one, and begged them for forgiveness."

Strange turned his back on Bart and addressed the jury. "But what happens? His family buys him a Chevrolet Yukon. They buy him a townhome in Willis, because they think he's going to Sam Houston State University, and on December 10, 2003, he kills his mother, he kills his brother, and he has his father shot. And make no mistake about it—he did this so he could inherit money. And then it just gets worse. Within a few months, he's trying to bribe a witness, Adam Hipp, to lie to the police. Within a month, he's up at T.G I. Fridays talking with Steven Champagne about having to finish the job and killing his father. Then he steals ten thousand of his father's money and runs to Mexico. And you wonder why this is a death penalty case?" Strange could not fathom how anyone could think otherwise.

"His girlfriend told you that he looks for people with low self-esteem. He looks for people that are looking for something in their life. And that's the amazing thing about him." The attorney turned and jabbed an index finger in Bart's direction. "At some point, Bart Whitaker somehow developed the skill to evaluate people. He can take a person that's in some type of turmoil and size up what that person needs in their life, and he gives it to them. It's as plain and simple as that.

"Look at all the different faces of the defendant we've seen. You heard his former fiancée testify that she knows 'Family Bart.' The Bart that loved his mom, the Bart that loved his dad, the Bart that was very, very protective of his brother, Kevin, because that's the face he wanted her to see.

"Adam Hipp got to know 'Financial Adviser Bart' as they used to sit around in the upstairs lifting weights together, talking about their trust funds. He knew that was compelling to Adam Hipp.

"The people in Waco got to meet 'Nerdy Bart,' that spent all of his time playing video games and basically almost flunked out of school. That's the face he showed Justin Peters and Will Anthony.

"The people in Willis and the Bentwater Country Club, they got to know 'Party Animal Bart.' The party was always at his place every night.

"And what you got to see yesterday was 'On Trial for Capital Murder Bart.' The defendant looks for people with low self-esteem and he exploits it. The reason why this makes him a future danger is because these are exactly the type of people that he's going to be in prison with—people with low self-esteem, people who are less intelligent than him, people who are less sophisticated than him, people that he is going to be able to influence."

Strange went on to point out three instances of evidence that Bart Whitaker considered to be a joke: first, a picture, taken on the night of the murder, with Bart and Kevin, smiling together, and Bart flipping him off in secret; second, the Keyser Soze–addressed mailer envelope sent to Adam Hipp, with bribery money inside; third, the Christmas card to Fred Felcman. Of the latter, he stated, "Fred Felcman obviously knows what Bart Whitaker is capable of, so if I send you a card with an ominous notation to your family, it's going to ruin your holiday."

Strange turned back toward Bart and said, "There is a time in your life to lay low. When you have been caught committing capital murder, and you are going on trial for your life, there is a time to just shut up." A few snickers could be heard in the gallery. "He can't do it"—Strange turned to face the jury box—"because it's a compulsion. It's just who he is."

Strange was quick to dispel the idea that Bart suffered from the hard bigotry of high expectations. "He told you with his own mouth he planned on killing his family. Unless he kills his family, there is no inheritance. And we know that money was the motivation, not the Peter Pan fantasy he tried to sell you yesterday. You saw no evidence that was truly mitigating. He tried to tell you this irrational story that somehow his family's expectations of him—the fact that they treated him too well, the fact that they bought him too much stuff—made him hate his family and caused him to kill them." Strange practically spat the words out. "Folks, it was over the money. He wanted to inherit the money. The thing is, he understands that people who kill their mommas don't fare particularly well in front of Texas juries when they do it for money, so he had to come up with Plan B. That's why he made up the Peter Pan–like fantasy yesterday. He doesn't want you to think he killed his family over money, because you'll hold it against him. And you should. And he did."

Strange told the jury that he felt bad for the Bartlett and Whitaker families. However, "the fact that the families have forgiven him, the fact that the families don't want it (a death sentence) to happen, it doesn't fit in this equation." He added, "A legitimate purpose of the criminal justice system is to deter crime. Hopefully, by making an example out of a person, other people will know not to follow that conduct. And if we know anything else from the facts of this case, Bart Whitaker deserves to be made an example of. He should be the poster child for this."

Strange lamented Bart's choices in life: "He had the chance for a perfectly easy life. He came up here yesterday and tried to tell you that he has been spoiled rotten, that his parents have done so much for him that he resented it. That because they were successful, it raised expectations for him. That's offensive! That's basically blaming Tricia and Kevin for their own deaths!"

Strange was furious, as were many onlookers in the gallery. He continued, "The bottom line is he has absolutely no moral compass. He has remarkable ability to be all things to all people, and he has no moral compass."

The prosecutor was ready to finish his portion of the argument. "Just like every one of you people, I hope the world, this community, is a better place because I tread on this earth. I think any moral person would want the same thing. We want to make a better life for our children, and we want the world to be a better place. There are some people, however, like Bart Whitaker, that just take. And they take and they take, and they suck the life out of everything they come in contact with. You've had a chance to see that."

Strange paused, collected himself, and turned toward Bart. He then looked back at the jurors. "He killed his mother. He killed his brother. They both loved him. Without condition. And he killed them." Strange let that sink in. "When you look at the life of Bart Whitaker, the only thing he's ever earned himself is this trip to death row."

The gallery fell silent.

Randy McDonald was up next to speak on behalf of Bart.

"There is no question, no question at all, that this is a horrible, tragic, unacceptable crime." McDonald somehow wanted the jurors to stifle their emotions and, instead, focus on the task at hand, which was to assess if Bart Whitaker should be considered a continuing threat if he was to remain alive—one of the three criteria to determine whether or not he should be executed.

The defense attorney disagreed with Prosecutor Strange's conclusion that Bart killed his family for money. "The state has made a big deal about the money. The money was his tool," McDonald surmised, "the manipulation. Money was a tool for him. The bottom line is there was something wrong with Bart. No one does this without something being wrong with them. No rational person would do this."

McDonald tried to blame Bart's conspiratorial plans on his alleged lack of acceptance. "What you really see is an individual withdrawing from society. That's exactly what he did. His feelings were that he was off on this island and he doesn't have anybody that loves him. He somehow developed that into a hatred for his parents. There could be no other reasoning."

McDonald then resorted to the death penalty defense attorney backup plan: guilt. "I'm up here telling you that you will never make a more important decision in your life about whether to take another human being's life."

McDonald's next tactic was to comparison shop Bart alongside his co-conspirators. He seemed amazed that the prosecution plea-bargained with Steven Champagne. "Fifteen years on a lesser included of murder, all because they are so driven to seek justice with the death penalty in this case. No remorse from him whatsoever, and he gets fifteen years."

The prosecution's potential dealings with Chris Brashear were even more appalling to Bart's defense attorney. "Is there something maybe less blameworthy about Bart's conduct than Chris Brashear's?" McDonald asked. He then listed Brashear's actions the night of the murders. "Just another walk in the park. What does that tell you about that person? What does that tell you about his moral culpability? Is that actually greater than Bart's? They didn't make a decision to seek the death penalty for him, and it's the same conduct. He was, in fact, the shooter! Had Chris Brashear not pulled the trigger, we wouldn't be here today."

McDonald then acknowledged the uniqueness of the case. "I've never been involved in a case where the defense called the victims in the case to put their feelings before you. The reason I did it is that they tell you they don't want the death penalty [for Bart]. More importantly, the devastation continues for these victims. They want closure."

The defense attorney made his final plea to spare Bart's life. "For someone like Bart, who had every opportunity in the world, who had loving parents, he's thrown it away. For someone like him being in prison every single day for the rest of his life, and thinking about what he did, that is pretty serious punishment."

McDonald then attempted to convince the jury that Bart had changed. "The Bart Whitaker that committed this crime could no more have gotten up here and faced you and told you the truth and accepted responsibility for this than the Man in the Moon. There's no way he could have done that. Only by being in jail, only by being faced with this, is he able to actually come clean with you about it. He tells you the truth. He actually is remorseful."

McDonald trumpeted the Christian theme of forgiveness laid out by Kent Whitaker. "We all know from our religious beliefs that confession is the start. It is the start of forgiveness and redemption. That's what you're hearing his dad talk about. That's what he's interested in. That's what he's telling you about."

McDonald closed with a return to guilt. "Do yourself a favor," he said directly to everyone in the jury box, "depending on your decision, one day you're going to wake up, and you're going to read the paper that Bart Whitaker was executed. You've got to know that it was proven to you beyond a reasonable doubt, and that you didn't just do it because it is such a notorious, high-profile, ugly, nasty crime." Some of the jurors noticeably shifted in their seats. "Treat him the way the state of Texas wants you to treat him, following your oath to do justice. I think if you really, really look at it, there is absolutely no evidence that he is a continuing threat to society, once he's given a life sentence."

McDonald signed off with the following bit of advice for the jury: "Render a just verdict. If you can do that, you'll be all right with yourself in the morn-

ing. If you can't, you're going to have problems with
it. Thank you."

McDonald finished his closing argument and ADA
Fred Felcman immediately popped up from his chair.
He did not look happy.

"I always listen very intently to what the defense attorney has to say, and I listened for an hour, and I
have never heard such rambling and doublespeak in
all my life. Never does he talk about the defendant.
He never talks about the evidence." Felcman shook
his head at the thought.

"I don't quite understand this moral thing with
Chris Brashear, that because he pulled the trigger,
he is more evil or more heinous than the defendant.
The defendant took his family out and ate bread with
them, knowing full well they were going to be dead in
a few minutes, and brought them back to be assassinated. Chris Brashear was the weapon that the defendant used to kill his family. He could have substituted
another person in, but it's always the defendant bringing back his family to be assassinated."

Felcman spoke about the Christmas card Bart sent
him before the trial and how it was indicative of his
future potential as a threat. "I said to him, 'When you
sent me that card, what was that all about?' He said,
'Well, I don't dislike you, Mr. Felcman.' Ladies and
gentlemen, he has no reason to dislike his family," the
prosecutor stated, and turned to look at the defendant. "He had absolutely no reason whatsoever to hate
his mother or brother or father, but in his mind"—he
poked his temple to hammer the point home—"he
perceived in his mind that they had offended him in

some manner, even though it had nothing to do with reality whatsoever."

Felcman turned away from the jury to glance back at Bart. In a booming voice, he declared, "It doesn't matter if you treat this defendant with kindness, as Mr. Kent Whitaker does. It doesn't matter if you're the ideal father. In his mind, somewhere along the line, he perceives it differently. You are now in danger. And not only that, there's nothing you can do to stop it. There's nothing you can do to stop it, until he's in the grave."

Felcman took issue with Randy McDonald's guilt tactic. "I'm sorry Mr. McDonald said something about you killing him. Ladies and gentlemen, you're going to answer these questions, but the state of Texas will execute him, all right? It was shameful for him to put you in that position, absolutely shameful."

Felcman moved on to whether or not Bart Whitaker would prove to be a future threat. "He talked seven people, five on the murders and two on the burglaries, to do things with him. He manipulated a trained psychologist to write a letter that said, *Don't worry, he won't do anything like this again.* He even convinced Lynne Sorsby to marry him after he was a suspect in a capital murder case and had lived a double life in college. This is a good salesman. This guy could sell ice to an Eskimo. Even Lynne Ayres, the educational diagnostician, said, 'He looks at people as tools.' Now he's looking at you as a tool to try to get out of the death penalty."

Felcman continued to paint the picture of the real Bart Whitaker. "It doesn't take him long to develop the perception that he hates you, or somehow you have offended him, and you deserve to die. He only does things when it comes to his advantage."

The prosecutor had had just about enough of the defendant. "He's the most heinous, evil thing you can think of. Without him," he declared to the jurors, "you're not here, and Mr. Whitaker still has his wife and son. The only person who is morally blameworthy is the defendant."

Felcman had a final bit of advice for the jury panel. "Hug each other, make your verdict, and go home."

At 11:55 A.M., Judge Vacek instructed the jury members to head back to the jurors' quarters to begin deliberating the fate of Bart Whitaker, and whether he should live or die.

Five hours later, the jury had not reached a conclusion. As a result, Judge Vacek ordered they be sequestered for the night, and to resume deliberations the following day.

55

March 8, 2007
Fort Bend County Courthouse
Richmond, Texas

Judge Vacek took his seat at the head of the court-room. The members of the jury were quietly led to the jury box.

The judge wasted no time in getting down to business.

"Let the record reflect that we're here in Cause Number 42,969, the *State of Texas* versus *Thomas Bartlett Whitaker.* The jury is present. The state is present. The defendant is present in person and with counsel. I've received the court's charge on punishment from the jury. I will read the jury's answers.

"Issue number one. *Do you find from the evidence beyond a reasonable doubt that there is a probability that the Defendant would commit criminal acts of violence that would constitute a continuing threat to society?*

"Answer: *Yes.*

"Issue number two. *Do you find from the evidence beyond a reasonable doubt that the defendant actually caused*

*the death of the deceased, or did not actually cause the death
of the deceased, but intended to kill the deceased or another, or
anticipated that a human life would be taken? You are instructed that in answering this issue, only the conduct of the
defendant can be considered, and that the instructions per-
taining to the law of parties heretofore given you cannot now
be considered in answering this issue.*

"Answer: *Yes.*

"Issue number three. *Do you find from the evidence,
taking into consideration all of the evidence, including the
circumstances of the offense, the defendant's character and
background, and the personal moral culpability of the defendant, that there is sufficient mitigating circumstances or circumstances to warrant that a sentence of life imprisonment,
rather than a death sentence be imposed? You are instructed
that in answering this issue, you shall answer the issue yes
or no. You may not answer the issue no unless the jury
unanimously agrees, and you may not answer yes unless ten
or more jurors agree. The jury need not agree on what particular evidence supports an affirmative finding on this
issue. The jury shall consider mitigating evidence to be evidence that a juror might regard as reducing the defendant's
moral blameworthiness.*

"Answer: *No.*

"*We, the jury, having answered the foregoing issues,
return the same into the court as our verdict.*

"Ladies and gentlemen of the jury, is this a unani-
mous verdict?"

"Yes," the jury members declared in unison.

"Thomas Bartlett Whitaker," Judge Vacek addressed
the defendant directly, "is there anything you wish to
say to this court before I pronounce sentence?"

"No, sir," Bart answered. He never showed any emotion upon hearing his fate.

"Then, in Cause Number 42,969, the *State of Texas* versus *Thomas Bartlett Whitaker,* upon the verdicts received by the court from the jury, rendered unanimously by the jury in this cause, that is the verdict of the jury unanimously finding that you are guilty of the offense of capital murder, as charged by the state in the indictment in this case, and their verdicts answering Special Issue number one unanimously yes, answering Special Issue number two unanimously yes, and answering Special Issue number three unanimously no. You are guilty of the offense of capital murder, as charged by the state of Texas, and that you be punished in accordance with the rules of Texas law. That is, that you be sentenced to death by means of lethal injection. Sheriff, you may take him away."

The courtroom remained silent as Bart Whitaker was escorted away to meet his final destiny.

56

Wednesday, September 19, 2007
Fort Bend County Courthouse
Richmond, Texas

Several months after Bart Whitaker was found guilty and sentenced to death, and after Steven Champagne was given a fifteen-year prison term, Chris Brashear finally entered a plea of guilty, as per his deal with the district attorney's office. In exchange, he was spared a death sentence and, instead, received life in prison.

During Brashear's hearing, Kent Whitaker was allowed to address the young man as part of the courtroom proceedings and offer up his victim impact statement. Many times, the statement can become a fiery scene between a murderer and the victim's family. Kent Whitaker was there, instead, to let Chris Brashear know he was forgiven.

"Chris, this is a horrible day for everyone." Kent nodded, almost as if he were embarrassed for both men to have to be where they were. "Not just for you, but also your family and loved ones, my family and loved ones, Tricia's entire family, and everyone who loved Kevin and Tricia. It is also horrible for me, as I have to once again face, in such a public way, everything that was taken from me on December 10, 2003.

"But, Chris, the truth is that it was your actions, and your actions alone, that actually took the lives of Kevin and Tricia, and it was you who tried to take my life as well. You located my gun, you loaded the bullets, and you pulled the trigger.

"I am not happy that you are standing here about to spend the rest of your life behind bars. I *truly* wish that you, Bart, and Steven had possessed the moral strength to recognize how wrong this was, and had never come to Houston that night. I wish you were out enjoying life, as you could have been, as Tricia and Kevin could have been. But the three of you chose to commit this heinous crime, and society must be protected from people who have such low regard for others.

"The night you shot me, as I lay in the hospital, trying to decide if I could ever trust God again, some things happened that changed my life on the inside, as much as you changed my life on the outside. I made a conscious decision that night to trust God, even though I couldn't understand why he would have let this happen. Amazingly, one of the results of my decision was that he gave me the ability to forgive everyone who was involved. This surprised me, because until then, I had been lusting for revenge, but the forgiveness was complete.

"You are facing many new challenges, and the road upon which you have placed yourself is dark and hard. But there are choices that can be made for great good, if you will ask God to give you the strength for them. I hope you will make those hard choices. Remember: *people can change*. That is the basic foundation of the Christian faith.

"The first step for all of you is to truly own up to what you did, and to accept *sole* and *complete* responsibility for your actions, without any conditions or limitations. Then you must ask all of us for forgiveness, including your parents. This is known as repentance, and it isn't real if the realization of the depth of what you did doesn't bring you to your knees. And while you are down there, ask Jesus to forgive you and ask him to take this and all your sins upon his back. Only when you do that can you, or any of us, expect to live a life of meaning.

"You took away the life of my wife and my son, and, in a real sense, you took my life as well. I have begun a new one, but it has been incredibly hard, and the loss is beyond your measuring. I choose to leave you with a gift to help make the building of your new life easier. You can accept it or reject it.

"Chris Brashear, I forgive you for everything."

Afterward, Chris Brashear's attorney, Edward Chernoff, spoke to the media plainly about his client, "He pleaded guilty today because he was guilty."

57

Kent Whitaker, in true witness form, has taken his story to the masses. His appearances on *Oprah, 48 Hours,* and *20/20* to promote his book have opened doors to thousands upon thousands of more people curious to hear his tale of tragedy and forgiveness. He has taken it a step further, and on a much more personal basis, and has begun giving speeches to various churches across Texas and Arkansas. He has also been a special guest at various Christian literary gatherings in Texas and Colorado.

Kent's story has been an inspirational anecdote for many who could not imagine the ability to forgive under such untenable circumstances. In an interview with Lauren Winchester, of the *Houston Chronicle,* Kent reiterated how God played the biggest role in changing his life: *"This was a gift I believe God gave me. The whole forgiveness thing was taken care of that night, and it was beyond what I could have done—but it happened."*

Kent added, *"I realized that maybe God had allowed me to live so I could display that unconditional love. By doing so, it surprised Bart. He could not believe that I hadn't turned on him."*

Kent then summarized the tale: *"If someone only sees the tragic events of the crime, then they miss the real story,"* he said. *"The crime is only the framework upon which the real stories of forgiveness and God's faithfulness are hung."*

On December 26, 2008, Kent Whitaker announced on his personal website that he would be getting re-married, to Tanya Youngling, a woman he met on a blind date. They were engaged on Christmas night.

The couple married on May 9, 2009. Kent told the *Chronicle* about his new wife, *"I am so grateful for Tanya. I had a wonderful life before the shootings, and have now been given a new one, full of hope and adventure; the way God has restored me should be an encouragement for every-one who faces hardships. Storms don't last forever. If you trust Him through it all, in time you will emerge into the sunshine as I have. Tanya is such a precious gift."*

After the wedding, Kent and Tanya moved back into Kent's home in Sugar Land, where his first wife, Tricia, and his youngest son, Kevin, were shot and killed by a friend of his oldest son, Bart, who had mas-terminded the entire plan.

Kent soon decided, however, that he and his new bride would finally sell the home and find a new place to start life anew.

"I'm moving because I'm married," he said, his mouth erupting in a smile. *"And that's a wonderful, won-derful thing."*

58

Bart Whitaker's time in prison since his conviction had been adventurous, to say the least. One of the first things he did, at the behest of his father, was to rediscover God. While most tend to believe he is merely another cynical prisoner with a "jailhouse conversion," so as to earn brownie points for parole appearances, his death sentence renders that point seemingly irrelevant. Of course, Bart Whitaker is much savvier than your average con. He seems to have a keen understanding of his place outside the walls of the Polunsky Unit in Livingston, Texas.

Bart's knowledge of killers and their placement on the pantheon of pop culture has held great interest for him. Inspired by the likes of Richard Ramirez, aka The Night Stalker, or his previously mentioned inspirations, the Menendez brothers (see Corey Mitchell's *Hollywood Death Scenes: True Crime and Tragedy in Paradise,* p. 232 and p. 81, respectively), Bart has cultivated a tiny following of sympathizers. In these cases, the killers' followers have been known as "death row groupies." Even though Bart's followers tend to avoid the term "groupie," their actions almost identically parallel those of Doreen Lioy, who married Ramirez, Anna Erikkson, who married Lyle Menendez, and Tammi Saccoman, who married Erik Menendez. About the only discernible difference at this point is that none of Bart's groupies have accepted a marriage proposal from the convicted murderer.

The reasons why some women choose to befriend, and sometimes even fall in love with, these convicted murderers is severalfold: some believe they can change the killer while he is behind bars; some believe they can help the killer find God; some merely feed off the notoriety of the case and the attendant attention they, too, may obtain as a result of it; others have no sense of self-worth and find that the fact that someone, anyone, is paying attention to them is acceptable; while others, as Houston Crime Victims Assistance director Andy Kahan is wont to say, "merely want to know where their man is at the end of the night."

Most of Bart's followers are female and range in age from their mid-twenties to their early fifties. Many proclaim to be anti–death penalty advocates who want to support Bart during his time of need while he awaits his final punishment. Others seem to have glommed onto him after his murder case appeared on CBS's *48 Hours Mystery* on October 20, 2007. Even more followers came out of the woodwork after Bart's father, Kent Whitaker, appeared on *The Oprah Winfrey Show*, on October 6, 2008, nearly one year later. Kent appeared on Oprah's nationwide broadcast to promote the release of his book, *Murder by Family*, which mainly discussed Kent's ability to forgive Bart for setting up and following through with the murders of Tricia and Kevin Whitaker.

Mention of Kent Whitaker's appearance on *Oprah* via this author's crime blog, In Cold Blog, led to several thousand more hits on the site, due to the large number of viewers of her program. Those who saw the program watched as the usually affable Winfrey grilled Kent Whitaker for his failure to see through Bart's fabrications, especially his inability to not know that Bart was not really going to graduate from college. The daytime talk show reigning queen seemed quite mortified that Kent was so clueless, and she raised doubts as to Kent's raising of his oldest son that may have led to the murders.

In addition, and also probably what led to a sizable increase in Bart's followers, was an interview with Bart himself by correspondent Lisa Ling.

The Bart obsession via *Oprah* continued with an Oprah Community message board. The comments seemed split down the middle as to whether Kent Whitaker was almost saintly in his ability to forgive his son, and disgust as to how someone could not see the signs that his own son would become a killer.

Most people were amazed by Kent Whitaker's ability to forgive, many wondered how he could forgive Bart, while still others doubted his sincerity. The majority of people who actually wrote about Bart were appalled by his callousness and his complete disregard for his mother and brother. They were also put off by how he was amazed that his father could forgive him. Others, however, sympathized with the young man and felt sorry for him.

Even more followers joined the Bart bandwagon after the Kent Whitaker interview was aired again on *Oprah,* in February 2009. That was followed by a new segment on *20/20.*

Bart's understanding of his presence in the pantheon
of notorious criminals was even more self reflective with
the introduction of his own personal blog. Entitled
Minutes Before Six, named for the time leading up to
an execution in Texas, it appeared on the Internet on
July 24, 2007, before the original airing of the *48 Hours
Mystery* episode that featured the familicide he orches-
trated. (Bart's website has since been transferred to a
blogging account on Blogger.)

Much to the surprise of many, Bart's blog entries
were actually typed up and posted by Kent Whitaker.
Since Bart did not have direct access to a computer,
he needed someone on the outside to input his pearls
of wisdom for him. In stepped his father. Once word
got out, however, about the blog, and that Kent was
participating in it with him, people were furious.
Sources say that members of Tricia's family were livid
that Kent chose to support Bart's endeavors. Given
the tenor of some of Bart's entries, it is understandable why surviving family members of the dead victims
would have been upset with his involvement. Much of
the blog is about Bart's opposition to the death
penalty, despite his claims otherwise, problems with
prison conditions, and a soapbox to complain about
the media coverage of him and his case.

Bart also announced to the world that he was
changing his identity yet again, that he would now be
going by his legal first name, Thomas, and leaving the
name Bart behind. He seemed to suggest that by
changing the name, he would also be removing a persona that he, and many others, found so repellent.

It was also disturbing to many for what it lacked—
any remorse whatsoever for his participation in the
murders of his mother and brother.

* * *

Bart's media savvy, however, does not end there. In addition to the television interviews and personal blog, Bart had accepted volunteers to act as front people for him on MySpace and Facebook. One such follower, Donna Wilde, aka Donna X, acts as Bart's de facto voice on both of the social networking sites, including a MySpace page listed as "Thomas Whitaker."

Crime victim advocate Andy Kahan had plenty to say in an e-mail to this author about Bart's media savvy:

Poor Bart, Thomas, or whatever he wants his minions to call him. He clearly is so delusional to believe that because he only planned the murder of his entire family and was not the shooter that his life should be spared. What a pathetic rationale by someone who clearly master-minded the cold blooded diabolical premeditated murder of the woman who gave him life, his brother whom he was obviously envious of, and now, on his website, he calls out to all the bleeding hearts—"Woe is me, poor little ole me—I am not the killer."

What a crock.

He is a pathetic lousy excuse for a human being who is under some false sense of delusion that he is now some kind of death-row philosopher who pontificates on all that he believes caused him to end up where he belongs, with the exception of the only person who truly deserves all the blame—himself.

He is truly a narcissistic psychopath who fails to

take any responsibility for his predicament. I notice on his various sites he never discusses his mother or his brother who lie, yes, Six Feet Under, to paraphrase his blog title. Amazingly, he has the audacity to ask others for money for his so-called defense fund using the bizarre logic that since he was not the shooter he should bear the ultimate premise.

Every one of his smiling photos which make him look like Beaver Cleaver asking Wally "Gee Wally, I didn't know killing my family would mean I would get punished." Bart seems to forget that his actions put him on Death Row, another person doing life, another one doing 15 years and, Oh, Yes!—a dead mother and brother.

How convenient for the new Plato. On death-row and now the big bad mean state of Texas plans on, Horrors!, punishing him.

What a manipulative, egomaniacal piece of work.

Some of Bart's followers have chosen to attack this author, well over a year before this book would be hitting the shelves. Bart's right-hand woman, Donna Wilde, had allegedly started up a petition that she planned on having Bart sign off on—not allowing the book to be published. Keep in mind, this was without having read a single word of prose in the manuscript.

We later corresponded with one another and she wrote, *I am no death row groupie. Thomas has been the subject of some online games, since the end of last year. The last thing he needs is any more bad press so to speak. I have been writing to Thomas for nearly a year, i find him a very inteliigent [sic] man. I am currently working towards an English Law Degree, with plans to move to Texas in 2012 to study an American Law Degree . . . and you guessed it hopefully work within the field of criminal defence [sic] and capital punishment. Thomas is my inspiration for that. He has given me the option of using his case as a case study if i wished, which i have refused, but he has also put me in contact with some very useful people. While i want to do what ican [sic] to help Thomas in his fight, this is also a learning curve for me, as Thomas will openly discuss anything that iask [sic] him.*

While Bart still had a handful of followers, usually females who oppose the death penalty, there were others who were once under his spell but now sing a completely different tune. Ronimal was one of Bart's penpals. She wrote to him at least once a week and used to receive lots of correspondence from Bart. She, too, stated how Bart had changed since the murders, not that she knew him back then, of course. However, he seemed like a genuine and caring individual. She added that he never spoke about the murders or even about his brother and his mother. She emphasized that he never once expressed remorse for his part in their murders.

None of these omissions deterred her. It was not until the Bart Groupie gossip mill began to go into overdrive that she became disillusioned with Bart. She began to hear grumblings through the various social networks, personal e-mails, and correspondence from

Bart that he was not quite the person he claimed to be. Apparently, one of the various incidents involved another woman, who had fallen hard for Bart and proclaimed to be his bride-to-be. Ronimal did not care about that so much, as she harbored no romantic feelings for Bart. However, the supposed relationship was causing tension among the various groupies.

Ronimal also stated that she was getting upset with Bart personally. She wrote, *My good friend got a letter from Thomas. He's pissed off. Something about you getting copies of the Facebook group I started? If you ask me, he's starting to become a real dick to his "Friends."* She added, *He is apparently very upset with me because the prison has blocked me from contacting him. Somehow that is my fault. He wrote a very nasty letter to our mutual friend, chastising her for not being "the right kind of friend." I'm thoroughly annoyed.*

59

Bart Whitaker was presumably annoyed on the morning of Wednesday, June 24, 2009, because his death sentence was upheld by the Texas Court of Criminal Appeals after considering an appeal filed on his behalf. While he did not contest his guilt, Bart argued that his death sentence should be tossed because it "wasn't proper because his court record doesn't include a plea offer he made to prosecutors." Bart, of course, wanted prosecutors to remove the possibility of the death penalty before trial and was willing to accept "as many life sentences as the state wanted . . . to spare his already victimized family the ordeal of a trial." Bart's main argument was that "the absence of the formal offer in the trial record impaired his ability to pursue a motion for a new trial."

The criminal appeals court disagreed with Bart and pointed out that the subject of the plea deal was discussed repeatedly during the penalty phase, specifically in the testimony of Bart's uncle, Bo Bartlett, and Bart's father, Kent Whitaker.

Bart's next biggest argument was that "the Texas

death penalty statute was unconstitutional because it failed to provide a consistent method for determining which cases merited capital punishment." Again, the criminal appeals court disagreed.

Bart Whitaker currently resides in the Polunsky Unit in Livingston, Texas, and awaits his unknown execution date. He still has the right to appeal his death sentence in the federal courts. To pass the time, he writes posts for his blog that focus on prison conditions, arguments against the death penalty, attacking any media coverage of his case, and mocking people who write him letters that are not deferential enough to him.

The greatest trick the Devil ever pulled
was convincing the world he didn't exist.
And like that, poof. He's gone.

—Verbal Kint (*The Usual Suspects*)

In Memoriam

Donald Mitchell

February 16, 1940–December 18, 2009

Acknowledgments

Savage Son is the first true crime book I have written where I wanted to leave the genre afterward. Bart Whitaker's cold, callous disregard for human life made it difficult for me to plant my butt in the chair and tell a compelling story that readers would want to spend time delving into.

I began researching this case just days before Thanksgiving 2007. Little did I know, my cozy little world in the field of true crime would soon be shaken up. It all started when I posted a humorous horror video on my own website, In Cold Blog. The Eli Roth-directed fake movie trailer upset a few of my contributors and a campaign to undermine my writing career, led by two people within my industry (later joined by a third non-blog member), was underway. I was stunned to witness the vitriol with which people, whom I considered to be my peers as well as my friends, went after me over a disagreement about the First Amendment.

I assumed that submersing myself into research for the Bart Whitaker story would shield me from the irrationality; however, I was in for another surprise. As soon as I was heavy-duty into my new book, one of my worst fears was realized: I received word that another person was writing a book on the case. I am not a fan multiple book releases on a fairly recent true crime story, so I proceeded with caution. To make matters worse, I assumed I was in big trouble when I learned who the author would be—Kent Whitaker. I later discovered that Mr. Whitaker would release his book through a religious based publishing house. I was relieved, as I believed his book would be a story more of redemption and forgiveness, whereas my version would be a thorough dissection of an amazing true crime story. I decided to continue on with the book, but also suggested to my publisher that I postpone the release of *Savage Son* so as to allow Mr. Whitaker's book more uninterrupted time on the shelves.

That winter, the fight between me and my former true crime genre friends reached a peak as one disgruntled former contributor (encouraged by her minions) attempted to smear my name among several victims' rights groups' charities even after I offered up a public apology. She was so obsessed with trying to make me look bad that she even publicly questioned the veracity of the rape of my late first wife, Lisa, and went so far as to stalk our friends through Lisa's online memorial website so she could question them as to whether or not she had been raped. This from an alleged supporter of victims' rights. Alas, her attempts failed, but I was flabbergasted that such venom could be spewed by a person whom I believed to be a purveyor of the most sacrosanct of American tenets—freedom of speech.

My disillusionment with true crime continued the following spring when a Houston television news reporter piggybacked on the upcoming release of my last true crime book, *Pure Murder,* in yet another attempt to smear my name. The reporter, possibly incensed that she would not be able to finagle her own book deal with a key participant featured in my book, used the power of the media to make me look bad. Her interview, with a parent of one of the victims, was to focus on a legal matter in the case, yet suddenly veered to the release of my book and led the parent to talk about the old anti-true crime saw, "blood money." I mistakenly assumed a television reporter, who had reported on murder cases for years, would understand that writing a book on a true crime case is not about making "blood money," but rather an attempt at finding the truth behind the headlines and sharing that information with a discerning public that deserves to know what goes on around them. Fortunately, the reporter's hatchet job was seen for what it really was, so I simply brushed it aside. *Pure Murder* was released months later and went on to become one of my most successful books. I later found out through a third party that the parent who decried my book actually read it and declared it to be excellent. Had that reporter not pressed her own agenda, I probably would have been able to include that family member into my book and made it even better.

After my *Pure Murder* book tour, I jumped back into the Bart Whitaker story. Meanwhile, the disgruntled former In Cold Blog contributors had moved on. Once they understood that I had already experienced the most horrendous day in my life with the death of Lisa and that nothing could ever make me feel any worse, they redirected their attacks on my editor at In Cold Blog. She had made the innocent mistake of defending me. Knowing full well that she had previously been a victim of violent crime, these people found it acceptable to make false accu sations about her and proceeded to unearth her personal information, including outing her once private persona, with the sole purpose of trying to break her down mentally, simply because she disagreed with them.

Needless to say, stepping out of a realm where people who disagree with you decide it is acceptable behavior to go after another person with the intent to shatter their life, into a different world where an egotistical, maniacal, control freak literally shattered other people's lives was not my idea of fun.

The more I learned about Bart Whitaker, the more I became repulsed by who he was as a person, by what he had become, and by the actions he had taken to solve his own imaginary problems. I have written about some of the most violent people in the world: Coral Watts, a serial killer who may have killed as many as one hundred innocent women; Anthony Allen Shore, a brilliant individual who raped his own daughters and strangled little girls; and Rex Krebs, a paroled rapist turned serial killer of college girls. Miraculously, I was actually able to find one redeeming trait within these wretched souls' lives. With Bart Whitaker though, I could not find it within my heart to locate a single iota of decency.

But that's when I remembered that true crime books are about so much more than just a killer and his gruesome crimes. They are about victims and their families, law enforcement officers who go above and beyond to catch these bad people, and the citizens who are adversely affected by murder and violent crime. These stories are the ultimate parables of good versus evil.

It was then that I remembered why I enjoy not only writing true crime books, but also reading them. No matter how tragic the circumstances surrounding the murder of a loved one, someone, somehow, always manages to rise to the occasion. In the Bart Whitaker story, that someone was Kent Whitaker. While I seriously doubt I could ever forgive someone who murdered my spouse *and* my child, I admire his ability to stick to his beliefs and stand behind his son.

Kent Whitaker has taken a lot of criticism for supporting Bart. He has been ripped to shreds online for his decision and called every name in the book, but he seems unfazed by the barbs. I'm sure they sting at times, but he has a higher purpose to serve. I truly admire him for that.

After watching the attempted evisceration of Kent Whitaker, it made me want to do two things: 1) detail his argument to free his son in this book at length; and 2) forget and forgive the people who have attempted to smear my name in this business.

For the former, I narrowed the trial information down to three people: Bo Bartlett, Kent Whitaker, and Bart. I wanted to show that no matter how horrible a person Bart Whitaker might truly be, there were still people out in the world that cared enough about him to argue on his behalf. I believe Bart's true, combative, egotistical nature comes out fully in his testimony, yet I believe I was more than fair in presenting his uncle and father's arguments for keeping him alive. It was the least I could do for Mr. Whitaker.

For the latter, it reminded me that nothing is more

devastating than losing a loved one. Also, I have long accepted the reality that people will do whatever they feel is necessary to tear down others to make themselves feel better about themselves, regardless of the consequences. Mere words and intentional disinformation, however, pale in comparison to murder—obviously. So, if Kent Whitaker could forgive his son for murdering Tricia and Kevin Whitaker, it was pretty apparent that my complaints were trivial in comparison.

Besides, life is far too short to concern yourself with spiteful individuals who seek to destroy others and refuse to build bridges for greater, more positive opportunities.

Again, I do not believe I could have done what Kent Whitaker did, but his actions are to be admired, not chastised.

I will continue to write true crime books as long as people continue to murder one another. These stories need to be told, examined, and shared. They need to be discussed at length, argued about, and held up as warning signs. Hopefully, I will continue to do justice to all parties involved in these devastating tales.

Thank you to Samantha Buxton, aka "Lady Long Legs," for providing the winning entry in my MySpace contest to name this book. You came up with the perfect title.

Thank you to everyone involved in the Whitaker case, especially Kent Whitaker, Fred Felcman, Judge Clifford Vacek, and Marshall Slot. This was a difficult book for me to get cooperation on, so to those several dozen people who had the courage to step forward, I truly appreciate your help and guidance.

Thank you, Karen Rothman. You are a sweetheart and one hell of a representative for all that is right in the justice system.

As always, Andy Kahan, you are an inspiration and a much-needed voice for crime victims across the globe. I am proud to call you my friend. Also, thank you to Wanda Greenbaugh. May you also succeed in assisting crime victims.

Thank you to Michaela Hamilton, Mike Shohl, Richard Ember, and everyone at Kensington for their continued support of me, even when I miss those pesky deadlines.

Thank you to Michelle McKee for running In Cold Blog and for being a fighter for what is right and just. Never give up.

Thank you to my mentor, friend, and fellow television mogul Dennis McDougal. Your friendship is invaluable. Putz!

Thank you to all of the wonderful contributors at In Cold Blog. It is my privilege to be able to work with so many talented and kind writers. You all are what make our blog one of the best.

Thanks to Vince Neilstein and Axl Rose at Metal-Sucks. It's nice to step away from true crime and talk about something fun like heavy metal! Also, thanks to Ben, Matt, and Gary Suarez.

Thanks to all of my friends, especially Peter Soria and Ray Seggern. It's nice to know you both always have my back.

Thank you to my good friend and attorney, David Schafer. More work coming your way.

Thanks to Brian and Amy Ditzel and the girls. It's

always special to welcome wonderful new people into my life.

Thank you to Dennis and Margaret Burke. We could not do this without your help and support. Much love from your son-in-law.

Thank you to Kyle and Ramona Mitchell, Darrin Mitchell, and Denise Burke. I am lucky to have such incredible siblings. I love you all, as well as my nieces and nephews Julie, Kaylee, Ronnie, Madison, Blake, and Leah.

Thank you to my mom, Carol Mitchell, for holding strong and staying tough all these years. I do not know how you did it, but you have kept this family together during twenty-eight very difficult years and somehow managed to keep your spirits up. You have made life fun for all of us around you. You are an incredible woman who I am constantly in awe of every day. I love you very much.

As always, thank you to my late wife, Lisa Mitchell. It is hard to imagine that you have been gone for more than eight years. I miss you every day and hope you are proud of what I have accomplished.

Thank you to my wonderful daughter, Emma. You are so brilliant it's scary. I have so enjoyed every minute I have been blessed to spend with you. I cannot wait to see you grow and blossom into the beautiful, funny, sensitive, and intelligent young lady I know you will become. But, no hurry. I love you, sweetheart.

Thank you to the newest addition to our family, Sabrina. Your mother and I are so thrilled to welcome you into this world. Don't let the subject matter of daddy's books scare you. It is a wonderful world out there and there is no need to be afraid of it. Aware, yes. Afraid, no. I love you, Sweet Bear.

Thank you to my incredible wife, Audra. It looks like our hard work is finally going to pay off. Either way, I am the happiest man alive simply because I get to spend the rest of my life with you. You are something to behold and I still don't understand how I was lucky enough to come into your life. Let's enjoy the fruits of our labor and laugh more and more together each day. Thank you for your intense support, devotion, and tolerance. I am madly in love with you.

My final thank you goes out to my dad, Don Mitchell. He passed away on December 18, 2009, at the age of sixty-nine, from dementia. Twenty-eight years earlier, he was diagnosed with an egg-sized malignant tumor in the frontal lobe of his brain. He was given anywhere from six months to two years to live after surgery, but he defied all odds and stuck around for twenty-eight more. He was a lover and a fighter, a jock and a sensitive man, an entrepreneur and a family guy, a frustration and an inspiration. He was everything that a young man would want as a role model, whether it came to his work ethic, how he respectfully treated women, how he fully enjoyed himself and his family, and how he had an incomparable lust for life. I could not have been luckier.

Thank you, Dad, for everything you taught me, showed me, argued about with me, revealed to me, and inspired in me. It is because of you that I am in any way, shape, or form a relatively decent human being. I will miss you more than you could ever imagine.

I love you, Dad.
Your son

Corey Mitchell, J.D., is the author of the best-sellers *Dead and Buried* and *Pure Murder*, as well as *Murdered Innocents, Evil Eyes, Strangler*, and the underground true crime classic, *Hollywood Death Scenes*. He is also the founder and executive editor of In Cold Blog, a collective of over twenty true crime authors and professionals, often regarded as the preeminent true crime blog.

Mitchell is a former contributor for the Discovery Channel and his work has appeared in Reuters, USA Today, UPI, AP, Examiner.com, Austin Chronicle, Houston Chronicle, San Antonio Express-News, Chicago Sun-Times, MetalSucks, Bloody Disgusting, and many more. He has also appeared as an expert on numerous national news broadcasts and featured on several television shows including E!'s 20 Most Horrifying Hollywood Murders and TV Land's Myths and Legends.

Mitchell has also worked with several charitable organizations to help assist victims of crime. He had the honor of introducing his book *Strangler*, at the twenty-first annual Parents of Murdered Children conference in Houston, Texas, as a Guest Speaker and workshop host. Mitchell is the only other true crime author, besides Ann Rule, to have ever been bestowed this honor.

Corey is surrounded by estrogen in the form of his lovely wife, Audra, and his two beautiful daughters, Emma and Sabrina, deep in the heart of Texas.

Follow Corey Mitchell on his website: www.coreymitchell author.com

In Cold Blog: http://incoldblogger.blogspot.com

Facebook: http://www.facebook.com/home.php#!/profile.php?ref=profile&id=660352330

Twitter: http://twitter.com/corey_mitchell

MySpace: http://www.myspace.com/coreymitchell